WOMEN THRIVE

VOLUME IV

Inspiring True Stories of Women Overcoming Adversity

Raimonda Jankunaite
Marci Hopkins
Karmin Reeves Jenkins
Theresa DeLorenzo
Kathryn Traff
Heather Hanson
Hayley Chambers
Mandy Merrifield
Pamela Spencer
Dr. Argie Nell Nichols
Barbara McAteer
Niobis Queiro
Anne-Marie Hughes
Amy Sanders
Kristi Brown

Women Thrive

Published by Women Thrive Media Ltd

This book compilation was initiated by Raimonda Jankunaite, founder of Women Thrive Media Ltd. If you would like to become a published author in our future book compilations, please visit www.womenthrivesummit.com/book or email us at contact@womenthrivemedia.com.

Paperback ISBN: 978-1-7384107-4-3
eBook ISBN: 978-1-7384107-5-0

Cover Art: Malena (@malena_lineart)
Cover Design, Interior Design, Formatting: Woven Red Author Services

Special thanks to the authors, mentors, editors, and the entire Women Thrive Media team for their invaluable support in bringing this book to life.

This book is dedicated to you—the woman who has faced life's challenges and emerged unbroken. You are strong and determined, even if you carry pieces of yourself that feel fragile or undiscovered. Within those shadows lie the seeds of transformation and growth.

This is for the woman who dreams of more—a life filled with purpose, freedom, and alignment—despite the struggles and pain that were meant to break her. Yet here you are, standing as a living testimony to resilience, courage, and what is truly possible.

Perhaps you've come across this book by chance, received it as a gift from a friend, or know one of the incredible authors who contributed their stories. Whatever brought you here, trust that you are holding exactly what you need at this moment.

This book is for the woman who wants to thrive and who seeks inspiration in the stories of others rising to their power and purpose. It's for the woman ready to step into alignment, live boldly, and unapologetically claim the life she was meant to live.

Remember:

"A butterfly cannot see its wings, but the rest of us can. You are beautiful, strong, and extraordinary, even if you can't always see it—know that we do."

If this book moves or inspires you, we would love for you to share highlights on social media using the hashtag #WomenThriveBook and tagging us at @womenthrivemedia.

To learn more about our authors or express interest in sharing your own story in a future volume, please visit our website below. Your story matters, and the world is waiting to hear it.

www.womenthrivesummit.com/book

WHY THIS BOOK EXISTS

At Women Thrive Media, we are dedicated to amplifying the voices of inspiring women who have faced life's adversities and emerged stronger. Our mission is to create a global platform where every woman has the opportunity to share her story, knowing her voice matters. Through our book series, we shine a spotlight on remarkable women from all corners of the world, celebrating their courage, resilience, and transformation.

Over the years, as we've collaborated with hundreds of women, one profound truth has emerged: our experiences, struggles, and traumas are more alike than different. These shared journeys remind us of the strength found in the community and the power of vulnerability.

By sharing our stories, we break the silence, liberate ourselves from shame, and empower others to embrace their truth. This book is a collection of deeply personal reflections—of life's challenges, inner dialogues, and incredible transformations. It is a testament to the healing and empowerment that comes from owning and sharing our journeys.

For the authors, the process of writing these stories has been profoundly healing and liberating. Today, as a reader, you become a witness to their courage and transformation, holding in your hands not just a book but a vessel of hope, connection, and inspiration.

This book was created to remind you that you are not alone. Through these stories, we hope you find inspiration, strength, and a sense of solidarity in your own struggles. Whether it rests on your bookshelf, your bedside table, or among your favorite coffee table books, may this anthology serve as a source of encouragement whenever you need it.

We invite you to gift this book to another woman—a friend, a sister, a colleague—so we can continue sharing these empowering stories of women who rise and thrive despite life's challenges. Together, we can spread the message of strength, resilience, and hope across the world.

Through our Women Thrive book series, we aim to provide as many women as possible the opportunity to share their stories and inspire others with their words. These are stories of overcoming, rising, and thriving, and they carry a message of encouragement for us all.

If you're inspired to contribute to a future *Women Thrive* book, we invite you to visit www.womenthrivesummit.com/book and complete our interest form. Your story has the power to inspire the world, and we'd be honored to help you share it.

INTRODUCTION

Dear Reader,

This anthology is a testament to the courage, resilience, and shared humanity of fifteen extraordinary women from across the globe. They come from diverse backgrounds, shaped by unique life experiences, yet united by one powerful purpose: to touch lives through the transformative power of their stories.

Within these pages, you'll find raw, heartfelt accounts—some shared publicly for the very first time. These stories are more than words; they are acts of bravery, vulnerability, and healing. Our authors have dared to revisit their most challenging moments, not only to find strength within themselves but to extend that strength to you, dear reader. Their hope is simple yet profound: that their journeys will spark inspiration, provide comfort, and offer valuable lessons to those who read them.

You may find yourself instantly resonating with some stories, while others might speak to a part of you that has yet to emerge. What doesn't touch you today might hold profound meaning in the future, providing the wisdom you need when life presents its own twists and turns. This is the beauty of these collective narratives—they are as timeless as they are transformative.

Life, as we all know, is a series of highs and lows. It can be breathtakingly beautiful one moment and unexpectedly challenging the next. Some of the women in this book faced adversity from the very start of their lives, while others were met with unforeseen trials later in their journeys. Regardless of when or how their struggles arrived, each of them discovered something extraordinary: purpose in pain, strength in vulnerability, and a path forward when it seemed all hope was lost.

As you delve into these pages, remember that you're not just reading stories—you're holding a survival guide, a source of encouragement, and a beacon of hope. Share this book with others, gift it to someone who might need it, and take a moment to reflect on how these accounts touch your own life. If an author's story resonates deeply with you, let them know. Your words of appreciation could be the greatest reward for their courage in sharing their truth.

Before you turn the page, take a moment to reflect on the image gracing the cover—a girl with flowing hair reaching upward. She embodies hope, resilience, and the unstoppable force of transformation. Her outstretched hand symbolizes the courage to rise, to reach for something greater, even when the path ahead feels uncertain.

The flowing hair represents the natural rhythm of life—the way we are carried forward by its currents, adapting, growing, and finding our strength in the flow. As you embark on this journey through the stories within, let this image remind you that growth is not always linear, and transformation often begins when we dare to reach beyond our comfort zones.

This cover is an invitation to rise above, embrace your own flow, and discover the beauty that lies within your journey. Every time you return to these pages, may it inspire you to keep reaching—toward your dreams, your truth, and the boundless possibilities of who you are becoming.

Let this anthology be more than a collection of stories. May it serve as a companion on your own journey, a reminder of the resilience within you, and a celebration of the strength we all possess to rise above life's adversities. Together, we can shine. Together, we can thrive.

With gratitude and hope,

Raimonda Jankunaite

TABLE OF CONTENTS

1

HAIRLESS AND FEARLESS: A NEW CHAPTER

RAIMONDA JANKUNAITE

Take Off the Mask

I stood in front of the mirror, clippers buzzing in my hand. My reflection felt familiar, like a version of me I had known all along but was just now meeting face-to-face with a new depth of intention. It wasn't intimidating or unsettling; it was inviting. It felt like an invitation to come home to myself, to strip away everything that wasn't truly me. For the first time, I wasn't just thinking about what I looked like—I was thinking about the deeper and more meaningful transformation. And I knew, with absolute clarity, what I needed to do. I needed to take off the mask.

I had been shaving one side of my head for 2 years now. It was an intentional decision, a small but powerful act of transformation and self-expression, and a bold statement of self-empowerment. After a painful long-term relationship breakup and self-reclamation, I decided to shave one side of my head to signify my inner change and the woman I was becoming, who was not afraid to stand out and be who she was meant to be.

Every time I shaved the left side of my head, it reminded me of my strength, and my ability to claim space for myself and step into the person I wanted to be: a bold, brave, and fearless leader. Today, I was not going to shave just one side of my head for a routine shave, I was ready to shave it all off and go completely bald.

I stared at my reflection for a long moment. My heart raced as I pulled a strand of my long, blonde hair to the side in an attempt to shave it off. The doubts started flooding in, louder than the hum of the clippers.

What if you hate it?

What if it doesn't suit you?

What will people think?

Will you still feel beautiful?

I let those thoughts come one by one, but I didn't push them away. Instead, I welcomed them like visitors—temporary guests who needed to be acknowledged before they could leave. I even turned on my camera and started talking to it, spilling out every fear, every hesitation, knowing that one day, I'd look back at this moment and remember the strength it took to move forward.

As I spoke, I realized that those voices of doubt weren't entirely mine. They were echoes of a world that tells women their worth is tied to their beauty—and their beauty is tied to their hair. For centuries, women have been told that long, luscious hair is the ultimate symbol of femininity, health, desirability, wealth, and power. I had spent years internalizing that message without ever questioning it until now.

For so long, I couldn't imagine myself without my hair. My thick, blonde locks had been my signature, my crown. It was the thing people noticed first and often remembered most. I joked that "blondes have more fun," and for a while, it felt true. My hair opened doors for me, brought admiration, and drew attention wherever I went. It made an impact and left an impression.

Especially when I traveled, people treated me differently because of my Eastern European features. Men would approach me, shower me with compliments, and sometimes even beg me to marry them. Yes, as drastic as it sounds, some men made it plain and clear of their intentions. At first, the attention was flattering, but over time, it started to feel suffocating. They weren't drawn to me—they were drawn to the image of me, the idea of a woman they held in their minds.

I remember when a friend referred me to a tech company founder for what was pitched as a well-paid project gig. At the time, I was doing consulting and project work in business and marketing. He invited me to attend a business conference with him in Barcelona, and I was under the impression that he needed my professional expertise to help promote his software. At first, it felt like an exciting opportunity—a chance to use my marketing skills and make meaningful industry connections at this great conference. But it didn't take long for me to realize his true intentions. He didn't value my insights or expertise. He wanted me to stand by his side as a prop to make him look good in front of his peers. It wasn't about collaboration or respect; it was just a cheap marketing ploy disguised as an opportunity.

For years, my hair—and my looks—shaped how the world perceived me. It wasn't just a part of my appearance; it influenced how I was treated. With blonde hair, people noticed me more. I often found myself pursued by men and gaining access to opportunities with surprising ease, all because of how I looked. My long, blonde hair became a symbol of femininity and desirability—a golden key that opened doors. Yet, for much of my life, I remained unaware of how differently I was treated because of it and the unspoken privileges it afforded me.

While I am grateful for those experiences, my hair also became a mask—a confining narrative of societal expectations. It became a look I felt compelled to maintain, a standard I felt obligated to live up to. Over time, it weighed on me, both physically and emotionally.

But on this day, standing in front of the mirror, everything felt different. I wasn't just shaving my head—I was reclaiming myself. With every strand that fell, I shed the expectations, the conformity, and the heavy weight of everything my hair had represented for so long. I didn't know exactly who or what I would find on the other side, but I was ready to meet her.

Let It Be Gone

The decision to shave my hair came from an unexpected, seemingly minor incident. I had booked a hairdresser to come to my house to color my hair. I'd taken a day off from my busy schedule and was genuinely looking forward to her visit. Doing my hair was always a lengthy process—it typically would take three to four hours. I would always try to enjoy it, as otherwise, it can feel like torture if I'm not completely comfortable with the stylist, which has been the case as of late. Trusting someone with my hair has always been essential for me to relax and let them do their job. In this case, while I wasn't entirely sure about my new stylist, her work on Instagram showed that she was one of the most experienced professionals I could find where I live.

In the coming weeks, my schedule was packed with interviews, podcasts, events, and media work, so I really wanted to feel confident and happy with my hair. This hairstylist was my last option after years of trial and error. I'd already gone through hell and back with all the best-recommended stylists in my town in Spain, each experience worse than the last. I'd dealt with burned hair, inexperienced professionals, and more tears than I care to admit. One particularly traumatic visit left chunks of my hair on the floor as the stylist tried to hide the damage by tucking it between her legs. I only discovered the extent of it when I ran my fingers through my hair and realized how much of my hair was falling out. After that visit, I spent double the original cost of the appointment on treatments to repair the damage, so by this point, I was extremely cautious and apprehensive.

When I could, I used to travel to London to see a stylist I had been going to for years. Those visits were planned around my other commitments, and they were exhausting and expensive. I was tired of it all. This new stylist was my last try and my last hope.

When the stylist arrived, she barely greeted me. Her cold demeanor and lack of concern set me on edge immediately. "I don't have any products for you, and I really don't have time to be here for hours today," she said flatly as if she didn't care about the appointment at all. She claimed she misunderstood our messages and was only willing to color my mum's hair and give me a cut, which I did not need. This attitude felt like complete disregard for me as her client. She knew from our previous conversation that I had been through bad hairstyling experiences before, yet her attitude only added insult to injury. It felt like the final slap in the face of a long saga of hairstyling woes. She simply didn't want to deal with me at all.

That was it—the last straw. I felt a surge of frustration and anger boiling inside me. At that moment, I decided I wanted to shave it all off. No more hairstylists, no more appointments, no more disappointment. I was done. Inside, I felt a deep desire to free myself from the cycle and stop fighting this losing battle. I needed a clean slate—literally.

I picked up my phone and called my boyfriend, knowing already what he would say.

"Babe," I said, "I'm going to shave off my hair. I can't deal with this anymore." I explained what had happened that morning, feeling anger, disappointment, and excitement about my decision.

"Do it," he said without hesitation. "You know I'll love you with no hair." His voice was calm and steady, full of reassurance. "But," he added gently, "if you're feeling angry right now, wait. You don't want to do something in the heat of the moment and regret it later."

His words made sense. Was this decision coming from anger and frustration in the heat of the moment, or was this my true, deep desire to go bold? Shaving my head was something I had considered before but had never had the courage to follow through till the end. I wanted to act on an impulse, but I decided to sit with the idea for a bit longer. I went out shopping with my mum to distract myself, but the thought consumed me the entire day. In the car, I finally brought it up. "I'm really thinking about doing it, Mom. Shaving my head."

My mom hesitated. "Are you sure? What about cutting it shorter first? Or trying a new style?" Her concern came from a place of love, and I appreciated her kindness, even though I knew she didn't fully understand the extent of it. She had seen me struggle with hairdressers for years, but this choice still seemed too drastic to her. After hearing my reasoning, she seemed to agree and my heart was settled that she approved. My mum has always been my trusted advisor, so her voice always mattered to me.

Later, I called my sister. Her reaction was immediate: "What? Are you crazy? Don't do it!" She was horrified, unable to understand why I'd consider something so crazy and unthinkable. My sister's hair was her pride—long, luscious, and perfectly gorgeous blonde. She had spent years nurturing it, and she couldn't imagine why I would willingly part with something so many women worked hard to maintain.

But this wasn't about anyone else. It wasn't about my sister, my mom, or even my boyfriend. It was about me—what I wanted, how I felt, and the freedom I craved. I could just imagine the feeling of freedom and a sense of empowerment, and deep down, I craved this transformation. I felt like a caged bird tied to my hair and letting it go was the ultimate feeling of freedom.

When the moment finally came, I was 100% ready and sure I was willing to go through with it. I sat in front of my phone camera in the bathroom, deciding to record the moment that meant so much to me. On another phone I had my boyfriend watching me do it in real time. He was the one to shave one side of the head already over a year ago, and that was the most intimate experience we shared so I wanted him to be part of this moment too. My hands trembled slightly as I smiled at my reflection. "You got this," I said aloud. "If anyone can do this, it's you," he added.

The clippers touched my scalp, buzzing as the first thick lock of hair fell to the floor. I still felt a flicker of fear, but there was no going back. Each pass of the clippers felt like shedding a layer of societal conditioning, external expectations, and conformity. It was liberating.

I picked up a handful of the severed strands and marveled at how something that had once been such a defining part of my identity could now feel so detached. It was just hair, now no longer part of me or an extension of me. With each pass of the clipper, the fear, worry, and regret vanished and were replaced by a sense of freedom and joy.

When I finished, I reached up and cradled my newly bare scalp with both hands. My head felt light—lighter than I'd ever imagined. I hadn't realized the weight I'd been carrying on my head for so long, both literally and figuratively. As my fingers traced the curves of my scalp, I felt as though I was discovering a new part of myself. I closed my eyes and let a wave of emotion rise within me: a deep sense of self-love, acceptance, freedom, and liberation.

For the first time in years, I felt whole. I wasn't hiding anymore—not behind long locks, not behind societal norms. It was finally me, and it felt so good. I looked in the mirror and fell in love with myself in a way I never felt before.

Unconditional Love

The next morning, my 1-year-old daughter woke me up as usual, her sleepy eyes blinking in the soft haze of morning light. When she saw me, her tiny hands reached out to touch my head, her fingers tapping and exploring the smoothness with innocent curiosity. She leaned in to give me her familiar morning kiss and a tight squeeze—almost like an extra hug as if to reassure me. My heart swelled with emotion. At that moment, I realized how pure and simple her love was.

She didn't care about my hair—or the lack of it. She didn't care about beauty standards, societal expectations, or what anyone else thought. To her, I was just her mama—the one who held her, laughed with her, and loved her more than anything in the world. Her unconditional love poured over me like a soothing balm, washing away any lingering doubts or insecurities. In that quiet moment, as I held her close, I let her tiny kisses and hugs remind me of a truth far greater than any fear I had carried: I was enough, just as I was.

Later, I called my boyfriend. When he answered, his excitement was immediate. "You look so beautiful without your hair," he said warmly. "I can't wait to see you and caress your head." His voice carried the steady reassurance I needed, reminding me that he had always seen me as I was—even before I could see myself.

We've known each other for over 15 years, and he has watched me through so many different stages of my life—the highs and lows, the changes, and the challenges. His presence has always felt steady and reassuring. Over the years, he has seen the parts of me that I've struggled to see in myself. Even when I doubted who I was or hid behind layers of protection, he saw me for who I was without judgment.

That conversation felt like a powerful reminder: the person I am today has always been there. I just couldn't see her because I'd been hiding behind a mask. That mask convinced me I needed to be beautiful to be accepted, that I had to look perfect to be loved. For so long, I thought people loved me because of how I looked. I assumed they couldn't see the real me, and, in turn, I began to hide her.

I built walls around my heart, layering on protection to keep people from getting too close. It felt safer that way—to let others see only the surface version of me. It was easier to keep the deeper, truer parts of myself locked away, out of reach. Sharing my dreams, desires, and vulnerabilities felt too risky. What if people didn't understand? What if they didn't accept me?

But in hiding the true me, I not only denied others the chance to see who I really was—I denied myself. I kept myself from being fully authentic, from speaking my truth, from embracing who I was beyond appearances. The world had taught me to stay on the surface, convincing me that no one would care about or understand the deeper layers of who I was. It was as though there were two versions of me: the one everyone saw and the one only a few people, if any, would ever truly know.

I spent a lot of time alone, often by choice. I became a bit of a loner and an introvert, retreating rather than risking vulnerability. But in doing so, I denied myself the chance to fully connect with others, and I denied others the chance to connect with me.

That moment, talking with my boyfriend, reminded me of what it means to be truly seen. Even when I doubted myself, he saw me—through the years, through all the changes, and through the masks I tried to wear. In that moment, I felt lighter, as though the weight of hiding was finally beginning to lift.

Ending My Hair Slavery

The next morning, when I stepped into the shower, I instinctively reached for a hair tie to pull my nonexistent locks into a bun—an old habit that made me pause mid-motion. I caught myself and laughed softly. There was no hair to tie, no more hair to wash.

I felt a renewed sense of excitement bubbling within me. Every movement felt lighter, and freer, as if I had shed not just hair but a lifetime of expectations. I felt deeply empowered.

As the warm water cascaded over my bare scalp, I felt a sense of relief and curiosity. This was my new, free, empowered self. My hands moved over the smoothness of my head, and instead of loss, I felt a strange, beautiful sense of gain.

After drying off, I looked around my bathroom and noticed the rows of expensive hair products lining the shelves—all types of shampoos, treatments, masks, and conditioners—all relics of the struggle I used to endure to maintain the image of my perfect hair. I had invested so much money, time, and effort trying to fit into a mold of beauty that I no longer cared about.

One by one, I began pulling the bottles from the shelves, filling a bag with every single product. I rummaged through cabinets and drawers, finding more of them than I'd even remembered owning. Hair treatments, one more expensive than other, oils, styling products, brushes, combs, clips, hair bands—they all followed.

As the bag grew heavier, I felt lighter. I wasn't just clearing out my bathroom—I was clearing out years of hair slavery, of feeling tethered to a beauty standard that drained more than just my wallet.

I had filled an entire bag with hair products, and as I stared at the now-empty shelves, I smiled and said to myself, no more hair slavery. Liberation had never looked—or felt—so good. I wished that every woman could feel the sense of liberation and empowerment I felt in that moment.

This wasn't just about hair; it was about reclaiming myself. My time, my energy, my power—all back in my hands. It was about not caring about what others expect, think, or want from us as women and truly doing something that made me happy.

My Reflection in the Mirror

The first time I saw myself with no hair in the mirror, it unearthed a memory from nearly a decade ago—a powerful, painful moment that still lingered in the corners of my mind. Back then, I stood in front of a different mirror, staring at a version of myself that others seemed to adore. My reflection in the mirror ten years ago showed a woman with long blonde hair, a radiant smile, and a physique that turned heads wherever I went. I was desired, admired, and envied.

But none of that admiration mattered because, in that reflection, I didn't see beauty—I saw a broken image of myself. Beneath the surface of what others celebrated was a woman battling the shadows of depression. I had just emerged from a toxic relationship that had stripped me of my identity, left me questioning my worth, and robbed me of my voice.

As I stood there, studying the woman in the mirror, I felt a deep disconnect. The reflection seemed like a stranger—polished, perfect, and hollow. I couldn't see who she really was. I couldn't appreciate or admire what others seemed to love. I wasn't kind to myself. My soul ached, and tears streamed down my face.

"Rai," I whispered to the reflection, my voice trembling, "please just speak. I need you to speak up, to find your voice, to restart your life after everything he put you through."

But the reflection gave me nothing in return. I was silenced by my own despair. I did not recognize myself nor see my purpose in life.

For years, I struggled to find my identity, to reconcile who I was with the expectations placed upon me. I couldn't see myself clearly, couldn't love or accept myself as I was. Instead, I gave all my love to others, hoping it would validate my worth. I cared for others more than I cared for myself, believing that if I poured myself into them, I could prove I was a good person, a good woman.

But time and time again, people took what I offered and left me empty. I was a vessel for their needs, their desires, and their expectations, and I had no room left for my own. Disappointment became a constant companion, a reminder that I wasn't living for myself—I was living for the approval of others. I became a reflection of what they wanted me to be, not who I truly was.

Fast forward to today, and the moment I looked in the mirror without my hair felt entirely different. This time, I wasn't searching for approval or validation. This time, I wasn't afraid of the raw, unfiltered version of myself.

For the first time, I saw myself clearly—no adornments, no masks, just me. And I didn't feel broken. I felt whole. The woman staring back at me was bold, unapologetic, and powerful. She carried the scars of battles fought and victories earned. She was someone I admired—not for her perfection but for her resilience, her bold courage, and her unapologetic sense of self.

I smiled at my reflection, not because I had finally become what others expected, but because I had become who I was meant to be. This was a moment of pure self-acceptance, love, and gratitude.

Gratitude for not giving up. Gratitude for taking a stand. Gratitude for empowering myself and healing my traumas and pains.

I no longer needed to be the woman who others approved of—I was the woman I approved of. As I embraced this moment of self-love, I knew I had found something priceless: the ability to see myself for who I truly am and to love her fiercely.

The Long Blonde Hair

Society has long placed a premium on a woman's hair as a marker of beauty and worth. It's woven into the fabric of our culture—hair is seen as deeply personal, a reflection of femininity, and often, a woman's pride. For many, it becomes an emotional cornerstone of identity, something we nurture with care despite the struggles it brings. Yet when hair care goes wrong—a bad cut, damage, or thinning—it can feel like more than just an aesthetic setback. It strikes at our sense of self, unearthing insecurities tied to societal expectations.

This weight of expectation was something I had carried for years, shaped in part by the quiet lessons of my great-aunt Adele. Adele was a remarkable woman, a symbol of strength and tradition in my life. She carried herself with grace, and there was one thing about her that everyone knew: her hair. It wasn't something she flaunted, but you couldn't ignore its presence. Her hair reached her ankles, always gleaming, always cared for with the utmost devotion. Every Sunday, she would sit with her comb and brush, tending to it in a ritual of care and respect. She would put oil in it until it shone, braid it tightly, and then coil it into a bun to keep it protected. Most times, wearing a headscarf as a sign of modesty for an older woman.

To Adele, hair wasn't merely an accessory or a matter of vanity—it was a symbol of pride, heritage, and femininity. She used to say, "Your hair is your crown. A woman's treasure is in how she nurtures it." She didn't preach this loudly, but through her actions and quiet words, she passed on this belief. I admired and loved her deeply, and so I carried some of her lessons with me into my adulthood.

As a child, I would sit on the floor and watch her long fingers skillfully work through the strands, wishing for hair as beautiful as hers. She inspired me to grow my own hair long, to see it as a prized possession, something to protect and nurture.

But as I grew older, that admiration turned more complicated. While Adele's lessons were grounded in tradition and pride, society amplified these messages into a rigid standard of beauty. Hair became less about personal pride and more about fitting into an ideal. Everywhere I turned, the world reinforced the notion that long, beautiful hair was essential to being seen as desirable, feminine, and worthy; it was no longer a choice—it was an expectation.

Modeling Career

When I was between 14 and 16, I tried my hand at modeling. At first, it seemed exciting—a world of professional photoshoots and opportunities that felt glamorous. But very quickly, I found myself dealing with photographers whose behavior made me uncomfortable. Some would push boundaries, suggesting things like nude photos, and I knew right then that modeling wasn't for me. I decided it wasn't a world I wanted to be part of, no matter how much potential it seemed to offer.

That said, I was proud of the work I did during the few professional photoshoots I participated in. But it didn't take long for me to realize I wanted to be known for more than just my looks. I began to see how shallow it all felt. Sure, beauty might get you noticed, but what I truly cared about was living with purpose and meaning—not being defined by appearances.

So, I turned my focus to education. I wanted to push myself as far as I could go. Over the years, I completed high school and earned two college certifications, a business management degree, and a law diploma. For a long time, I was a full-time student, investing in myself and building the foundation I needed to create the life I wanted.

It wasn't just about gaining knowledge—it was about proving to myself that I was more than a pretty face. As an immigrant in the UK, English was not my first language, so I had to work harder than most to attain any opportunities in life. I wanted people to respect me for my intelligence and what I brought to the table. But even as I pursued these achievements, I often found myself fighting against the same old narrative. No matter how much effort I put into proving my worth, it seemed like people still wanted to focus on how I looked.

Challenges in Business

In my mid-20s, as I began building my business, I threw myself into networking events, meetings, and coffee chats, hoping to form meaningful professional connections. But more often than not, these interactions didn't go the way I hoped. What started as business discussions would shift into comments, subtle innuendos, or even blatant advances.

It became exhausting. Every time I thought I was making progress, it felt like my efforts were being overshadowed by the way I looked. I had worked so hard to build my skills, refine my ideas, and present myself as a capable professional, but so often, I was met with ulterior motives.

The frustration really hit me when I started looking for funding for my business. I thought that securing investments would be about pitching my vision and proving my value as an entrepreneur, but instead, I found myself attracting the wrong kind of attention. Too many conversations veered off course, and it felt like people weren't interested in my business—they were interested in me for all the wrong reasons.

This cycle of feeling dismissed or underestimated for my looks took a toll. It started to chip away at my confidence and made me question if everything I had worked for—my education, my experience, my vision—was even worth it.

Women Thrive: Finding My Voice to Champion Others

When I founded Women Thrive Media, I had no idea it would become a movement—a space where women could come together, feel seen, heard, and celebrated. Initially, it was just an idea born out of frustration with the limitations I faced in male-dominated spaces. Time after time, my worth was reduced to my appearance, and my ideas were dismissed or overshadowed by ulterior motives. I realized something had to change—not just for me, but for the countless women who shared similar experiences.

Hosting my first Women in Business event was transformative. Surrounded by ambitious, intelligent women, I experienced a sense of belonging and mutual respect that had been absent in mixed-gender business settings. For the first time, I wasn't worrying about being objectified or underestimated. The energy in that room was electric—supportive, collaborative, and inspiring. It made me realize the power of women coming together to create a space free from judgment, competition, or societal expectations. I knew then that this was where my heart belonged.

What started as one event grew into a platform—a safe space where women could share their stories, ideas, and dreams without fear of being silenced. Women Thrive Media became a platform of empowerment, championing women's voices and encouraging them to embrace their authenticity, confidence, and unapologetic selves. It wasn't just about business or professional growth; it was about cultivating a movement of women who could rewrite their own narratives.

Shaving My Hair: The Catalyst for Speaking My Truth

Shaving my hair was more than just a personal transformation—it became a powerful symbol for the work I was doing with Women Thrive Media. Letting go of my hair liberated me in ways I hadn't anticipated. It was as if I had stripped away the final layer of societal conditioning that had kept me from fully stepping into my truth.

In the weeks following, I felt a new surge of confidence. I stood taller, spoke louder, and allowed myself to be seen—not for how I looked, but for what I stood for. The act of shaving my hair had given me permission to shed not only outdated beauty standards but also the lingering doubts and fears that I wasn't "enough" without the exterior trappings of femininity. I realized that by embracing my authentic self, I was modeling the same empowerment I hoped to inspire in others.

When I spoke with my clients in our group calls post-shave, I noticed that my message resonated more deeply. I saw the way women in the audience leaned in, captivated not just by my words but by the rawness of my journey. They weren't just hearing my story—they were seeing themselves in it. I spoke about the power of owning your story, of choosing to live authentically, and of breaking free from societal expectations. For many women, it wasn't just inspiring—it was a call to action to evaluate how they are showing up. Inside, I felt more empowered and determined than ever before to speak boldly and unapologetically. Anything that was holding me back was gone. My new bald crown has become my new source of strength and inspiration.

A Movement of Unapologetic Women

Through Women Thrive Media, I've met women from all walks of life—entrepreneurs, artists, activists, and everyday heroes—each with a story worth telling. What I've learned is that our power lies in our diversity, in our willingness to embrace who we are, flaws and all, and in the courage to speak our truths. But too often, women are conditioned to silence themselves, to shrink, to conform. I've made it my mission to change that.

Shaving my hair wasn't just a personal act of rebellion; it was a commitment to being unapologetically me, to showing up as my truest self. And in doing so, I found that I could empower others to do the same. It became a reminder to every woman I met that they are more than enough just as they are—that their worth isn't tied to their appearance, status, or the expectations of others.

With every event, podcast, and story we share on Women Thrive Media, I see the ripple effect of empowerment. Women are stepping into their power, using their voices, and embracing their authenticity. The movement has grown beyond me—it's now a community of women lifting each other up, sharing their truths, and championing one another. Together, we are dismantling the barriers that have held us back for generations.

Shaving my hair taught me that true power comes from within. It reminded me that being seen isn't about fitting into a mold—it's about showing up authentically, even if that means defying expectations. That act of letting go helped me unlock a new level of courage and clarity, enabling me to step fully into my role as a leader and advocate for women everywhere.

Today, I look in the mirror and see a woman who is fearless—not because she's without fear, but because she chooses to face it head-on. A woman who no longer hides behind her looks, her achievements, or anyone else's approval. A woman who stands boldly in her truth and encourages others to do the same.

Through Women Thrive Media, I've found my purpose: to amplify women's voices, to create spaces where they can feel safe to be themselves, and to remind them that they are worthy, powerful, and capable of anything. As I continue this journey, I carry the lessons of my own transformation with me—a reminder that when we let go of what no longer serves us, we make room for something greater.

This isn't just my story. It's a story for every woman who has ever doubted her worth, questioned her path, or felt the weight of societal expectations. It's a reminder that we all have the power to rise above, to reclaim our voices, and to thrive unapologetically.

RAIMONDA JANKUNAITE

Raimonda Jankunaite is a speaker, visibility expert, best-selling author, and serial entrepreneur. As the founder of Women Thrive Media, a global platform dedicated to empowering women, she has built a community of over 600,000 followers worldwide. Raimonda is also the visionary behind the Women Thrive Summit, an annual event held in March to honor Women's History Month, bringing together thousands of attendees and showcasing inspiring female voices.

Her passion lies in helping women step into the spotlight, share their stories, and claim their place as thought leaders and speakers. Having overcome her own challenges, including trauma that once took her voice and confidence, Raimonda now empowers others to reclaim their power and live unapologetically.

Through her books, retreats, and programs, including her signature coaching program, UNAPOLOGETIC, Raimonda has helped countless women build visibility, refine their messaging, and create lasting impact. Her work celebrates resilience, community, and the transformative power of storytelling.

Her message is simple but profound: Your story matters, and the world needs to hear it.

Website: www.raimondajankunaite.com

2

BREAKING THE CHAINS: CREATING A LIFE WORTH LIVING

MARCI HOPKINS

"Rock bottom became the solid foundation on which I built my life." - J.K. Rowling

The journey of life can often feel like navigating a maze—filled with unexpected turns, heart-wrenching walls, and sometimes, the disorienting thrill of descent. My journey led me to a point where I could either choose to wither away or rise anew and for me, that decision was etched in time precisely on October 3rd, 2015.

My Last Day of Drinking: A Day Like Any Other

I was pursuing a career in modeling and acting—a dream I had as a teen but was now chasing in my 40s. It felt crazy to fulfill this dream at an older age, but the light inside me never dimmed; it was finally my time to go for it. In the beginning, it was exhilarating, but soon, the weight of being judged in auditions began to take a toll on me. Balancing it all became a struggle. I lived in pain and anger, burdened by the trauma of my past, pushing my feelings deep down while I sought validation and fulfillment through the modeling dream I had always held.

As a mother to my two children, I desperately wanted to shield them from the feelings of abandonment I had experienced from my own parents. I pursued a career I believed would bring me happiness, but it only deepened the self-hatred I felt because of my lack of self-confidence and trust in my own abilities. I often felt like a victim; my husband worked long hours, leaving me feeling alone and overwhelmed. The facade I maintained was exhausting—appearing to have it all together while crumbling inside.

Yet, this day held promise; I had booked a gig (a modeling job) at Short Hills Mall, and I needed to put on a brave face. To model clothes and present the mask of confidence, I shoved aside the chaos in my mind and decided to pretend that everything was just fine. I meticulously arranged my essentials—my outfit laid out on the bed, accompanied by my thermos filled with all-too-familiar liquid courage: wine.

I say goodbye to my children, their innocent faces unaware of the storm brewing beneath the surface. I remember kneeling to embrace them, breathing in their sweetness, and wishing for just a moment that I could be the pillar of strength they needed. As I close the door behind me, I silently hope that perhaps today would be different, that I could momentarily escape my demons.

As I drove towards the mall, I approached the day with a mix of anticipation and dread. Short Hills Mall shimmered on the horizon, a beacon of possibility. I could envision the buzz of excitement, the laughter of friends, and the sound of music setting the stage for my moment on the runway. As I parked the car and gathered my belongings, I was feeling very nervous but I convinced myself that today, I wouldn't need the wine. I could do this. I'd made it through tough situations before; after all, I was a survivor.

The Gig: Spiraling Through the Fashion Show

As I come up the escalator, I start to feel a mix of nerves and excitement. The hustle and bustle of shoppers fills the air, but as I reach the second floor, an unsettling realization awaits me. The atmosphere is eerily quiet. Where are the throngs of people? Where is the music that should be heralding the fashion show? A sinking feeling settles in my stomach, and as I approach the nearest sales representative, my heart races in unimaginable directions.

"Excuse me, where is the fashion show?" I ask, desperately hoping for a glimmer of hope.

His answer rushes over me like icy water—there is no show at this mall. Instead, the event is an hour away at Riverside Mall. I read the email incorrectly from my agent and went to the wrong mall! I live in a constant fog and am so upset with myself for missing that very important information. Time now works against me; my world spins on the precipice of chaos, and long-buried feelings of inadequacy creep back with vicious fervor.

"You will make it," I tell myself, but fear tightens its grip.

I jump back into my car and frantically call my agent, my nerves frayed. After a flurry of conversations, plans are hastily laid out, and I just have to get there. I punch the gas, shifting into a mode of reckless determination.

In the passenger seat sits my thermos filled with liquid courage—aka a water bottle filled with wine. I'm not thinking about any outcome; I'm just thinking I need to settle my nerves. I feel overwhelmed and upset with myself for messing up yet again, so I begin to drink, a quick decision that further entangles my fate.

I finally reach the Riverside Mall, feeling tipsy from the wine but ready to face the job I am booked for: modeling clothing for a high-end clothing brand. I race up the escalator and narrowly make it in time to change and step onto the runway amid cheers and applause. It is only then that I realize those cheers are for me—someone who seems to have everything together but is really drowning inside.

manage to finish the show, thinking I've done a great job, and now I am ready to reward myself. I always do this after an audition or a gig: go for a glass of wine and a meal as a sort of reward. My friend comes to the fashion show to support me, and afterward, we head out for an afternoon filled with lunch and drinks. Although I barely consume any food, I drink enough to forget what I want to escape. In those days, I drank my calories instead of eating them. As I nibble on a piece of fish, I succumb to another drink. I feel like I am spiraling down, but in my intoxication, I am buoyed by a façade of confidence.

When my girlfriend suggests one last drink before parting ways, despite knowing it is the last thing I need, I hopelessly agree. I am not in a position to make rational decisions; my judgment is compromised.

The Wrong Turn

As I sip the last glass of wine, everything begins to blur. The last thing I remember is saying that I need to eat something. My friend must step away because before I know it, I stumble out of the restaurant, my mind engulfed by darkness.

The next moments are a whirlwind—a blur of red and blue lights flashing, voices demanding my attention. Police officers found me parked on the side of the road in my hometown. Someone has noticed my erratic driving and reported me. I am in a blackout; I have no memory of how I got there.

When the officers begin a field sobriety test, I know I am going to fail; I feel so much fear and shame. I get arrested. My heart pounds—not just because of the consequences but also because of how mortified I feel about my actions. Will my husband find out? I am petrified that if he discovers this, he will leave me and take the children. How could I possibly explain this to him? I can't even explain it to myself. I can't understand how things have gotten so bad.

I remember calling a friend—a drinking buddy—hoping she could help me navigate the fallout, wanting to believe in some semblance of a rescue. I do not want my husband to know. I think somehow I will be able to hide what I have done. But soon, I see my husband through the window. He is there to pick me up from the police station. How can this be? I feel betrayed, angry, and afraid. I have so much anger in me from the abuse of my past and live as a victim. I have lost control of the situation, trying to control the outcome of an uncontrollable situation. The familiar waves of anger consume me.

"Why are you here?" I shout at him, anger bubbling over. "How did you find out?" In that moment, the rage I feel overshadows the shame. The police called him to pick me up without my knowing.

We drive home in silence, the weight of unspoken truths pressing heavily in the confined space. Walking through the door of our home, I whisper a hollow apology to the babysitter and say goodnight to my children. I feel ashamed, frustrated, and utterly alone. Embers of anger simmer within me; how can this be my reality? I go to bed, a victim, wondering how this could have happened to me again. I feel like life is always working against me. I do not take responsibility for my actions but instead blame my husband for what has happened. If he had been there more for me, I would not have drunk so much. I feel the burden of the world on my shoulders, trying to pursue a career, caring for my children, and feeling so alone because my husband is always working. I seek every excuse for my drinking instead of facing what is truly at the core of my chaos.

The Cycle of Victimhood

For much of my life, I had played the victim card, often reflecting on my childhood experiences. When I was six years old, I would wake up earlier than my mom and her boyfriend, leaving me to entertain myself. One morning, I found a Tootsie Roll can in their roommate's room and, thinking it was filled with candy, eagerly opened it. To my surprise, it was a bank filled with coins. I decided to take the silver coins, believing they were more valuable than the copper ones, but at that age, I had no understanding of their actual worth. About an hour later, my mom's boyfriend walked into the room, gripped the can, and shook it, noticing it was light. He looked inside and asked me where the money had gone. Terrified of getting in trouble, I played dumb, but he didn't believe me. Ironically, he had intended to give me that money. In a fit of anger, he grabbed my arm and dragged me down the hall to his bedroom while I screamed for him not to hurt me. He ended up beating me right in front of my mom, who just lay in bed as it happened. I was consumed by fear and pain. Afterward, my mom told me it would be okay, reminding me that I shouldn't have taken the money and to stop crying. That day, we were supposed to go to my grandparents' house for a party, and I was instructed to keep the beating a secret. But the pain and hurt became too overwhelming, and I ultimately confided in my grandparents. They responded by kicking my mom and her boyfriend out of the house.

I was given the option to live with my grandparents or go back with my mom—a huge decision for a six-year-old. I opted for my grandparents' home so I could feel safe from my mom's boyfriend and her party lifestyle. You see, my mom was young, drank a lot, and there wasn't much room in her life to care for a child. Because of this, I felt abandoned by my mom, and my dad was never around. My mom and dad got married when I was born to try to be there for their newborn baby, which was me, but they divorced a year later. I never saw my dad until late in life. I lived with my grandparents for safety, but I always dreamed of being back with my mom. All I ever wanted was my mom, her love, and a family— that fairy tale life: me, my mom, and a dad, even if it was a stepdad.

At twelve, when my mother married a man who appeared to be our savior, I thought my dreams were finally coming true. It was shortly after their wedding when I remember going to see the movie *Porky's* with him, a film crafted for adults that I felt special to watch alongside him. His arm wrapped protectively around me; I was only a small 12-year-old, 5'2" and 100 pounds, while he towered at 6'1" and 250 pounds. Safety enveloped me in his presence—how lucky I felt to have such a strong man in my life.

But that moment of comfort turned sinister when I felt his hand slide onto my knee, slowly, in that dark theater. A second later, as if a switch had flipped, fear seized me. I froze. His hand began to wander down my leg. The sensation of safety morphed into raw panic. I pushed against him, but he merely pushed back, attempting to touch me between my legs.

In a rush of adrenaline, I bolted from the seat, tears streaming down my cheeks as I fled the theater. He followed me outside, immediately apologizing, swearing it would never happen again, begging me to promise not to tell my mother. His voice was laced with desperation that echoed within me; somewhere in the depths of my heart, I wished to believe him.

To calm me, he offered a gift, a way to buy my silence—the chance to go on a school trip to Europe, which he had previously deemed unattainable. At that moment, I clung to his reassurance, believing this would be a singular incident, something we'd never revisit. In my youthful mind, I forgave him and placed my trust in him once more.

We went shopping for luggage, a physical representation of my new secret, an unspoken agreement that this would not happen again. I felt elated, but somehow, I also felt the weight of a secret that I couldn't share with anyone. Little did I know that this was only the beginning.

As time moved on, the abuse continued. My stepfather would try to watch porn while I was in the room with him. He would make comments that if I looked a certain way, he would leave my mom for me, and I knew he was doing things to me in my sleep. It was a guttural feeling; my intuition knew, but I just didn't know for sure. I reached a breaking point one day when we went on vacation to Hong Kong. My mom, my stepdad, and I all went by the pool for the day. My stepdad and I left the pool earlier than my mom because I wanted to get dressed for dinner. While he watched TV, I got into the shower. I was in a big glass shower when I looked towards the door and noticed him peeking at me under the slats. Perversion and violation ignited a storm within me, and I jumped out of the shower, outraged and terrified.

My mom came in not too long after. I was acting like nothing happened because I did not know what to do and I was putting my makeup on. I still needed to do my hair. My stepdad wanted us to leave, and my mother complied. I was devastated; you see, I was broken on the inside, but I thought if I could keep myself looking perfect on the outside, I could somehow hold it together. My mom said we could find a place to do my hair. We never did, and we got into a huge fight. I was taking all of my pain out on my mom. The fight got so bad that she started strangling me, and I looked her in the eye, in tears, and shared my fears about the sexual abuse with her, hoping she would finally protect me from this monster. Yet her response shattered me. She did not know what to do at that time and just told me to wear more clothes. So I did.

Like I said, I knew I was being touched during the night; sometimes, I would wake up feeling disoriented. But one fateful night proved my worst fears true—waking up to find his hand between my legs was a violation I could no longer ignore. I turned away in horror, but it left a deep scar.

That experience followed me into school the next day, where I felt like a hollow shell, combating waves of shame and anxiety. Every day had become a relentless battle, a struggle to mask the pain inside. Home became a battlefield of emotions, and I felt desperate to escape. I contemplated ending my life many times, feeling utterly defeated.

That day, when I came home from school, my mom could tell that something was very wrong. I finally confided in her about that most recent incident, hoping she would finally leave him. Instead, all I got was a call to a helpline. I thought she finally recognized the urgency.

However, when my stepfather denied everything, suggesting I had wanted it, my mother's loyalties felt divided. I was left wondering if she truly believed me, and ultimately, we didn't leave. She stayed with him, and a few months later, we relocated to a different part of Houston, The Woodlands, moving yet again. I had moved so many times in my life. I could not believe I would have to start over again, but I did.

In my new environment, I struggled. I didn't recall much about that house with my mom and stepdad—it was as though I existed in a fog. All that mattered was the façade I needed to maintain—if I looked perfect on the outside, perhaps the pain and destruction raging within me could remain hidden. My mom had done it for so many years; why couldn't I?

My mother finally divorced him just before my senior year. I was relieved yet still unsettled by the years of upheaval. I begged her not to move from The Woodlands and uproot us again. I longed for stability in my final year of high school. I just couldn't start over again. She agreed to stay so I could finish my high school years in The Woodlands, and we settled into a small home, but my mom's drinking spiraled out of control. She had always been a drinker, but she had always had someone else caring for her, like a boyfriend or a husband. Now, it was just her and me. I found myself playing the role of caretaker—taking on responsibilities in a house where I felt isolated and neglected.

I despised my mom for the way she was. She was so consumed with her own pain and addiction that she had no capacity to care for me. I never wanted to be like her, yet I found myself on a similar path, using alcohol as an escape from the chaos of my life. I thought it could mask the overwhelming emotions and feelings of hopelessness. For years, I struggled with addiction until I reached a point of reckoning the moment I wound up at my rock bottom.

The Day I Surrendered and Felt True Love

When I awoke the morning after my DUI, everything felt surreal—waking up in a haze of regret and self-reflection in the guest room. As I navigated through agonizing pain, I faced a stark truth: I was an alcoholic. With this admission came a wave of clarity, as if unveiling my true self for the first time.

I knew I could no longer avoid confronting my husband. The weight of my actions loomed, and I had to face the music. Slowly, I walked down the stairs, each step feeling monumental, my heart racing as I approached the living room.

My husband Ray sat there, and the tension hung thick. I thought he hated me, would scream at me, and never forgive me. I sank into the couch and burst into tears. The anger from the previous day had dissipated, and a profound sense of defeat took over me. For once, I acknowledged, "I'm an alcoholic."

His arms enveloped me in a much-needed embrace, and at that moment, I felt a release—a pouring out of all the pain I had harbored. I no longer had to pretend. There, in that space, entirely stripped of pretenses, I was safe. I surrendered.

The tears flowed as he held me tightly, conveying the type of love I had longed for my entire life. I had been drowning in a sea of chaos, but here was my opportunity to rise anew. I was struck by the revelation that amidst the years of pain and turmoil, I had overlooked the very person who stood by me all along. In that moment I felt the weight of the world fall from my shoulders, and a warmth overcome me that I never knew was possible. It was the feeling of love-the one thing I had sought all of my life, and I was finally feeling it for the first time. It was magical.

The Awakening

With that embrace, I made an irrevocable commitment. I would no longer indulge in the temporary relief that the alcohol provided; I would get sober—for me, for him, and for our children. This was a pivotal awakening—a crossroads in my life that promised renewal and hope.

The journey ahead wouldn't be easy. Numerous challenges awaited me, but for the first time, I felt the faint glimmer of optimism cutting through the dark clouds that had overshadowed my existence.

My Healing Journey Began

The very day I made that commitment marked the beginning of my healing journey. I was filled with a mix of fear and determination as I sought help. My first step unfolded as I attended an Alcoholics Anonymous meeting. Ray drove me, our children in tow, as my heart raced with trepidation.

Upon arriving at the meeting space, I felt a whirlwind of emotions weighing heavily on my shoulders. The air felt thick with stories of struggle, pain, and, ultimately, the promise of recovery. As I stepped inside, I was met with familiar faces, including Debbie, whom I had met during a previous attempt at sobriety. Last year, I tried to get sober, but at that time, I didn't truly believe I had a problem. I compared my story to others in the room, which swayed my judgment. I thought to myself, 'I don't drink like them, so I must not be an alcoholic.' It's easy to get caught up in your own head and convince yourself that you don't have a problem with alcohol, and that's exactly what I had done. So, I began drinking again, and it was worse than ever before. I needed a huge consequence to finally accept that my drinking was not normal and I had an addiction. This time, I was ready to do the work-whatever-and I fully believed that I had alcohol use disorder.

She greeted me with warmth and kindness that infused me with a sense of belonging—even as I felt utterly broken inside. I was hungover, but my spirit yearned for connection and healing.

"I'm here," I whispered to myself as we began our journey.

Every face in that room carried stories of hardships and resilience. I introduced myself as an alcoholic, a gesture that felt crucial to my adolescence of healing. I was not alone; we were kindred spirits woven together by the threads of shared experiences.

As I listened to other participants share their journeys, I began to reconnect with the parts of me that had been lost to alcohol. I felt the fog of shame begin to lift; I was not unique in my struggles. Surrounded by others who were going through the same challenges, I understood that I was not alone in my addiction.

The Weight of Shame

I soon realized that the weight of guilt I carried was a burden I had imposed upon myself. How many nights had I laid awake, grappling with shame and self-loathing? It was in the fellowship of that room that I began to unearth the roots of my pain.

I sat with my eyes closed, absorbing the collective strength of each person's story. Their words resonated within me, pulling back the layers of my own trauma. I remembered the feelings of suffocation and blame I had harbored for so long.

Deep down, I knew these emotions had been stifling, and the ritual of sharing was slowly unraveling the weight of the story that I carried for so long. I had been taught to keep my feelings and experiences quiet, which only kept me sick. The more I shared, the more I let down the walls I had built, and the more I began to heal. I was finally in a place where I was encouraged to speak, and the more that I listened to others share, I found the voice I had lost so many years ago.

Embracing Vulnerability

Each subsequent meeting illuminated different facets of my soul. I began to open up, share my story, and connect with those who understood. I bonded with Debbie and established a path of accountability; she became my guiding light, ushering me through the steps of recovery.

As weeks morphed into months, I discovered the art of vulnerability. I learned to express my emotions—to not shy away from feelings I had previously drowned. For the first time, I felt growth and healing intertwining. I was embarking on a journey toward becoming my true self.

But healing often felt like peeling back layers of an onion; each tear brought discomfort accompanied by more profound revelations. I was unearthing memories and emotions that had been festering, and often, I felt the weight of this discovery overwhelming.

Challenging the Past

One day, during a particularly poignant meeting, someone spoke about breaking free from generational cycles. Their words echoed in my mind for days, stirring memories of apprehension and vulnerability. I realized my parents' relationship, my experience of abuse, abandonment, and their addiction had shaped my perceptions of relationships and trust. The unhealed wounds from my childhood were influencing how I navigated my interactions in adulthood.

The past had a powerful hold on me; it was a story I had used as my shield. However, the truth of my experiences had become a part of my identity. It was time to challenge my belief that I had put up a front and acted strong when, in reality, I was struggling to manage the pain deep in my soul. I began to embrace the idea that I could rewrite my story.

I began exploring deeper paths of self-discovery through meditation, journaling, reading books on recovery, and engaging with other individuals who offered hope. Each step demanded honesty, accountability, and introspection.

The Divine Connection

As I began to deepen my understanding of recovery, I felt my spirituality change. I turned to prayer, establishing a connection with a divine force. During quiet moments, I would visit the chapel attached to the meeting hall. The silence enveloped me, providing a sense of safety and hope.

In those sacred hours, I would kneel and pray at the altar, pouring out my heart to God, speaking the things I had longed to voice—my fears, anguish, hopes, and desires for change. I fervently asked for guidance and, perhaps most importantly, solitude from the grip of alcohol.

Within that sacred space, nestled amid soft candlelight and the playful dance of shadows, I allowed myself to open my heart to the possibility of renewal. The stained-glass imagery of Jesus cradling a lamb began to symbolize the sense of protection I longed for.

In my prayers, I envisioned myself as that sheep—tender, vulnerable, and seeking guidance. I begged for strength and promised to rekindle my connection to the spirit if He could help guide me through this phase.

Finding My Purpose

As I navigated the waters of recovery, I realized the importance of purpose. My journey became more than personal; it evolved into a mission I felt compelled to share. Stories of resilience from the people in my meetings stirred something profound within me.

I felt called to help others, so I launched my talk show, *Wake Up with Marci*. My show is dedicated to sharing inspiring stories of triumph to spread hope and remind others that they are not alone. Today Wake Up is airing in New York and New Jersey on WLNY-TV, Hulu Live, Fubo TV, and in other markets such as Palm Springs, Santa Barbara, and Idaho Falls.

From Trauma to Triumph

As my mission and healing grew, I felt guided by God to write my memoir, *Chaos to Clarity: Seeing the Signs and Breaking the Cycles*. I poured my heart into the pages, expressing the intricacies of my journey through trauma, alcohol use disorder, recovery, self-love, and a newfound spiritual connection. This book became my catharsis, a powerful medium through which I could shed the burdens of my past and drive meaningful conversations about trauma, recovery, and the importance of breaking generational cycles.

Within those pages, I revisited my childhood and the myriad experiences that shaped me. I wrote about my alcoholic mother, the first moments of betrayal by my stepfather, the confusion I felt, and the misplaced trust that turned into anguish. I explored how these early experiences led me down a path of addiction, unhealthy relationships, and confusion.

At the heart of *Chaos to Clarity* is the message of overcoming adversity and finding light amid chaos. My book sheds light on the dark realities of sexual, physical, and mental abuse and how I transitioned from victim to survivor, ultimately living a life beyond my wildest dreams. I weave my story of recovery throughout the pages, inviting engagement, reflection, and introspection as I create a pathway to healing for readers seeking more joy through the recognition of their own worth. I offer insights for mindset growth through gratitude, forgiveness, and daily meditation.

A Path to Self-love

Through my healing journey, I learned the immense importance of self-love. It became clear that I had to confront the patterns of self-sabotage tightly woven into the fabric of my being. The voices of negativity and doubt that echoed from my past could no longer dictate my present.

I began a daily practice focused on gratitude, intentionally articulating three things I was thankful for each morning. I would write them down, perhaps reflecting on the warmth of sunlight spilling through my window or the laughter of my children that echoed in the halls. This process grounded me, anchoring my thoughts as I embraced the day ahead.

Meditation became a cornerstone of my recovery, a quiet time where I could connect with my higher power. In those moments of stillness, I learned to quiet the chaos, to listen to the whispers of my spirit that longed for authenticity. As I embraced mindfulness, I slowly let go of perfectionism, realizing that life was imperfect, and so was I.

With this newfound courage, I began facing my fears head-on. I no longer saw them as insurmountable walls but rather as barriers I could chip away at, piece by piece. I spoke openly about my past and my struggles, baring my soul to friends and family, and inspiring them to share their own stories as well. We formed a community of support, celebrating each other's milestones and bolstering one another during challenges.

Breaking Generational Cycles

As my understanding of generational trauma deepened, I vowed to break the cycles that had plagued my family for years. Looking into the eyes of my children, I felt a swell of responsibility—a fierce determination to cultivate an environment that might shield them from the pain I had endured.

I realized it was my responsibility to create a different narrative for my children; I would nurture an environment of love and acceptance they deserved. Throughout this process, I learned that love begins with oneself. Through the practice of self-compassion, I could foster healthier relationships—not only with my children but also with myself.

As I embraced vulnerability, I became a source of strength for my children. I intentionally created spaces for open dialogues, allowing them to voice their feelings, and their worries—teaching them that it was safe to express their emotions. We'd share moments at the dinner table, discussing our highs and lows of the day, knitting trust into the fabric of our family dynamics, allowing my kids to see me evolve from a woman lost in her struggles to one striving for personal growth and healing.

The Road Ahead

Reflecting on the winding path I've walked thus far, it becomes apparent that healing is not linear. Each day presents new challenges, fears, and realizations. But beneath the surface, there exists a beautiful tapestry of growth and transformation sewn together by love, forgiveness, and understanding.

Through my work, my writing, and my show, I began to create a movement—one that embraced transparency and support. I rediscovered my voice, realizing that my purpose was to empower others who were struggling, to uplift them, reminding them that they are not alone. These newfound connections became my lifeline; the relationships I cultivated were rooted in genuine understanding and empathy.

Soon, I was invited to speak at conferences, workshops, and schools, sharing the lessons I had learned and the importance of seeking help, breaking cycles, and fostering a spirit of resilience. Every story I shared felt like a piece of a greater puzzle—one that celebrated survival and tenacity. I wanted to plant seeds of hope in the minds of others that there is always a way out of darkness, a route toward the light.

To All the Women Out There

To all those navigating their own personal battles—be gentle with yourself. Open your heart to the love surrounding you, for it is through vulnerability and surrender that true healing begins. Embrace the journey towards self-discovery and empowerment. Remember, your past does not define your worth; it offers a chance to build a foundation rooted in strength, resilience, and unwavering self-love.

As I engage with individuals from all walks of life, I continually find inspiration in their stories. This exchange of narratives—rich with pain yet overflowing with courage—fuels my own journey and reassures me of the human capacity for healing.

The most beautiful part of this ongoing journey is recognizing that we are not defined by our trauma; rather, we are shaped by how we choose to rise from it. Sharing our stories is an act of rebellion against the silence that so often accompanies pain. In unraveling our truths, we provide comfort to others—whispers of hope that they, too, can transcend their struggles.

Today, I stand before you not only as a survivor of my past but as a beacon of hope for others. My rock bottom may have marked a painful chapter of my life, but it has also paved the way for my metamorphosis into a woman of strength and conviction. I invite you to join me on this journey of recovery, self-love, and empowerment—the stories we share, the lives we touch, will resonate far beyond our understanding. Together, let us forge paths of healing and light, illuminating the way for those who may still find themselves lost in the darkness.

MARCI HOPKINS

Marci Hopkins is a multifaceted powerhouse in the media world, renowned for her transformative impact as an award-winning TV host, creator, executive producer, author, motivational speaker, inventor, and mental health advocate. As the driving force behind the acclaimed talk show "Wake Up with Marci," she has earned multiple accolades, including three prestigious Telly Awards and two Anthem Awards, solidifying her status as a leader in inspirational broadcasting. Marci is also the acclaimed author of the International Impact Award-winning book, "Chaos to Clarity: Seeing the Signs and Breaking the Cycles," which has made waves by ranking as the #1 new release on Amazon in the 12-Step Recovery category. This memoir explores her journey through addiction, recovery, spirituality, and self-development, providing readers with tools to break free from their own cycles and find clarity.

Through her work, Marci not only entertains but also empowers, guiding individuals on their paths to healing and personal growth. With her infectious passion and unwavering dedication, she ignites the spark of possibility in everyone she encounters, inspiring them to embrace change and live their most authentic lives. Her fearless and engaging presence on screen allows her to delve into a diverse array of topics on her show, ranging from mental health and women's health to self-improvement, social impact, and wellness. Through candid conversations with her guests, Marci's mission is to inspire and empower her audience while instilling hope and happiness.

Beyond her professional achievements, Marci is a devoted mother, philanthropist, and survivor of sexual abuse. With over nine years of sobriety, she is dedicated to helping others lead fulfilling and joyful lives. Marci Hopkins exemplifies strength, resilience, and a relentless commitment to making a positive impact on the world.

Website: https://wakeupwithmarci.com

3

THE POWER OF ABUNDANT RELATIONSHIPS AND THE PERSONAL TRANSFORMATION THEY BRING: HEALING AND THRIVING BEYOND TRAUMA

KARMIN REEVES JENKINS

My Formative Years

A sense of emotional scarcity marked my childhood; I often felt undervalued and struggled with low self-esteem. I sought acceptance from men who frequently placed conditions on our relationships, unaware of my love languages, which included words of affirmation, quality time, and physical touch. When I was eight years old, I learned that the man I loved as my father was not my biological dad, which shattered my sense of stability.

After my mother separated from my stepfather, I met my biological father while he was in prison. Our meetings ignited a curiosity and desire for connection, but the disruption of my family structure deeply impacted my academic performance and emotional well-being. Insecurity led to my having an abortion during my high school years.

At school, I faced numerous challenges. I struggled to express myself and felt isolated from my peers, many of whom had present father figures. The tumultuous relationship between my biological parents filled our home with tension and conflict, leading to police visits during my middle school years, which left me feeling embarrassed and ashamed.

As I grew older, I learned I had siblings from my biological father's previous marriage. Although we met several times, I struggled to form meaningful connections with them, which deepened my rejection, especially since I did not share my father's last name.

Despite these challenges, I found comfort in building relationships with extended family members. Ultimately, my journey reflects the transformative power of relationships, which have shaped my path to healing and self-acceptance.

My mother and stepfather separated when I was about eight or nine years old, and they never reunited. I saw my stepfather a few times after their split but eventually lost contact with him. Not long after their separation, I began to build a relationship with my biological father. I met him for the first time while he was in prison. He was a handsome man with a dark chocolate complexion, and I noticed some resemblance in his eyes, nose, and smile, which felt fulfilling.

I remember him asking me many questions and showing genuine interest in my life. As I continued to visit him, my curiosity about our connection and similarities grew.

My mother and I would take a Greyhound bus to see him, and I spent the entire journey thinking about what I wanted to say and the topics we would discuss.

Over time, I began to have regular contact with my biological father while he served his prison sentence. After his parole, he moved in with my mother and me.

The disruption of our family structure significantly impacted my stability during my developmental years, especially in school. I struggled with memorization in math, science, history, grammar, punctuation, sentence structure, vocabulary, printing, and cursive writing. To this day, I still face some academic challenges. Although I love learning, test-taking and writing papers remain particularly daunting.

Despite facing significant challenges, I am proud to have earned a master's degree in Social Sciences, become a published author and speaker. I retired as a Major in the United States Army Reserve, while holding a senior pay grade with the federal government.

I kept my thoughts and emotions to myself for much of my life. I often felt like I had lost my voice and seldom communicated my feelings to others. As a child, I was very observant and generally kept my opinions and desires to myself. I felt like what I wanted would not matter.

I was about 13 years old when I discovered that my biological father had three other children living in our city and that he had been married to their mother when I was very young. I learned that I have a sister six days older than me.

My siblings never accepted me as a sister; as I matured, it became less important to have contact. Tragically, my youngest sister and brother have since passed away, leaving me with deep feelings of rejection because they did not take me as part of the family.

I moved forward without having any sibling relationships and bottling up my related emotions. I told myself it was okay if I could not be a part of their lives, but I was lying.

Growing up without siblings made me feel like I didn't belong and left a hole in my heart. This emphasized my feelings of not fitting in.

Like many young girls of that time, I kept a diary recording my hopes and dreams. I envisioned a husband who would love and understand me, a partner for life, one set of twins, a fulfilling job, and a lovely house.

Like most teenagers, I experienced typical childhood moments; my parents rarely had to discipline or scold me for not completing tasks.

Although I was not a perfect child and did have my share of disobedience, there were things my parents never knew about me.

After attending eight different schools from elementary through high school and enduring sexual abuse and abortion during my sophomore year, I found the resilience to graduate from high school in June 1978.

My beloved mother and my uncle, her youngest brother who had served in the Army, devised a plan for me to join the military after graduation. They pooled their ideas and met with a recruiter to discuss my options. A month after graduating, and completing initial military training, I found myself heading to Berlin, Germany.

At that time, I was emotionally and psychologically immature, intellectually naive, and spiritually vulnerable. I was venturing into the world alone, having never spent more than a week away from home, and it felt like I had to grow up overnight.

I participated in activities that brought me joy, especially track and field. My favorite events were the 200-yard dash and the 4x400 relay. Occasionally, my high school coach would place me in the long jump and high jump to help our team earn points in various competitions.

Being part of the track team taught me many valuable lessons, such as the importance of preparation, developing skills and talent, understanding my limitations, maintaining a healthy diet and structured exercise, and staying focused.

I also learned the significance of consistency, resilience, reliability, dependability, teamwork, following guidance, persistence, and finding satisfaction in doing my best. At the time, I didn't realize that these lessons would be essential in my adult life.

My early experiences in sports helped prepare me for my service as an Army soldier and my work with government and non-government organizations. I also learned the importance of being part of a unified group, which helped me navigate marriage and parenting.

I remember my first leadership assignment in Germany, where I served as the administrative leader for the OB-GYN Clinic. The skills and resilience I developed through my family life and athletic involvement equipped me to lead effectively and persevere during challenging times.

My Adult Years

I carried a lack of confidence and unhealthy coping behaviors into my Army career. It took me about five years to adjust to the military culture and embrace my adult self. Throughout my mid-20s, I mourned my childhood, the family I didn't have, and the time I spent away from home.

I struggled to reconcile the conflicts between my needs, the realities of the distance between myself and my siblings, and the relational conflicts in my family. I yearned for close relationships, friendships, and healthy kinships.

The little girl inside me sought unconditional love in all the wrong places and struggled to understand how to find it. Although intimate relationships were uncomfortable, I still longed for a boyfriend, engagement, marriage, and starting a family.

During my first four years of military service, I faced racism, sexism, sexual harassment, and two instances of sexual assault. These experiences deepened my low self-esteem and caused me to withdraw further into myself. I became short-tempered and impatient with others; I felt seen but not heard or respected. I completed my job satisfactorily but contributed no more than what was required.

I developed a love for music and dancing during my teenage years, which became essential to my coping mechanisms. I enjoyed hanging out with friends and dancing.

Joining the Army allowed me to drink alcohol at 18, which I used as a way to cope and feel like I fit in. Drinking alcohol and smoking cigarettes helped me be more social and connect with others who drank and smoked. Every military assignment in the first 9 years of my career was close to a club that served alcoholic beverages.

The time I spent away from home was extremely challenging. I focused too much on trying to meet expectations, being overly social, fitting in, and seeking unconditional love, acceptance, validation, and significance. I became a combination of the healthy and unhealthy aspects of my childhood. I was an overachiever, self-critical, success-driven, emotionally gated, and insecure woman. I had promised not to allow anyone to hurt or mislead me like in previous occurrences.

Then, I met the man who would become my spouse. We were both in the Army. He was the first man I felt could be serious about being in a committed relationship. During one conversation, he said, "You are better than the life you're living." Those words touched my heart in a way I couldn't even describe.

He encouraged me to quit smoking, spend less time in local clubs, go to college, and plan for a better future. His words changed my perspective. For the first time, I began to see myself as beautiful, capable, and worthy of things I had not recognized in myself before. No man since my father or grandfather had ever spoken to me so meaningfully. Not long after, I quit smoking and only consumed alcohol occasionally.

Healthy relationships became more important than fitting in with a social group. For the first time, I truly felt seen and valued by someone outside my family. I was happy in our dating relationship, which lasted about two years before we married.

In March 1987, I had the opportunity to participate in a Reserve Officer Training Corps (ROTC) program, which was a valuable choice. However, returning to Cleveland, Ohio, and getting married later that same year felt overwhelming. When you're young, it is easy to develop an invincible attitude that can cloud reasonable decision-making.

My college studies were completed in May 1990, and I moved to West Point, New York, to join my spouse. Later, he received an assignment in Korea, and we agreed that I would use that time to return to Cleveland and complete a one-year Masters degree program in Social Science Administration.

Our first child was a toddler at the time, and I was juggling a long-distance marriage, my studies, and a part-time job.

As adult responsibilities piled up, they highlighted my strengths and some unresolved issues, leading me to seek individual therapy and later marital counseling.

The Mid-Life Years

Our second child, a son, was born in January 1997. Despite the multiple challenges of a military lifestyle and frequent adjustments, we overcame many obstacles.

After many years of sacrifice, struggle, and joint commitments, in 2019, my spouse and I separated after 32 years of marriage.

I had never felt the depth, degree of defeat, anger, and undeserving of the situation up to that point. I felt robbed of the love we once shared and utterly hopeless and powerless to move forward.

My internal resources, coping skills, and positive self-talk let me down. The methods I had relied on to face life's difficulties no longer worked. I felt empty, having exhausted all my resources.

I reached a point where my whole world collapsed. I concluded that we had been busy doing and getting things, missing the essential elements of building a cohesive marital relationship.

The reality was that there was nothing more I could do to save our marriage, and I thought there was no reason to continue living. I desperately wanted to be a wife and to share our lives; my heart was in great pain, shattered beyond my ability to piece it back together. The hope I had clung to that we would overcome had faded in the distance, as did our marriage.

I did not realize for so long that my love for him was no longer enough to keep him connected to me. At this point, nothing would salvage my heart, mind, or emotions.

My spouse now knows that I secretly took several pain pills, hoping to end my life about a year before his moving out of our home. I just wanted the pain and disappointment to be over. I had stopped fighting for myself and our marriage. I couldn't see the point of living.

I'm still alive and have stayed in our house, which now feels like home.

My first experience going to a monthly food bank was during the first three years of our separation. I frequently shopped at thrift stores and consignment shops and had to cut back on many self-care activities such as manicures, pedicures, and haircuts.

Often, I found myself choosing between paying bills and nonessentials. Eventually, I learned to handle much of my beauty care and limited other luxuries.

By 2024, my financial situation, emotional well-being, and spiritual health have significantly improved. I have resumed attending dinners, going to the cinema, and enjoying monthly self-care sessions.

I now have a strong fearless sense of self-love and embrace everything about who I am. The first few years of separation were emotionally challenging for me, filled with constant reminders of what once was and financial difficulties. I was grateful that my spouse continued to cover most of the bills until we could establish new economic arrangements. Even today, he still helps with the mortgage and some other expenses.

Since fully retiring, experiencing marital separation, and navigating the societal changes brought on by COVID-19, I have learned to live with less and find satisfaction in that simplicity. I plan solo vacations and engage in regular activities because I know I am worth it.

Forgiveness has been a crucial component of my relationships throughout my youth and adulthood. I have learned that holding onto resentment can prevent us from living abundantly.

I had to start by forgiving myself for all I had internalized as my fault, and then I needed to forgive my spouse. Initially, this process was challenging. At 59 years old, I found myself living alone and restructuring my life from what it had once been as a married woman. However, with the support of my close friends and family, I managed to make this transition.

After letting go of the past and embracing my truth, my spouse and I began interacting cordially.

As part of this transformative process of forgiveness, I reflected on my parents' roles in my life. I realized that leaving home was one of the best opportunities I could have received. The love my mother gave me played a significant role in my healing.

It became clear to me that she wanted a better life for me than the one she had, which marked a pivotal shift in my mindset. In her words, "Karmin, you are my greatest accomplishment."

I miss my parents' physical presence, especially on birthdays, holidays, and other special occasions. During difficult times, I can hear their voices in my heart and mind, imagining what they would say, which comforts me.

For a long time, I resented my mother for encouraging me to join the Army. I didn't fully commit and held on to some anger. However, as I matured and saw the military's opportunities, I embraced the culture and resources. During difficult times, I can hear their voices in my heart and mind, imagining what they would say, which comforts me. My mother was strong, intelligent, intuitive, wise, and loving.

Although I did not understand and appreciate many things as a young girl, once I married and had children, I began to value her presence in my life. I often wonder what my life would have been like if I had stayed in Cleveland, Ohio. Would I have found stable employment, completed a college degree, been a wife, and had the wonderful children and grandchildren who are now part of my life?

My relationship with my biological father was positive. I am grateful he lived long enough to walk me down the aisle on my wedding day. Although he had some emotional challenges, he gave what he could and was there for me when it mattered most. Unfortunately, he didn't live long enough to meet my children or grandchildren, but I know he would have cherished the role of grandfather and great-grandfather.

As my mother aged and required 24-hour care, I felt honored to provide and coordinate her care. She had dedicated her life to giving me the best possible opportunities, and I could do the same for her.

I will never forget her sacrifices or how her eyes would light up when she spoke about her daughter becoming an officer in the Army. Before she passed away, she had no regrets and was happy being a grandmother. During that time, we were able to mend cracks in our relationship and heal together.

All the men I have mentioned so far as caretakers, spiritual supports, and my spouse came into my life at critical times when I needed more stabilization. My biological father provided the fatherly figure I required during my upbringing, my spouse was a life partner, my Bishop served as an elderly male figure, and my Senior Pastor was like an older brother.

Now, the wisdom, protection, security, and love they offered is gone.

They have all departed from my life as dependable emotional-spiritual supports, either through death or by conscious choice.

Interpersonal connections like these have significantly enhanced my life and filled the gaps from my childhood. Thus, helping other women develop healthy mother-father-daughter relationships is essential for me because I understand the challenges and benefits involved.

Confidently and intentionally, I know my purpose is to assist women, military women veterans, and parents of adult daughters to thrive in their identity and lifestyle. Now more than ever, I recognize that the quality of relationships matters more than the quantity of people in my life. I have much to be thankful for and a wealth of wisdom to share with others.

My family research has taught me about generations that have overcome substantial opposition; the genealogical exploration led to tracing my lineage back to 1860. This exploration of my family history has instilled in me a profound appreciation for the era in which I was born.

Interpersonal connections like these have significantly enhanced my life and filled gaps from my childhood. Helping other women develop healthy mother-father-daughter relationships is essential because I understand the challenges and benefits.

I know a lot about the power of abundant relationships and the personal transformation they bring.

Today, I have restored my purpose: to assist military women, veterans, and parents of adult daughters in thriving. Now more than ever, I recognize that the quality of relationships matters more than the quantity of people in my life. I have much to be thankful for and a wealth of wisdom to share with others.

My family research has taught me about generations that have overcome substantial obstacles, allowing me to trace my lineage back to 1860. This exploration of my family history has instilled in me a profound appreciation for the era in which I was born.

Although my life has not turned out as I imagined it would when I was a little girl, I am genuinely grateful for the life I have.

As a child, I struggled to navigate life and carried a lack of emotional strength into adulthood. However, I now feel empowered to overcome any obstacle.

Choosing a career in social work was no coincidence; providing life coaching feels part of my destiny.

I am intrinsically motivated to confront challenges and strive to be my best self for myself and others.

My pursuit of self-improvement and authenticity led me to participate in several weeks of Axiogenic Coaching in January 2024.

Axiogenics is a science-based approach that measures and enhances the quality of thinking and performance by integrating mind-brain science and value generation.

This coaching experience was invaluable for exploring my emotional and social intelligence and understanding how these factors influence my behavior. I gained tools that transform negative thought patterns and feelings into positive outcomes. Instead of ignoring my challenges, I have learned to turn them into assets and focus on value-added solutions.

A key takeaway from my coaching is a central question I ask myself daily regarding all relationships: "What choice can I make? What action can I take now to create the greatest net value?" With this mindset, I can respond and move forward as my best self, integrating the principles and theories from this experience into my coaching style.

As an empowered life coach and licensed clinical social worker, I prioritize self-care and abundant living. This includes having a personal coach and seeking clinical counseling to enhance my mental health and well-being.

Life continues to present challenges. On November 2, 2024, while driving home alone from a social gathering, I was involved in a three-car accident on a major interstate, thankfully resulting in no fatalities.

My 2015 car was totaled, and I sustained a mild concussion. Additionally, my right eye was injured, requiring sutures for a laceration and surgery to repair a fractured occipital bone.

Whenever I reflect on the accident, my heart skips a beat, my eyes sometimes well up with tears, and I smile with gratitude for what could have been.

I am incredibly thankful for my life; the only loss was my vehicle. I am grateful that I did not lose any limbs, my vision, or another life wasn't taken.

Kintsugi, or kintsukuroi, is a traditional Japanese art form that translates to "golden repair." This technique involves fixing broken pottery by mending the fractured areas with urushi lacquer mixed with powdered gold, silver, or platinum.

The philosophy behind Kintsugi is phenomenal because it considers that what was broken can be repaired and become something beautiful. Kintsugi restores objects regardless of their flaws and does not try to disguise any aspects of them. In life, various perspectives exist regarding the value of broken things; often, we discard items without considering the potential for restoration.

Unfortunately, in some societies, people are treated as disposable. I feel an overwhelming sense of gratitude for having come to understand my worth, value, and life purpose.

I have forgiven myself and my spouse for the state of our marriage. I have learned to enjoy life without approval or the conditions placed on me by others. I love myself for who I am, and I don't feel alone. I travel on solo vacations, dine out, watch movies, attend events, and participate in entrepreneur gatherings.

I refuse to be bound by societal norms, expectations, or trends; instead, I choose to live as God (Yahweh) intends.

For a long time, I felt uncomfortable being around other couples without my spouse, including family members and acquaintances who were aware of our situation. I perceived myself as a failure, and being in their presence presented a psychological challenge.

However, that is no longer the case. I consciously choose to invest my energy in the positive aspects of my life.

My mindset, emotions, and heart posture have transformed for the better. Most of my thoughts are now positive. I used to feel disadvantaged because I tried to hold on when I needed to let go. I have become a great example of how to bounce back from adversity. My journey to achieving a healthy emotional lifestyle has been unconventional yet successful. I am determined to move forward and be a true reflection of the God in whom I believe — unapologetically and authentically.

My focus and passion lie in helping other women recognize and believe in who they are meant to be. Whether through mindset work, transformation, manifestation, relationship coaching, or other avenues, I meet women exactly where they are, guiding and equipping them to progress toward a better, more fulfilling life.

My life purpose is to empower women to overcome adversities and encourage them not to settle for ordinary living but to strive for extraordinary, victorious, and empowered lives from the inside out.

The strong relationships I have built within my family, church, and local community have been the foundation for reshaping my current life. The support from both men and women during my transition from married life to living solo has made this journey much more manageable.

I love what I have now and am excited to see it improve. I know that my best days are still ahead of me.

1 John 5:4 has taught me that I am born of God to be victorious, continuing as a world conqueror. My persistence in faith empowers me to overcome the world's challenges and receive everything that God has in store for me to live abundantly.

I lived in untruths, self-doubt, and discouragement for a long time, falling short of my potential.

I believed I only deserved what I received until I began to think differently and adopted a new perspective.

The challenges to my psyche during my formative years and beyond were tremendous. If it hadn't been for God sending people who could see my wounds and knew how to uplift me, I would not have blossomed into the woman I am today. At one point, I didn't know how to live free from negative feelings, nor did I know how to escape unhealthy experiences.

My heart is full of love, and I no longer fear being unloved and alone. I did many things to keep people in my life, even when they mistreated me. I desperately wanted my marriage to work, to be repaired, and to have another chance to be a wife worthy of love.

Unfortunately, that was not the outcome, and it has taken years for me to gather the pieces of my heart and strengthen my mind and soul. I could not have moved forward without the support of a dear friend who spoke loving truths to me, affirming that I am worthy of the love I desire.

I am still learning to love myself, to fill my heart regardless of what others say or do, and to honor my life.

The courage, fortitude, and strength required to navigate narratives filled with economic and emotional deprivation, hostility, opposition, violence, and hardship are remarkable. It astonishes me that I am one of those people—a testament to human resolve, resilience, and perseverance.

Pursuing significance and cultivating relationships that provide abundant exchanges have become essential to my healthy sense of self. Healthy relationships hold immense power.

In every interaction, I aim to move forward—not to struggle to be someone I am not, but to thrive as my true self. I have worked to overcome my people-pleasing tendencies and self-doubt. I am dedicated to being authentic and avoiding pretentiousness.

Living abundantly and exploring the power of meaningful relationships has been rewarding, empowering, and fulfilling for my mind, heart, and spirit. I aspire to help as many women as possible achieve the same. By being honest about the areas of my life that need repair and ongoing maintenance, I have acquired the essentials for survival. I rely on specific people who can guide me through challenges and help me overcome adversities.

Healing has involved repairing my mind, emotions, will, and spirit and identifying what hinders holistic progress within me. I have spent many years focusing on my heart, attitudes, values, morals, biases, beliefs, prejudices, mental health, physical health, emotional intelligence, and overall well-being.

My actions are motivated by my desire to live in serenity. I engage all aspects of myself to achieve the most significant gains. I have come to understand that I am not defined by my past experiences, my actions, the titles or degrees I hold, or the roles I occupy.

My past is behind me; the present is perfect, the future is promising, and the best is yet to come.

I discovered that Karmin means garden or splendor, while Simone means to hear or listen.

She is loving, caring, compassionate, and thriving. She deserves a deep love that completely nourishes her—one that is patient and kind, free from insecurity or envy, not prideful, does not dishonor her, is not easily angered, keeps no record of wrongs, rejoices in her truth, protects her, trusts her, hopes for the best, and aims to preserve the relationship.

I await the upcoming year with great expectations of greater business opportunities, personal fulfillment in unexpected areas, and the showering of bountiful blessings, unlike any other time in my life.

I see the earth opening up experiences for me; I would have needed to find them otherwise strategically.

In the Bible, St. John 10:10 (Amplified Version) says: The thief comes only to steal, kill, and destroy. I came that they may have and enjoy life, and have it in abundance [to the full, till it overflows]. I thank God my life has transformed from despair to abundance, fullness, and overflowing goodness.

I am pursuing a life of fearlessness, nurturing the many loving relationships I am fortunate to have, and embracing the personal power that comes from within.

References

What Are Piaget's Stages of Development and How Are They Used? Medically reviewed by Karen Gill, MD. Ashley Marcin's article was updated on March 29th, 2018 [healthline.com].

Answering The Central Question (How Science Reveals the Keys to Success in Life, Love, and Leadership) by Peter D. Demarest and Harvey J. Schoof, MS, published December 14th, 2010

Kintsugi- Wikipedia

Karmin Reeves Jenkins

Karmin Reeves Jenkins is a certified Abundant Living Coach who helps women, military women veterans, and parents of adult daughters develop strategies for living abundantly from the inside out. As a Licensed Independent Clinical Social Worker, Karmin helps her clients rewire negative thoughts into positive ones to help them engage in healthier behaviors. She helps them change their life stories and create new narratives impacting their relationships with others.

She is an empowering woman who supports transformation in relationships. Her company, Inner Healing For Abundant Living, Inc., aims to help women live abundantly despite life challenges by using a unique Neuroplastic and Multigenerational Family Systems Healing Framework. Karmin is the proud mom of two, one bonus son, and a loving grandmother of three.

A Licensed Independent Clinical Social Worker with a Supervisor designation, a retired government social worker, a former Major Army Reserves, a Certified Life Coach, a Co-Author, a TEDx speaker, a lead Intercessor with Kingdomsake Ministries International, an Elder at New Dimension Worship Center, and a board member of Crossed Bridges Inc. She holds a Bachelor of Science degree from Cleveland State University and a Master of Social Science Administration from Case Western Reserve University. She is a member of Cambridge

Who's Who and Marquis Who's Who in America. Her purpose is to help women strategically live Abundantly, regardless of challenges.

Website: https://www.ih4al.com

4

HUNGRY

THERESA DELORENZO

Trichotillomania

It was evident from an early age that I liked things neat and tidy and was verging on obsessive-compulsive. One of my favorite 'toys' as a toddler was Tupperware. I would take the lids off, fill the containers with things I found around the house, stack them, empty them again and have hours of endless fun. When it was time to learn to fingerpaint in art class at school I panicked. Getting paint all over my hands seemed terrifying. To comply with the assignment but comfort my fears, I dipped the very tip of my pointer finger in the paint and created my artwork from that, careful not to get paint on any other fingers. When it snowed I got very upset when the paperboy would walk across our lawn, ruining the perfectly white blanket that covered OUR yard. I loved collecting things like candles and stickers, but I never wanted to use them because then they would be, well, used; not neat and in their original form.

When I did my hair for gymnastics it had to be absolutely perfect. Not one bump or one hair out of place was tolerated. I often preened the ponytail 10 times to get it smooth enough for my liking.

As I got older, anxiety ensued. I wasn't nervous about anything in particular but always felt anxious. I resorted to pulling my eyelashes out to ease the anxiety, a disorder called trichotillomania. Once my eyelashes were gone, I turned to my hair. Until my teen years though, food and my weight were never a concern.

Gymnastics

When I was six and my sister was three, my parents signed us up for gymnastics. Apparently, they were tired of us flipping around on the furniture and thought we would do well with the sport. They were not wrong. We started on a small local team and eventually outgrew it. The coaches thought my parents were putting too much pressure on us but it was all my sister and I wanting to succeed. We eventually left and joined a more competitive team.

Our dreams of excelling were granted. We competed all around the Northeast, landing ourselves spots on the podium regularly. There were numerous coaches and during the school year, we practiced 3 hours a night four days a week. During the summer we practiced from 9-5 Monday through Friday. We loved it at first...

During the summer between 7th and 8th grade, things changed. It was early July. We arrived at the gym for an hour of warm-ups and then proceeded by rotating through all four events as the temperature of the day and in the gym grew unbearably hot. As we finished up our time on the beam, my least favorite event, we packed up and got ready to move to the uneven parallel bars. Coach Bobby was leading bars that day. I chalked my hands and stepped to the bars to practice my release from the high bar to the low bar. I worked on this particular sequence for a few weeks and struggled to perfect it. As I re-chalked between skills, Bobby looked at me and admonished that he struggled to spot me very successfully because I had gotten so big. I stepped away stunned. The memory of this moment is still crystal clear despite the decades that have passed. All of the other gymnasts swung from bar to bar perfunctorily. Was I that much bigger than them? I stumbled to the bathroom utterly confused and hurt. How could I have let this happen? I stared at myself in the mirror in the bathroom and thought, "he's right!" I am not scrawny anymore!" I have boobs. No one else has boobs! I pulled at my thighs making desperate attempts to pull them off. I had never had an issue with what I saw in the mirror until this day. I had never really even thought that much about it. At the age of 13, that changed.

Section 1: 32 Strands

"Girls, dinner is ready." I walked to the table as the smell of freshly sauteed garlic overtook me. I knew we were having spaghetti and meatballs because knowing what was for dinner was essential before I consumed anything for the day. It all had to fit together. The rest of the day was planned around what my mom was making for dinner. Occasionally, she changed the plan and my anxiety overtook me because I had already eaten meals that "fit" with what she originally told me. Today, she thankfully stuck with the plan.

I approached the table cautiously, knowing I had to stay in control. Spaghetti was tricky. It was delicious and hard to stop after my allotted 32 strands. Eating more was not an option even though I never got full after lunch and dinner was half an hour later than I was originally promised. My stomach grumbling loudly, I sat down at the table, moving the tiny, delicious strands around to take up time so it appeared to take the whole dinner time to eat 32 strands of spaghetti. I took a tiny bite of my meatball, my stomach wanting more. Ten minutes into dinner I was nearing my quota of pasta so I went to the bathroom to waste some time.

At 15 I had maintained my weight at 87 lbs for two years. Each morning I surreptitiously took the scale out of the bathroom closet, gently placing it on the floor, careful to not make noise, nervously weighing myself while the shower water was running so no one knew. My plan of staying at 87 pounds couldn't be found out because they would make me stop. They would make me eat more and there was no way I was doing that.

As a child, one of my favorite foods was mashed potatoes. So prior to the issue at hand, I would eat several servings. More than one serving was naturally not feasible anymore. "I feel like Theresa doesn't love mashed potatoes anymore," my sister announced one night. Oh no! They are noticing! I was terrified. "Eat enough!" my dad admonished. If only it was that easy.

Breakfast was always a chocolate chip muffin with orange juice. Sugar helped me feel full and eating the same thing every day helped me feel safe. Lunch was a garlic bagel with cream cheese and an apple. Snacks were meticulously calculated; 48 cheerios, 16 grapes, or 20 teddy grahams. Each day I was permitted two snacks.

My eating plan was a delicate balance. Going to friends' houses became stressful. At a friend Erin's house, her mom prepared us hot dogs for lunch. I panicked and made sure she knew I didn't eat hot dogs. She asked what I preferred. "Could I have yogurt and a banana?" Yes, that's exactly how I eat. Whew. That was close. Looking back, I realize Erin's mom might have restricted her eating. Social events became less and less frequent. The stress attached was just too high.

As I entered ninth grade, lying awake at night was an unfortunate pastime that worsened as my disorder worsened. Eating at restaurants became increasingly difficult. I struggled to fit the meals I typically ordered into my new shrunken daily allotment. Some restaurants stressed me out because what I typically ordered was not going to be able to squeeze into my newly created rigid food rules. I feared that if I veered from what I normally ordered I would tip off my family to know I was up to something. As a child, I had always ordered a hamburger and French fries almost everywhere we went. Red meat, two carbs at one meal, and fried food I lamented! No way. I had to figure out a new plan. My head spun trying to figure out how I could eat things that I liked and appear to be normal, yet not go over my allotment. I got anxious when my mom would buy more than one snack option at the grocery store because the choices overwhelmed me. Sometimes I merely opened the package and smelled it instead of eating it when it didn't fit into the day. It made me sad that I couldn't allow myself to eat it but it also felt gratifying to put it back in the container, successfully refraining from eating any.

There were days when I gave in and ate an extra few bites of something because I was just too hungry to resist. It felt dangerous to not compensate for this "extra" food. I planned to make up for it the next day. But, because my allotment was already so low, I often took days to compensate for “overeating”. In my mind, I failed until I counterbalanced my day of “overconsumption”.

Sugar

Because I wasn’t consuming enough calories, I craved sugar, usually in the form of chocolate. We were having a holiday party at gymnastics, and I planned to eat brownies and only brownies. I loved brownies. I missed them. I figured out how many brownies I could eat for a meal equivalent. I skipped lunch and counted the brownies as my meal. I thought of one for each bread equivalent and one for the inside of the sandwich. My friend Erin noticed my odd behavior and commented that she had never seen me eat so much before. I explained to her that I hadn’t eaten anything else. In my mind, it made perfect sense. I’m not sure she agreed.

I was babysitting one day in tenth grade. The mom left out chocolate chip cookies for me and the child to have as a snack. I decided to have one. I couldn’t stop. I ate cookie after cookie. Later, I skipped dinner and told my parents that I ate dinner with the child I had been babysitting. Technically, I ate. I couldn’t bring myself to eat more after all of the cookies. If I allowed myself to eat to fullness at my meals, I wouldn’t have been so tempted by sugary treats. Sugar felt so satisfying at the time on my hungry belly but weighed heavily on my mind afterward. Even though I had eaten all of the cookies, I should have had a healthy dinner. I wasn’t so logical at that time in my life. Binging is a result of filling our body with something that’s missing. Underfueling leads to overindulgence. You can employ all the willpower in the world, but until you are properly nourished, your body will win.

Broken

During the winter of my sophomore year of high school, my restrictive eating caught up with me. It was a Wednesday night. We were at gymnastics, as we were most nights of the week. I made my way over to the uneven parallel bars, my last event for the evening. Exhausted from the three-hour practice and not taking in enough calories for several years at this point, I wrapped my grips on my hands, chalked up, and began my routine. My lack of energy was paramount as I swung from low bar to high bar and back again. My limbs felt heavy as I prepared for my dismount, a giant into what was supposed to be a piked position flip. Completely out of energy, I bent my knees and crumbled to the ground, my ankle crushing underneath me.

My tendon grew black and blue and was extremely swollen. The diagnosis was badly sprained. I spent months in the gym while it healed, doing what I could to desperately stay active, but nothing that required putting weight on my foot. I lifted weights to maintain my upper body strength, I sat in splits on each side for ten minutes at a time to maintain my flexibility, and hundreds and hundreds of crunches to keep my physique under control.

Six months later, finally cleared to return to all activity, I injured myself again just three weeks into my return. I jumped to catch the bar and jammed the fingers on my right hand, breaking all of the bones across that hand. After years of under-fueling, my bone density had diminished significantly. I realized gymnastics might not be realistic anymore. I kept getting hurt and needed something safer for my frail body. Meanwhile, I wrote all of my 9th-grade final exams with my left hand.

In the fall of Junior year, I joined the diving team; similar movements to gymnastics, but a softer landing. The inward dive was my favorite. Standing with your back to the water, jumping backward, and flipping towards the board. This became my best dive. In the reverse dive, when you jump away from the board and flip backward towards it, I hated it. It seemed perilous to throw your head backward towards the diving board, but it was required, so I did it. The swimming and diving team went to a bagel shop before practice every day. I wanted to fit in, so I got a salt bagel with nothing on it. It scared me to add this to my diet, but I also was growing tired of the isolation that my food rules had forced me into. My weight inevitably started to creep up. I hit 90 pounds and decided I needed to add something else to my exercise regimen.

In the spring of my Junior year, I joined the track team. My uncle had always been a runner and was always urging me to join him, but gymnastics had consumed so much time and energy that I never entertained it. Better late than never. At the start of the season, the other track members and I ran through the halls of the school since we live in upstate NY, and the ground remained snow-covered. We eventually went outside, and I began to find a rhythm with a small group of girls. Finding running more arduous than I had predicted, I trailed behind my teammates. I felt like my legs weighed a thousand pounds each. Getting through the workouts seemed almost impossible. I ran the 800-meter in races and struggled to finish. Not only was I struggling from undereating, but I also developed mononucleosis. (most likely from under-eating and having a weakened immune system). Mono is a viral infection that causes extreme fatigue, a devastatingly sore throat, and swollen lymph glands. This illness took me out of track for a month. I felt so weak that my dad had to read my homework assignments to me. Finally, I went back to school after three weeks and resumed running track, but not for long. Apparently, too anxious to refrain from exercising, I ended up with walking pneumonia. "It seems as though it's time to hang up the shoes for the season." That was my coach's response when I informed her.

College

As high school came to a close, it was time for college. I chose the University of Rhode Island due to its ideal location on the beach in Narragansett, Rhode Island. Not surprisingly, I decided to study dietetics. I spent so much of my teen years learning about food and nutrients, it was the natural choice. I gradually relaxed some of my restrictive habits towards the end of high school and developed a strong network of friends. However, I was still very interested in food and nutrition and wanted to learn more.

I moved onto campus, started my classes, fell into a group of friends, and was having a great time. However, studying nutrition day in and day out while being under my own roof sent me backward in the natural recovery that I had experienced in my senior year of high school. I could choose to eat however much or little I wanted at the cafeteria. URI had a beautiful gym that I could work out in as much as I wanted. I found myself spiraling back into my restrictive ways.

I got certified to teach aerobics during my freshman year of college. One class a day turned into four, which eventually led to working at all of the local gyms and teaching not ten but fourteen classes a week. As if that wasn't enough, I would arrive early for my classes to do extra cardio and stay after to do crunches. I became known at the URI gym, where I attended college as "ab girl." I walked to all of my classes. The URI campus was not small. This amounted to a lot of walking.

The gym manager at one of the gyms I worked at recognized I was in danger and cut me off. I was riding the stationary bike one day after teaching my third aerobics class for the day. "Go home, you have done enough!" I was no longer allowed to use the exercise equipment outside of teaching my classes.

When I came home from college, I took walks to simulate the amount of walking I did on campus from class to class. I got a job teaching aerobics at my home gym and filled in the gaps with the cardio machines. I was terrified that if I decreased the amount of movement my body was used to, I would gain weight. All of this exercise equated to about four hours each day between all of the different activities. Exercise is good for you. That much is not.

I also grew obsessed with water. Water regulates body temperature, prevents constipation, flushes out waste products, and allows organs to function properly. If I could flush out waste products with water, then I wanted to make sure I had flushed out ALL of the waste products. Some people are germ-phobic and clean their hands and everything around them constantly. I wanted to clean the inside of my body constantly. I decided I needed two gallons of water per day to do the trick. That equates to 256 ounces. The general recommendation is 64 ounces. I was of the mindset at the time that if some was good, more was better.

I frequently got together with my group of friends from my senior year of high school when I came home from college for the summer, but I made sure to do my workout first. I wouldn't let the fun get in the way of my prescribed exercise regimen. When we stayed up late, they would often order pizza. I would stare at it longingly, wishing I could allow myself to have some, obviously hungry since it was several hours after dinner. A few times, I couldn't help myself and indulged, making sure to skip a meal the next day to compensate.

December 18, 1998

I am so frustrated. I just want to be able to stick to my daily eating regimen, but it's so hard. I feel like I'm always making up for extra food that I consumed the day before. This shouldn't be that hard. Just stick with the plan! How am I ever going to feel comfortable with my weight if I keep eating this way!? I have been eating way too much chocolate. Maybe I'm stressed. Ugh. I need to go back to filling up on vegetables and stop eating so much chocolate. I have to fix this now. I need to work out extra to compensate for all of the extras I've had over the past two weeks. The plan is less caffeine, less chocolate and more beans and veggies. Just do it!

The Beginning of Recovery

The summer after my sophomore year of college, I knew I needed help. I finally revealed to my parents that I was struggling. I went to a therapist, Erica. She diagnosed me with obsessive-compulsive disorder and put me on Prozac to help regulate my obsessive thoughts and anxiety.

Through my work with Erica and studying nutrition at URI, I learned that OCD and eating disorders commonly co-exist. They are both a result of an imbalance of the neurotransmitters dopamine and serotonin. Dopamine regulates our motivation, movement, and pleasure. Serotonin regulates our mood, appetite, and sleep. Dopamine causes hunger, while serotonin suppresses it.

Ninety percent of our serotonin is produced in our gut. It then travels from our gut to our brain via the vagus nerve, keeping us calm. However, this connection relies on a healthy gastrointestinal system. Stress breaks down the gut and flattens our intestinal villi, the absorptive finger-like projections in our gut that secrete digestive enzymes, making serotonin's journey less successful. Starvation breaks down the gut and flattens the villi also impacting the transit of serotonin from the gut to the brain. What came first: the stress or the starvation? One worsens the other, and it's a vicious cycle.

There are certain nutrients that help preserve the integrity of the gut, such as magnesium, omega-3 fat, tryptophan, pre and probiotics, and zinc. Chocolate is a rich source of magnesium. We often crave the foods our body needs.

Recovery is Not Linear

Therapy and medication helped a lot. I relaxed my food rules and decreased my exercise. I had friends and a social life. However, stressful events in life caused me to regress. After college, I became a Registered Dietitian as planned. I moved out to Colorado after completing my required dietetic internship. As a new grad, I falsely assumed that I could just move and find a job anywhere. I resorted back to teaching aerobics as I had in college.

"Take a seat on your mats and close your eyes." Said the instructor at my first yoga class. Trying to stay true to my recovery, I decided to add yoga to my schedule.

"Take several deep breaths, filling your lungs with each inhale and letting everything go with each exhale." "Seriously!?" I thought. When do we start moving? Growing more and more anxious, I opened my eyes to find everyone else all zenned out. "Take five more breaths and then slowly open your eyes," she instructed. "Oh my goodness, you have to be kidding me. This can't be for real." I was getting annoyed now. How was this possibly beneficial?" I thought, panicking. "I need to move my body." "How was yoga T?" my roommates asked when I returned to our home in Fort Collins that we rented together. "Horrible, ridiculous! I can't even believe that it is considered exercise!" Little did I know at the time yoga held so much more meaning than just burning calories. Apparently, college coming to a close and embarking on the real world, unable to secure a full-time job, had sent me backward a little bit.

After a year in Colorado, I realized finding a job in a health-saturated state was futile. Teaching aerobics all day was not helping my exercise obsession. I looked for jobs all over the country and went wherever the best offer was. I ended up in South Carolina. I spent two years working in clinical dietetics and made the best friends. It was a great place to start my career and be freer than I had ever been because of my isolation and food rules. I grew eager to go back home where I was from.

I secured a job at the hospital where I was born. I worked as a NICU dietitian, went back to school to get my doctorate in nutrition, met my husband, and got pregnant. Getting pregnant sent my brain into a bit of a spiral. I knew I had to gain weight to keep the baby healthy. It was a mental battle. I had to stop my medication. My doctor told me it wasn't safe to take while pregnant. I convinced myself it was the healthy thing to do for my baby. I would just fix it after she was born. But it became a mission that grew perilous.

"How long after I have the baby can I resume exercise?" I asked my doctor when I was pregnant with my first child, Rose. Even when I first had children, my exercise obsession had not waned yet. "We will do a checkup around six weeks and then clear you for exercise." Was her reply?

Six weeks!!?? I was horrified. I was able to exercise through the whole pregnancy, and then after I had the baby, I wasn't going to be able to? "We have to make sure you are healed." "I can do yoga, though, right?" I asked in desperation. "No, yoga would be harmful and could cause you to tear, but walking will be ok."

So I walked and walked and walked. Lots and lots and lots of walking. With Rose in the stroller, I headed out for a walk each morning... and each afternoon... and each evening. When I was finally cleared to exercise again, I tried to make up for lost time. I added yoga. I added Urban Rebounding, a mini trampoline workout I had learned in college. I exercised until there was blood in my stool. I developed micro-tears in my GI tract from exercising too much. "T, do you think maybe you are doing too much?" my friends lamented.

"Probably," I thought, but I was having trouble not being active. I felt like I needed to make up for the lost time. I finally was able to resume my medication and regain control over my thoughts. The hormones of pregnancy, combined with the weight gain and not being able to take my medication, caught up with me. As the hormones settled and the medication kicked back in I was able to cut back down to a moderate amount of exercise.

Yoga to the Rescue

Although I didn't appreciate yoga when I tried it in Colorado, One of the classes I took during my doctorate focused on integrative approaches to health. I did my final project on the health benefits of yoga and fell in love with it. I wasn't ready for it the first time around, but at the age of 30, I was able to appreciate it for its benefits. But just practicing yoga occasionally with my OCD brain wasn't feasible. I practiced daily. I got a yoga teacher trained. I went on yoga retreats. I got certified in aerial yoga. I converted my basement into a yoga studio and had my dad hang six aerial yoga swings so I could hold classes. Yoga helped me feel calm, and the swinging motion of the aerial swing helped even more. It brought me back to my gymnastics days, too, with the upside-down poses. If it helped me, I thought it would help others, too. I enrolled in a yoga therapy program so I could work with individuals one-on-one and help them heal pain, anxiety, body image issues, insomnia, and other issues using all of the elements of yoga. The more I practiced yoga, the more I was able to connect with my body and honor it vs. punishing it as I had years ago. It helped me learn what my body was asking for when it needed to rest and what I wanted to eat. It helped me to abandon my food rules and connect with what my body needed instead.

Running Round Two

Two years after Rose was born, my husband and I got pregnant again and had our daughter Julia. Unfortunately, right after she was born was the demise of my marriage. We fought and no longer saw eye to eye. When Rose was five, and Julia was two, I got divorced. It was a tumultuous process that took a year to culminate. We had shared custody, which left me living alone again at the age of 36. I needed something to do to fill my free time, so I started running. As you may have learned by now, when I do something, I don't just occasionally do it, but I dive head first and do it all the time. Doing 5k's turned into 10k's and then half marathons. After six half marathons, I decided to embark on a full marathon, despite the fact that I said I would never do one. I completed the first marathon and felt like I was on top of the world. I was hooked. I did two marathons a year for three years, qualifying for Boston twice and recently completing my ninth full marathon.

Running this time around, though, was not like it was when I attempted it in high school. When I ran in high school, I did it because I wanted to burn calories. I did it to change the way I looked. I also was severely undernourished, so it was much harder. Running this time around was enjoyable. It gave me a sense of accomplishment. I knew if I didn't fuel correctly, I would get hurt and not be able to do it. I fueled so that I could run instead of running to get rid of the fuel I had taken in.

Coalescence Method

As I became more entrenched in the running community, other runners started asking me for nutrition advice to help them with their running. At this point, I had moved out of working in clinical dietetics and was working in academia, which was a much more flexible schedule. I missed directly working with people on their nutrition, so I started my private practice, Nutrition for Optimal Performance. I quickly learned that many people in the running community also struggle with under-fueling and body image conditions. I launched my signature program Coalescence Method.

The Coalescence Method includes nutrition counseling to work on why the image exists, what they struggle with, and how to work through it. It also utilizes yoga therapy to help clients who are struggling to learn how to listen to their body again vs. the diet culture telling them what they should and shouldn't eat. It helps them reconnect with their hunger cues, their fullness cues, and their cravings. It allows them to honor all of these things without feeling guilty. We also use journaling to work through triggers and things that come up during the program. My Coalescence Method is how I found peace with food and my body and how I led others to do the same.

THERESA DELORENZO

Dr. Theresa DeLorenzo is a Registered Dietitian and owner and founder of Nutrition for Optimal Performance, founded in 2019. She has been practicing as an RD for 23 years. She is the author of the newly released book Crave and has spoken at numerous conferences locally, nationally, and internationally, most notably, the World Conference on Pediatric Obesity in Rome, Italy. She has worked in various settings as a dietitian, including the neonatal intensive care unit, outpatient pediatric nutrition centers well as in academia. She currently serves as the program director for the Masters Program in Nutrition and Human Performance as well as the Masters Program in Applied Nutrition and Dietetics at Logan University.

Dr. DeLorenzo works with athletes to help them make sure they are eating the correct proportion of macro and micro-nutrients to perform their best, come up with a race day nutrition and hydration plan to feel and perform their best, as well as improve their gastrointestinal health. She also works with individuals with body image disorders. Her signature program, the Coalescence Method, is a uniquely designed program that helps individuals reconnect their bodies and minds to ditch food rules, learn to identify their cravings and honor them without guilt. She combines nutrition counseling, yoga therapy, food therapy, and journaling to help those struggling to find peace with food and their body.

Dr. DeLorenzo received her Bachelor of Science in Food Science and dietetics from the University of Rhode Island and her Masters and Doctorate in Clinical Nutrition from the University of Medicine and Dentistry of New Jersey. She is a 200-hour trained yoga teacher and holds a certification in yoga therapy with an emphasis on improving body image.

Website: https://nutrition-4-op.com

5

BEYOND THE BOTTLE: FROM THE SHADOWS TO THE SPOTLIGHT

KATHRYN TRAFF

A 17-Hour Wakeup Call

A 17-hour marathon in the operating room changed my life forever. Before that day I was in love with my career working for a surgical technology company. The operating room was my stage to share with some of the brightest minds in medicine. In places like Mayo Clinic and Stanford, it was my job (and privilege) to run the cutting-edge imaging systems my company produced. The sense of purpose and fulfillment I received from being a part of the patient's care team ran deep.

I was one of about 500 people in the world who knew how to do what I did. The deeper I delved into this rarified world doing my job, the more my identity was woven around that work. To this day, people still marvel when I share what my life was like. They all react in the same way: "Wow, that's amazing!" But in rare, honest moments I had to acknowledge I had no life.

What stopped me from leaving that career? Two things:

1. I had no idea who Kathryn was outside of that world. If I wasn't that person anymore, who was I? That question scared me the most. If I didn't do that work anymore, was I worthless? In some ways, I told myself, yes.
2. The role my ego played. When people understood what I did it usually took over the conversation. It didn't seem to matter if I wanted to talk about them, they wanted to talk about *me*. It created a belief in me that the work I did made me more important. It was addictive to my ego.

To avoid facing those two uncomfortable truths about myself, I stuffed those two things down. Despite the growing exhaustion, I clung to the illusion of purpose, fulfillment, and importance, driving me to persevere.

Bottle Therapy for Burn Out

That rocket ship ride of a career I enjoyed started to sputter and run out of fuel. I stayed beyond burnout, convinced no other path could offer me this sense of purpose. If I couldn't find that purpose I truly believed I would lose my mind.

As the demands of being on call intensified, my mind raced incessantly. My body ached with chronic muscle tension. Looking for relief, I turned to quick fixes to quiet my mind and relax my weary muscles.

A glass of wine (or 2 or 3) became my nightly ritual. The first glass while I made dinner. Then I would say to myself, "Hey, that felt pretty good. My muscles are starting to relax." Then I would say to myself, "Let's have a glass of wine with my dinner too." "Okay, I'm starting to get to the point now where everything's relaxed! Woo Hoo!"

But there's a problem with that; the 20 to 40 minutes of being in that place, *never* lasts. The price I paid for that 20 to 40 minutes of quiet in my brain was enormous.

Every night that I drank to that point, I woke up at 2 or 3 in the morning, heart racing, sweating, with "hang-xiety". It *always* showed up. The effects of the alcohol wearing off along with the chemicals released by the brain to counteract the depressing effects of the alcohol would jolt me awake. I also woke up to the voice of the meanest version of me yelling and criticizing me. She was brutal. She would say things like:

"What the fuck is wrong with you, Traff?"

"Why the fuck do you keep doing this to yourself, Traff?"

"When are you gonna fucking learn your lesson, Traff?"

This is how I spoke to myself. The sense of shame around this cycle was intense. Why couldn't I stop doing this to myself? Then the guilt would set in. The only person I had to blame was myself. What was wrong with me?

It wasn't easy to go back to sleep with Mean Girl screaming at me. It made waking up most mornings brutal. When I didn't get enough sleep, I wasn't always able to function so I loaded up with coffee, energy drinks, B vitamins, whatever I could think of to get me through the day. On top of that, menopause hell was setting in! The brain fog was crippling.

The Worst Day of my Career

Mean Girl started yelling at me about 3:00 this morning.

"Why were you drinking last night?"

"This is exactly what happens to you when you have anything to drink!"

"What's wrong with you? Are you a moron?"

The alarm goes off at 4:00. Despite the fuzziness and fogginess in my brain, my mind starts racing. While throwing on my scrubs and making coffee, I calculate how many things could go wrong today. That's my normal way to start any day, it's how I stay in control—at all times. I hit the road by 5. The hour-long drive to the hospital doesn't do anything to calm my racing mind. I keep playing out potential disaster scenarios trying to plan for anything that can go wrong.

As I rush into the hospital questions are plaguing my mind.

"How will I manage everything in front of me today?"

"How in the world am I going to be in two places at once?"

There are 3 surgeries (cases) I am responsible for helping with that day. Two of them will be happening at the same time!

A series of "What if" questions keep looping through my mind. I'm already feeling the knots in my stomach.

There are only 15 minutes to coordinate with five different people to ensure everything is ready for the surgeries. A single misstep on my part will derail my entire day. I had to do everything "perfectly" in order to succeed. At least that's what I told myself.

The first sign of trouble shows up when I arrive in the operating room (OR). Instruments that are critical to the case are missing. Without those instruments, the case will have to be canceled. That's completely unacceptable in the world of surgery. Despite it not being my direct responsibility I volunteer to find them. I have to keep things on track, there's too much going on. I go on the hunt for them.

As I search for the instruments, I walk by the OR schedule board and see a fourth case has been added that will use my systems. My heart sinks. It's a very long, complex spine case that will likely keep me in the hospital until about 10:00 that night. But that's the way my life is, my schedule is never my own. It's always dictated by the surgeon's schedule. How long could I keep up with this life?

It's my job to operate a specialized, million-dollar imaging and computer system (kind of like GPS) that creates a 3D model for the surgeon. It's a lot like playing video games for removing a brain tumor or placing screws and rods in the spine to stabilize it with the utmost precision.

The first case goes smoothly once I locate the missing instruments. Now the challenge is to manage two operating rooms simultaneously. The hospital has 2 sets of the imaging and computer systems I run. It's my job to get both sets in both ORs, booted up, and ready to go. It's close to noon now. I've been on the go for more than 8 hours.

The two surgical suites I'm working in are on opposite ends of the surgical floor. Yikes! I will literally have to sprint between the two operating rooms. Patients are on the table, the clock is ticking, and the longer a patient is under anesthesia the more risky it becomes for them. The case can't proceed until I'm there to run the systems.

As I explain to both the neurosurgeons why I can't be in two places at once, neither of them is happy with me or the situation. They both believed their cases were more important than the other surgeons. All my diplomacy skills are necessary to smooth things over. That tension between all of us sets the tone for what happens the rest of the day.

In room number 1 it's time to start taking pictures of the patient's spine. The imaging system moves into place. Damn it! The system won't take the pictures! "Are you kidding me?" I scream to myself. It's my job to fix it—now. The clock is ticking, I have been called to the other room! If the systems aren't working the case has to be aborted. This would create enormous expense and trauma to the patient without any positive result. It takes me 5 minutes but feels like 5 hours, but I managed to get the system up and running again. I tell room 2 I'll be there as soon as I can.

We have the pictures now but something is preventing them from being transferred to the GPS computer system. Before the surgery, I specifically checked to make sure this problem wouldn't occur. "Now I look like a moron who doesn't know how to run the system," I tell myself. I have to reboot the computer. That takes 3 more minutes. The surgeon asks me why he bothers to use the systems if I don't know how to run them. My face is getting hot and I'm angry but I try to calmly explain what the problem is. He doesn't want to hear it.

In room 2 the surgeon's frustration with me is growing. There's a phone call on the hard line of room 1 asking where I was. My text messages on my phone are also blowing up. I stop trying to fix the system and answer the call. I explain the nature of the problem I'm fixing and give an estimate of when I'll be in the other room. I'm sweating and shivering at the same time. My thoughts are racing to figure out why this is happening. It feels like my mind is stuck in a loop.

As I burst through the door of the second room the surgeon gives me an earful. He wants to know why I didn't arrange to have someone help me, he also tells me I am the problem and all I'm doing is slowing him down. The harangue continues until I get the imaging system into place, take the pictures, and get the pictures transferred to the computer so he can start that portion of the surgery. Finally, his focus shifts away from me and I can breathe for a few minutes.

As the surgeon starts using the system he's not clear on the information my system gives him about the patient's anatomy. While I'm explaining to him how to interpret the information he blows up. The surgeon isn't a fan of women in the operating room outside of certain roles. He insisted I call my male counterpart, and put him on speaker to explain what I had just explained. That's what finally got the surgeon to accept what I told him. I was angry, but the patient on the table was my primary concern so I let it go.

Despite how much I have to juggle, the hours are dragging by. It's nearly 4:00 but the day seems like it will never end. The nurses in the room with me are changing shifts. They are also arguing with each other. No one wants to be in that room with *that surgeon*. Truth be told, not a lot of people enjoyed working with him because he's so volatile.

As the chaos of the shift change ensued the instruments needed for the surgery are dropped on the floor, slowing us down. I race to the area where clean instrument sets are to try to find what we need. It's all taking too long. I have to be in another room now to start that complex spine case. It feels like I am running on fumes. "When did I last eat?" "When was the last time I went to the ladies room?" I wondered.

It's 4:30. The last case of the day, a complex spine case is finally starting. This is not the ideal time of day to start a case like this. There are so many variables that can throw the case off and cause problems.

The case starts with a disagreement between the surgeon and the anesthesiologist about how to proceed in the case. I am unable to share more information with you here about that argument. But what I can share is it is heated and it sets the tone for the rest of the case. The tension and chaos in the room is palpable. "Please God, I just want to go home."

Most of the things that could go wrong do. My system starts acting up—again. "Why is this happening?" I scream to myself. I have to reboot it—again. My heart is pounding, my shoulder muscle is so tight it's causing me tremendous pain, it's hard to think.

The night shift surgical team has limited experience in this type of complex surgery. Their inexperience slows us down by *hours*. A case that normally takes 8 hours is now taking almost 12.

It's after midnight. Finally, it's time to remove both systems from the OR. As the imaging system was being removed it's misdirected and crashed! As I review the damage I realize it would not be fixable until parts arrived a day or two later. Now I was going to have to come back to the hospital later in the morning to inform the surgeons who wanted the imaging system that it wasn't available. That was going to be an ugly conversation. The thought filled me with dread.

I walked into the hospital at 6 a.m. thinking I would be home by 6 p.m. It was after midnight now. All day long as I was berated, running, fixing, I said to myself "I will buy my favorite, expensive bottle of wine as a "treat" for everything I had been through. But I never got that drink, I just went home and went to bed.

That was my Day 1 in my new alcohol-free life. Then Day 2 came—I was too tired to drink. Then Day 3 would change my entire life.

Now is the Time

On Day 3, when I arrived home after another long day in the OR, I realized there was no wine to be had in my house. For a long time I sat on my couch staring out my window contemplating if I should leave my house to buy the favorite bottle of wine I had promised myself two days earlier. Truth be told it was a serious tug of war in my mind. "Should I stay or should I go?" Back and forth, back and forth. As this tug of war continued I heard the Holy Spirit speak to me and say "Now is the time." The Holy Spirit showed me what my life would look like.

If I don't do something about my Gray Zone drinking problem *now*, if I don't walk away from this career now, I am on the path to destruction. I would develop a serious alcohol problem. At this point I was 55 years old, the risk of having a stroke, developing breast cancer, etc., was all too real because I was consuming alcohol on a regular basis. That Gray Zone was enough to put me at serious health risk. But how could I give it up? During Covid I had given it up but only made it 30 days before I went back to my "daily treat".

There was a time when I thought of myself as just a social drinker. But I've learned that a Gray Zone drinking problem can sneak up on you at any point in life. It doesn't take a lifelong struggle to find yourself there—sometimes, it's a tough divorce, children leaving home, or the pressure of an all-consuming career. Life throws challenges at you, and suddenly, you're standing in a place you never imagined, questioning how you got there. I never saw it coming. It blindsided me.

Every evening, when I turned to wine to quiet my mind, I'd tell myself, *"Today doesn't matter. It's just a glass or two."* But that was the lie I told myself every single day, for four long years. When I finally decided it was time to stop, I always promised, *"I'll start Monday. I'll take a break."* But Monday would come, and I wouldn't follow through. For so long, I felt like I was the only one struggling—like I was alone, or somehow *not normal*. The question that haunted me was always the same: *"What is wrong with me?"*

You're probably wondering what I mean by a Gray Zone drinking problem. It's a term I use to describe the area that exists between no drinking problem and a problem so bad that it lands you in places like rehab and 12 step programs. In our culture we're told you have no problem or you have a problem only if the alcohol you're consuming wrecks your life and your health.

What's important to note is millions of people who are in the Gray Zone don't need alcohol to function. They're doers, achievers, winners. They use alcohol to turn off their mind or turn down the volume in their heads. They even view it as self-care. I sure did.

Good Help is Hard to Find

The reality of where I was in my life started to set in. The pit in my stomach grew when I thought about giving up my "treat", my "reward". It felt like that was all I had to keep me going.

But I knew I had to try. Like so many other people I started to search online for things like:

"How do you know you have a drinking problem?"

"How do you know if you're an alcoholic?"

"How much is too much to drink?"

There was all kinds of help for people who wanted to "cut back" or who had serious addiction problems. But that wasn't me. Plus I didn't want labels, meetings, or to be told I have a disease. I knew that wasn't who I was.

There were times in my life where I could take it or leave it. For instance when I quit during Covid. The problem was I rarely "left it" anymore. While I didn't drink large amounts, it was rare to not even have 1 glass in an evening.

On about Day 4 or 5, I came across an online course that ran six weeks. The course didn't refer to my type of drinking as Gray Zone drinking, (that's my term) but the approach it offered was, "Your life doesn't have to be boring without alcohol." It was intriguing because I was convinced life would be boring without alcohol.

The person offering the course was on social media, living what appeared to be a fabulous life. The thing that fascinated me most about the course was it presented the most current data about the effects of alcohol specifically on women. That was incredibly appealing to my nerdy, neuroscience geek brain.

After completing that course I found myself wanting more. I was 8 weeks into my new alcohol-free life and loving it. So I launched into reviewing new studies and various brain scan studies of moderate drinkers. As part of my career, I had rigorous training in how to understand and interpret studies. The information I was uncovering was the very best and most reliable of any other studies.

Around the time I finished the on-line course I came across the work of Dr Daniel Amen, one of the preeminent psychiatrists in the US, who's done more brain scans and studying of brain scans than any other physician in the world. Dr Amen scared the hell out of me with a SPECT scan of a moderate drinker vs. a non-drinker brain.

The scan, which shows blood flow in the brain, was frightening. At that moment, looking at the scan, I knew that's *exactly* what my brain looked like thanks to years of Gray Zone drinking. At that point, I knew I could never go back to drinking. I didn't know how I was going to do it. I didn't know *if* I could do it, but I made the decision, I'm never going back. I wanted my brain to heal.

Thanks to my new knowledge from the updated studies I started to understand what had been happening. It made so much sense now! I wasn't angry at myself anymore. All the shame, blame and judgment was gone.

What I uncovered was that all the big beverage companies have this new data. They bury it! Then they sell us a lie. It's not a "celebration" if you don't have alcohol in the glass, alcohol is 'liquid courage", "alcohol makes things more fun!" The marketing to women has been stepped up significantly in the last 2 decades! We're told it makes us "sophisticated", "sexy", "funny".

While I poured through the information it occurred to me there's nothing wrong with me or anyone else. There was everything wrong with this crap drug called alcohol. The sense of relief and liberation I felt was enormous. *I wasn't the problem!*

The Power of Patterns

Not long after I found the studies, I also came across the works of people like Byron Katie, Louise Hay, Dr. Bruce Lipton, David Bayer, Dr. Caroline Leaf, and the list goes on. As I studied how neural pathways are formed in the brain, I started to understand that many of the things I was struggling with in life were simply patterns of behavior I had learned as a girl.

Because I understood neuroplasticity (your brain can make new pathways at any time) I finally realized I had the capacity to retrain my brain in areas that no longer served me!

For instance a limiting belief is "I'm not good enough". So many women struggle with this. This belief usually shows up in childhood because an adult treats you or tells you something to make you believe this. You absorb it into your subconscious. That sets up a pattern of behavior, known as a psycho-cybernetic loop. What does a loop look like?

1. Limiting Belief
2. Thought created by the belief
3. Feeling created by the thought
4. Action created by the feeling
5. Result created by the action
6. Result reinforces our beliefs

When I learned I could harness the power of neuroplasticity to completely rewire, reprogram, and retrain my brain I started to explore what types of patterns in my life held me back. What kept me stuck in my Gray Zone drinking pattern?

One of my most harmful patterns stemmed from the belief that I had to do everything on my own and couldn't rely on anyone else. This belief took root as a teenager, when my father's death from pancreatic cancer plunged my family into financial chaos. For a time, that mindset served me—it helped me get into college and excel in my career. But it also isolated me, overwhelmed me, and ultimately played a role in my divorce.

The epiphany I had was the Gray Zone drinking problem wasn't the problem. It was the limiting beliefs and the patterns of behavior from those beliefs that led me to the place of wanting to turn off my mind.

With Truth Comes Clarity

Now that I knew the truth about my patterns, the truth about what alcohol does in the body, especially after menopause, it freed me to develop a new way of thinking. That new knowledge helped me build a framework to get to a point that I never miss alcohol. To this day I never had one slip or have gone back to drinking. *Because I don't miss anything about it!*

My chronic high blood pressure and sleep problems are gone. My skin looks better, too. It's incredible how the body repairs itself when you stop poisoning it! Now that I'm sleeping well, I wake up motivated to work out—something I never used to do. Today, I'm on a three-year journey to be in the best shape of my life by 60.

As I learned more, I began to really like the person I was becoming. With a clearer mind, I started asking big, scary questions—like, "*What if I changed careers?*" For the first time, I trusted my judgment. That trust led me to make the boldest decision of my life: resigning from a role that had defined my identity for nearly two decades.

These days I have no shame or judgment about where I am now. The old patterns I followed once served me—they drove me to achieve success I never thought possible, but it was all out of fear. By the time you hit your 50s, fear takes its toll. You can't keep pushing the same way; you're burned out, exhausted, and tired of living in constant anxiety.

When I reclaimed the time lost to the drinking I had time to spend on figuring out what was important to me now. I had more energy, I had new ideas, I took some classes to help discover the next path to take in my career.

You deserve the freedom, the peace, and the lightness I feel. All you have to do is start recognizing your patterns then get to work developing new ones. Truth be told it wasn't easy work, I worked on it daily, but it is worth every second you devote to the work.

New Brain, New Life

When those new pathways and new patterns of behavior were established I started to get new, better results. Those changes led to remarkable coincidences happening in my life. It felt like I had a superpower.

The right people at the right time were showing up to support me, the money, the right opportunities at the right time were happening (Being asked to write a chapter in this book is one of them). Why was this happening? Because a part of my brain called the RAS (reticular activating system) had been altered by all the work I did. It's the filter through which your brain sorts all the information it receives.

Here's an example of a limiting belief I had: "When I go out with friends, I won't have a good time because they're drinking and I'm not." "I'm going to be viewed as boring". So I asked myself the question, "What if the opposite is true? When I go out with my friends, I don't need alcohol to be fun." In fact, because I was fully present with my friends they found me more fun to be around because I wasn't constantly repeating myself.

When I made the decision to change that limiting belief to "Life is exciting without alcohol"—I was able to find evidence in my life that it was true with examples like this: When I was a teenager and I would go to the movies, to a county fair, whatever it was, with my friends, none of us had anything to drink. Ever. We laughed the hardest we've ever laughed. Some of my best memories of my young life are the times I spent with my friends at birthday parties or sleepovers, with no alcohol.

That new decision created a beautiful surprise. When I shared with my friends, "I'm not drinking anymore. I feel amazing and this is what I order instead." Then I showed them a drink recipe written up on a mini Post-it note that I would give to the server. I also asked for the drink to be served in a pretty glass. That way it looked like I was having a cocktail as well. I never stood out.

To my surprise my friends stopped ordering wine and asked for what I ordered. I never expected that! Because I had the courage to flip the script in my brain, I turned myself into a non-drinker, who never misses alcohol.

Letting Go, Living in the Light

In the last four years, I've intentionally let go of anything that no longer serves me—starting with leaving my city, career, and social circle three years ago. A year ago, I ended a relationship with the man I once thought would be my lifelong partner. But the most transformative change was quitting my Gray Zone drinking habit. That one decision changed the entire trajectory of my life.

The purpose of sharing my story is to be your emergency brake, your safety net to let you know you can do something ***now***. You don't have to wait until your life is in tatters or your health is compromised to walk away from alcohol and not miss it.

The reason I'm at peace, at 58 years old, is because 3+ years ago I had the worst day of my entire career. THE WORST. It felt like an awful setback but it was actually an epic ***set up!*** Volumes of space, opportunity, and people started to show up in my life to help me get to where I am now.

Today I run a coaching business and a ministry to help women at the midpoint of their lives walk away from alcohol and not miss it. They learn how to train their brains to work for them in alignment with who they want to become. This is truly the most rewarding work I've ever done. Working in the OR is now a distant second.

My story is meant to serve as evidence, a blueprint, or even a beacon for anyone stuck in their own Gray Zone, especially when it comes to drinking. But maybe your Gray Zone isn't about alcohol at all—it could be something else. Perhaps you've stopped living in full color. What if you stepped out of your own Gray Zone and embraced the most powerful version of yourself? What could your life look like?

The mission that drives me is to bring that message to anyone who is open to it. You, too, can have new beliefs and patterns that serve you. Embrace your pivot point.

Get out of your Gray Zone and come into the Light. ***Now*** is your time.

Reach out to me. Let's create a plan for how you can start living a life beyond your wildest dreams. All my love to you. God bless you.

KATHRYN TRAFF

Kathryn Traff is a dynamic brain health mentor, speaker, entrepreneur, author, and coach with over 20 years of experience in neuroscience. After leaving a successful career in surgical technology, she transitioned to coaching, helping women give up alcohol and not miss it. Kathryn's passion for this work stems from her own struggle with a Gray Zone drinking habit.

Kathryn combines neuroscience, mindset techniques, and faith to guide her clients in identifying and reshaping the thought patterns that no longer serve them. She empowers them to understand how the brain works and to actively rewire those patterns, enabling lasting transformation without shame, blame, or judgement.

As a coach, speaker, and author, Kathryn provides practical tools and strategies for personal growth, teaching individuals how to master their behaviors and build resilience. Through her work, Kathryn has helped countless people reclaim control over their lives and unlock their true potential of who they were created to be.

Website: https://revivesoberspirit.com/

6

BENEATH THE SURFACE: HEALING UNSEEN SCARS

HEATHER HANSON

What I once fled, I now face. I dive into the darkness, seeking freedom from the chains that have bound me for a lifetime.

At the tender age of 18, I made the heart-wrenching decision to leave my family behind, shielding them—and myself—from the unspeakable events that transpired within the walls of my parents' house. The weight of unspoken truths pushed me to create distance, severing ties without explanation as I sought solace from the pain.

Yet, as my story unfolds, you'll uncover a profound truth: evading the shadow of our struggles does not equate to resolving them. Unattended wounds have a way of resurfacing, yearning to be acknowledged and, ultimately, healed.

Before examining deeper, it's essential to understand that this narrative is a reflection of my journey, seen through my eyes. It explores how I intentionally chose a different path and life than the one I observed and inherited from my parents during my upbringing. This story is not to throw blame, but proof that it is possible to heal from scars that cut deep into our souls.

Invisible Noose

I was born a red-haired, green-eyed baby whose face was smashed with forceps during birth. This distorted the soft cartilage of my nose, caused my right eye to droop and damaged the retinal cells in my right eye so that I never developed much sight in that eye. Despite this, my grandparents, aunt and uncle loved me dearly. I never had a doubt about that for a second. They took care of me when I was a tiny baby, showed me that I was special, and showed up as examples of the type of person that I wanted to be. Kind, strong, loving and gentle. I spent as much time at my grandparent's house as I could. I was the oldest grandchild and loved living next door to them and capturing their attention.

In stark contrast, my parents were not endowed with nurturing instincts. Both incredibly young and unfamiliar with each other, their journey into parenthood commenced abruptly. They had known each other merely two months before entering into marriage, and just ten months later, I made my entrance into their world. From what I've heard, I was not an easy baby, and that complicated the situation.

There is no doubt that I was a stubborn child with a mind of my own. I ran away from home at the age of four. I vividly remember grabbing a brown paper sack, filling it with underwear and heading through the yard to my grandparent's house, a place of safety and love. It was inevitable that I'd be found, and thus, I was expected to return to the oppressive environment of my parent's home, which I likened to a chamber of torment with immense fear of my father.

If the walls of that house could speak, they would echo with my cries and the countless tears I shed. There were distressing moments etched into my memory, such as when my father would envelop me in a blanket, trapping me despite my desperate cries and pleas for release. He repeatedly subjected me to this torment, even displaying it to his friends as if it were a joke. For him, it was amusement; for me, it was sheer terror.

Another chilling memory involves him lifting me onto a precarious, three-inch ledge within the stairwell. He would instruct me to grasp onto imaginary handles before releasing me into fear's grasp, only to catch me when I faltered. Again and again, he pushed me back against the wall, insisting I hold onto nonexistent supports, as my tears flowed freely. "Hold on to the wall, Suzie" (his nickname for me). To him, it was a source of entertainment; to me, agony.

Reading *The Body Keeps the Score* by Dr. Bessel Van Der Kolk gave me clarity. The book explains that when someone is trapped or prevented from taking protective action—whether in war, accidents, or abuse—the brain continues firing stress signals, leaving lasting scars.

This insight helped me understand why the repeated incidents of my childhood and teen years left such deep wounds. Unable to protect myself, the trauma lingered, pulling me back into darkness like an invisible noose.

Silenced by Fear

A month after I started kindergarten my life was turned upside down and the darkness really crept in. My parents, my brother and I moved unexpectedly to another town about 15 minutes from my grandparents. I overheard my dad say we moved because my Pap was "too nosy", as he would call or come to the house when he would hear me crying and screaming and my parents "needed their privacy".

I was so sad that I had to move away from my grandparents and leave my kindergarten class. I vividly remember feeling lost, lonely, and disconnected in school. Kids teased me relentlessly, calling me a witch because of my crooked nose and red hair. I was awkward and clumsy, especially because I had to wear really thick glasses and a patch over my "good eye". I fell down the stairs often and got into more trouble for breaking my glasses.

After moving to a dreary old house, I started to develop mysterious health issues. The longer I lived away from my grandparents, the more problems I developed. Hives, rashes, other skin problems, warts, poison ivy over and over. I frequented the small town doctor's office, although most of the time, he just went to the cabinet, put some pills in a small envelope and said, "Try these".

Looking back, these health issues are directly tied to a haunting memory of that rundown house. One that refuses to fade and revolves around a recurring, disturbing scene from my childhood. My parents would take me into their bedroom, stripping away my innocence, where my father would violate me physically and emotionally. His actions were ever accompanied by my mother's presence, her voice cautioning him not to leave visible marks as I was set to visit her parents overnight. The stark reality that my mother witnessed these moments and never intervened is a betrayal that echoes deeply within me. She chose not to protect me, which left me feeling alone and abandoned.

I was only 25 pounds when I started kindergarten, tiny and underweight. By 6th grade, everything changed. I gained weight quickly, my face puffed up, especially around my neck, where a thyroid goiter grew. I entered 7th grade, weighing 158 pounds—more than I was when I had my first child. At school, the insults became unbearable. I was called "fat", and I still hear my father's cruel words echoing, "No one wants a fat cunt."

At home, I lived in constant fear, walking on eggshells. My dad's moods dictated everything. If he was calm, I could relax a little, but if he was angry, a heavy dread settled in my stomach. Would it be just yelling or worse? The fear of what would happen next kept me silent, trapped in shame. I couldn't tell anyone, too scared of what he might do. So, I buried my feelings and clung to whatever semblance of normal I could find.

The Illusion of Control

I didn't realize until I was 49 that my need for control was rooted in childhood survival. This core program kept me safe and made me a strong, independent woman who refused to let anyone tell her she couldn't achieve something. If someone said, "I don't think you can," I was determined to prove them wrong.

But this need to control also wreaked havoc on my life. By 15, I struggled with severe body image issues and an eating disorder. I hated my body and just wanted to be normal, pretty, and accepted.

The disorder was both a burden and a twisted source of confidence. As I ate less, inflammation decreased, the weight dropped, and people noticed. Compliments rolled in— "You look great!"—but inside, I felt ugly, sad, and broken.

I'd go days without eating, then binge, only to restrict again when I felt puffy. On dates, I refused to eat, terrified that any weight gain would make me unwanted.

From One Cage to Another

In my junior year, I met a 21-year-old man who made me feel seen for the first time. At 17, his compliments on my thin waist and long legs filled a void I didn't even realize I had. Instead of joy, though, his words brought pressure. I didn't dare gain weight. By the time he proposed a year and a half later, I said yes—not out of love, but out of fear that no one else would ever want me. At 18, I thought settling for "better than my dad" was enough.

But as my senior year was ending, doubts crept in. Feeling suffocated, I broke off the engagement, ready to leave for the Army Reserves. That resolve only strengthened when my father assaulted me in a fit of rage, shoving me against the wall and choking me. The next morning, I packed my things and moved in with my ex-boyfriend until graduation.

Freedom was short-lived. At the Military Entrance Processing Station, I learned I was two weeks pregnant. My plans crumbled. Though my ex-boyfriend, the father of my baby, urged me to consider adoption, I chose to keep my baby. He promised to stand by me and enlisted in the Army, and we married in a courthouse ceremony before moving to Colorado.

Living with him was a harsh awakening. He resented me, spent our money frivolously, and was drunk the night I went into labor. Even after our son was born, he prioritized games and friends over family. Yet, I convinced myself to persevere. Divorce wasn't an option in my family. I vowed to give my son the love and protection I had never known.

Behind closed doors, I struggled. My then-husband's obsession with thinness fueled my eating disorder. Starvation, binging, and laxatives became my coping mechanisms. At one point, I weighed only 90 pounds, my fingertips able to meet around my waist. My health spiraled—autoimmune thyroiditis, debilitating periods, and chronic fatigue—but I soldiered on, believing control over my body and environment was my only refuge.

Escaping the Noise

The drive to control didn't end with my eating disorder—it spilt into every corner of my life. I was overworked, overexercised, and overgave, desperately trying to prove my worth through constant motion. Helping others became my escape, and nursing felt like the perfect outlet for my need to pour myself into something meaningful.

When my son was just a year old, I started night classes, determined to be a great mom *and* an exceptional student. A 4.0 wasn't a goal; it was a requirement. I must be at the top of my class; it was non-negotiable. Then, a year before graduation, I decided to have a second baby—because isn't that what married people do? I convinced myself it was the "right time", even though my schedule barely left room to breathe.

The truth? I wasn't just chasing success; I was running—from the noise inside me. The voice that whispered, *You're not good enough. Not smart enough. Not pretty enough.* I buried those feelings beneath an avalanche of accomplishments, but my body wasn't fooled. It responded with unexplained health issues, one after another—a physical rebellion against the emotions I refused to face.

Breaking Point and New Beginnings

In 1997, at 38 weeks pregnant, we moved to Fort McClellan, AL, where I gave birth to my second son. I promised myself I wouldn't fall back into starving my body—not while he was a baby. But at my six-week checkup, the scale read 138 pounds, and panic set in. I spiraled back into calorie counting, eating just enough to sustain breastfeeding, terrified of gaining weight.

When my baby was 14 months old, I took my first job as a nurse at a family practice office. The stress was overwhelming—it felt like living in my parents' house all over again, walking on eggshells every day. My health began to unravel. My periods grew heavier and more painful, headaches and fatigue took over, and bloating made me look pregnant again. I even went 14 days without a bowel movement once. A GI doctor's advice: "Drink milk; it might give you diarrhea." Seriously?

Years of binging and restrictive eating had taken their toll, and my body couldn't keep up. Things worsened after I got breast implants—another effort to fix what felt broken, this time at my husband's request. Our marriage deteriorated. He spent his time gaming while I struggled alone, and every time I brought up leaving, he threatened suicide. I stayed out of fear—fear of failure, fear of what others might think.

At 25, I hit my breaking point. Doctors found a dermoid tumor binding one of my ovaries to my uterus, and surgery was scheduled to remove the ovary and tumor. But when I woke, I learned the procedure had revealed severe endometriosis. They had to perform a hysterectomy as well.

I was left with an incision stretching from hip to hip and doctor's orders to take six weeks off to recover. But there was no time to rest. My husband was absorbed in his gaming and offered no help around the house or with the kids. The internal medicine practice I worked at insisted they couldn't manage without me and called me back to work just two weeks post-surgery, leaving me physically and emotionally drained.

To protect my children, I decided early on they would barely know my parents, ensuring the cycle of harm ended with me. My role as a mother was clear—to create a safe, nurturing environment for my kids, one completely different from what I experienced growing up.

But it wasn't just my parents I had to protect them from. My children's father, who should have been their ally, became another source of instability and betrayal. One evening, my husband called, telling me to park down the street and hide under a hoodie because he lied to his Sergeant, claiming I'd abandoned the family. His scheme? To get a family hardship discharge from the army, divorce me, and then remarry once he was out.

He underestimated me. My strength, my resolve, and, above all, my instinct to protect my children outweighed everything else. That night, I knew it was time to leave the marriage.

I wrote a detailed letter to his First Sergeant, explaining his struggles with depression and suicidal threats, hoping they would help him get the support he needed. Instead, they transferred him to Korea. In 2001, as my boys and I watched him board the plane and wave goodbye, I knew it wasn't just the end of his assignment—it was the end of our marriage. We never saw him again.

From that moment forward, I fully embraced my role as both protector and provider. I was determined to build a life for my boys that was grounded in strength, stability, and love. No matter what it took or how difficult the path, I would ensure they were safe, nurtured, and free from the cycles of pain I had endured.

I'm forever grateful for the strength God gave me and the blessing of my two sons. It wasn't easy, but it gave us all a chance at a better life.

A New Chapter: Love, Trust, and Healing

A few months later, fate set me up on a blind date with an incredible man. Neither of us wanted anything serious—just a light connection. But the universe had other plans, drawing us together and revealing the true meaning of love and trust.

He became everything my children needed: a father figure who was hardworking, confident, and loving. The boys bonded with him instantly, telling me they wanted him to be their dad. He loved them as his own, adopted them, and admired me, cherishing my role as their mother.

His commitment to us never faltered—not for a second. Twenty years later, on his wedding day, our youngest son said something that still echoes in my heart: "The best decision you ever made for me was marrying my dad." His words reminded me how deep our bond runs, how love can heal, and how choosing the right person can change everything.

Even though I was married to an amazing, supportive man, my struggles continued. I battled with deep-rooted beliefs that I wouldn't be loved or wanted if I gained weight, fueling my cycle of binging, restricting, and overexercising. It wasn't because of my husband—it was because of the tight grip those beliefs had on my mind.

With these health problems plaguing me, I longed for someone to listen and guide me toward feeling better. After a devastating gynecologist visit, where he suggested immuno-suppressants because he "didn't know what else to do," I threw my medications in the trash and decided to find my own way to heal.

I realized that on days I didn't eat, I felt better, so I began exploring the cause of my issues. Reluctantly, I went gluten and dairy-free, a rare choice in 2002-2003. I was told it was all in my head, but the symptoms—headaches, bloating, fatigue—proved otherwise. It took years, but by 2011, I had fully eliminated gluten and discovered an allergy to cow's milk.

A Bold Shift: From Traditional Care to Root-Cause Healing

During my nine years at a family practice, I built deep, trusting relationships with patients who often felt stuck. Many, in their 30s to 50s, were resigned to fatigue, high blood pressure, diabetes, or high cholesterol, believing these were inevitable signs of aging or genetics.

Because I had transformed my own health, I knew there was more I could do for those patients. That realization led me to make a bold move—I shifted my focus to teaching patients how to eat, exercise, and take control of their well-being.

At the time, I thought it was that simple, but I quickly learned there was much more to uncover. I became certified in First Line Therapy, a 12-week lifestyle program that helped many patients reduce or eliminate their need for medication. Seeing these transformations was inspiring, but I was even more intrigued by those who didn't see results. They drove my deeper exploration into root-cause healing, leading me to pursue advanced education in holistic nutrition, functional medicine, and trauma healing.

This journey was also personal—it led me to discover that my oldest son had celiac disease, a condition that had gone undiagnosed for years. It became clear to me that symptoms are the body's way of communicating that something is wrong, and addressing them at the root level is the key to lasting health.

In 2019, I took a leap of faith and fully committed to my own practice—a decision that has been the most rewarding of my life.

Today, I specialize in crafting individualized, transformative plans for clients, helping them uncover and address the true causes of their symptoms. One high-achieving client came to me feeling utterly burned out and betrayed by her body. Exhaustion, bloating, and weight gain had taken a toll on her physically and emotionally. Together, we uncovered the underlying stress and unresolved emotions disrupting her gut health. By addressing these root causes, she eliminated bloating, regained mental clarity, and reclaimed control of her life. Seeing transformations like hers reaffirms my mission: healing is possible when we address the whole person—mind, body, and spirit.

A Letter That Changed Everything

A pivotal moment in my healing journey came in 2007. I sat down, heart pounding, and poured every ounce of raw, honest emotion into a letter addressed to my parents. In that letter, I laid bare the pain I carried, the hurtful actions that had shaped so much of my life. It wasn't about accusing or seeking their validation—it was about giving myself permission to release the burden of guilt and responsibility I had been shouldering for far too long.

Whether they read it or not didn't matter. That letter was for me—a declaration that I would no longer let their actions define my life or dictate my healing. Writing it allowed me to step firmly into my truth and begin the process of letting go.

It wasn't easy to confront those emotions or to acknowledge the boundaries I'd placed to protect my children. But through that raw honesty, I found clarity. I realized healing wasn't about fixing what had been broken in the past but about claiming my power in the present. As long as I stayed true to myself and the journey I was on, I could create a legacy of love, safety, and strength for my family.

The Breakthrough: Confronting the Past to Embrace the Future

COVID changed everything. My clients were overwhelmed, grappling with the resurfacing of unresolved emotional and physical traumas. For the first time in my career, the root-cause methods I had relied on for years—methods that had always worked—seemed to fall short. Nothing I tried brought the breakthroughs they desperately needed, and I felt powerless to help them.

Doubt crept in so deeply that I even considered leaving the field altogether, entertaining the idea of switching to real estate, which felt like running away from the passion that had driven me for decades. It was a moment of profound uncertainty, forcing me to confront not only my professional challenges but also the personal blocks that were holding me back.

It became painfully clear after my grandfather's death, which left a deep void in my heart. Losing him was like losing a connection to a source of light in my childhood. His absence left me grappling with layers of grief, guilt, and unresolved pain—feelings that had been buried under years of self-protection. I had distanced myself from my family to shield my own children from the trauma I endured, but that decision came with its own cost.

The aftermath of his death, coupled with painful encounters with my parents, intensified the weight I was carrying. Questions that I had long suppressed began to surface: *Who am I? What is my purpose? Why can't I help my clients?* I felt like I was failing—not just myself but the people who depended on me.

Then, two dear friends invited me to a 3-day event called **The Powerful Living Experience**. Skeptical but desperate, I hesitated, but the tagline "Grow your business by changing your mindset" piqued my interest. As I stood in line on the first day, I whispered to a stranger that I would leave if it didn't resonate. Doubt consumed me: *Why am I here? Am I wasting my time?* Yet, something deep within urged me to stay.

What I now know is that God guided me to that pivotal moment. That event introduced me into a container that became a sanctuary for confronting my deepest limiting beliefs. One exercise, in particular, reshaped my life in an instant. Through visualization, I faced my parents—not with anger, but with gratitude. I thanked them for everything they had done to me because, through it all, I had become a strong, independent woman. Saying those two words—*thank you*—altered my very being. It didn't excuse the past, but it allowed me to release its hold on my present. For the first time, I felt an intense sense of peace.

That moment marked the beginning of a transformative journey into healing. I immersed myself in practices like **Transformational Mindset, NLP (Neuro-Linguistic Programming), Neuroscience, Murray Method Trauma training**, and other healing modalities, delving into the depths of my trauma and finally emerging with clarity, resilience, and purpose.

Beneath the Surface: Tying Auto-immunity to Trauma

In September 2023, I attended a 3-day immersive mindset retreat, part of my business coaching program. We focused on a 12-step process to identify our *Core Program*—a deep-seated belief shaped by our parents' belief systems, often passed down through generations. Unlocking it is essential to reaching our full potential.

On Day 1, during Step 4, I confronted my deep-rooted resentments. I thought I had none, believing my hardships had shaped me. But there it was in writing: *Resentment #1: My mother did not protect me.* Seeing it on paper shocked me. It was hard, but I was determined to release this emotional baggage once and for all.

On Day 2, under the humid Costa Rican sun, I worked out and soaked in some vitamin "sea". The waves crashing against the rocks brought life to every cell in my body, carrying some of my burden away.

Walking into my first embodiment session, I felt butterflies—nervous, excited, maybe even terrified. Others spoke of feeling lighter and more grounded after. My need for control tightened my stomach, but stepping into the unknown required me to trust someone I barely knew.

I started off laying facedown on the massage table and was instructed to just let my body move intuitively through the process. My arms and torso were moving with any conscious effort. I could feel the intense energy within my body, although I did not understand what was happening, and I did not need to know; I just needed to breathe. Halfway through, I was told that it was time to roll over and lay on my back. As I moved to my back, he whispered that we would be going through a process to release the stored energy from my body. "Put your hands on your neck and say, 'Sometimes I do not feel safe'," he said. As I placed my hands on my neck and listened to his words, I was paralyzed. I watched two slow movies flash vividly before my eyes. First, my thyroid goiter, then my mother being dragged up the stairs and choked on the bed by my father. Water poured from my eyes and I was so deeply ingrained in these movies that I could not speak or even respond to him for what seemed like minutes, although it was probably seconds. I was finally able to speak and move through the remainder of the session. It's difficult to explain. I felt like I was giving birth to pain that had been trapped there since childhood. Water streamed down my face, and my body moved to expel trauma energy that had been trapped for over 45 years. Never in my life have I ever experienced anything like it.

When he said the session was complete, I jumped up, eager to leave. I couldn't handle those intense, uncomfortable feelings—I wanted to shove them down. He gently touched my arm and said, *"I know you want to get on with your day, but you just went through a lot. You need to lie down and let the process complete."*

With mascara running down my face and messy hair, I made my way back to my room, grabbed a beach towel and went out to the garden to lay on the ground. A flood of tears streamed from my eyes, and I felt this immense shift in my body. Thoughts raced through my mind. "Was I what trapped my mother in this abusive relationship"? "Did she hate me because she had such a difficult delivery? Did she believe what my dad said, that I "ruined her"? "Was it easier for her to let him abuse me so that she would not reap his blows? "Maybe she did not know how to protect me." Years of pent-up energy were released from my body through tears as I was connected energetically to the earth and to God. I connected to a God that I had not trusted in many, many years because I thought I could not trust him to protect me, and here I was, surrendering to him. I could not and did not want to carry the burden any longer.

Uncovering Trauma's Whisper

I've known for a long time that trauma affects the body. Sending that letter to my parents years ago was a first step, but it wasn't until recently that I connected a specific incident from when I was three to my thyroid goiter and autoimmunity. My unconscious mind knew the trauma link was there, and at 49, I was finally ready to face it.

We can only connect the dots by looking back. For years, I stuffed down childhood trauma, moved away, and tried to live my life. But if you don't deal with trauma, your body eventually starts screaming—manifesting symptoms and creating difficult circumstances until you're forced to listen.

I've questioned whether my parents truly loved me. How could love coexist with such cruelty? They weren't impaired by alcohol or drugs, yet their actions left me burdened with guilt and shame. I've since made peace with them and let go of anger and judgment.

The truth is, while I thought I was helping others, God was guiding me to help myself—to face the damage I buried. This was the root cause of my symptoms, and confronting those deep-seated beliefs was the most life-changing transformation of my life.

I realized I was never really in control. The things beyond my control shaped me and spurred my growth. The only way out of chaos is through it. When life feels unbearably hard, you must keep going. Breakdowns lead to breakthroughs, but only if you face the discomfort head-on.

Your Symptoms Are Messages—It's Time to Listen

All that I have been through in my life has prepared me to help women heal, I know this deep in my soul. If your body is crying out with symptoms—fatigue, brain fog, bloating, weight gain or chronic pain—know this: these are not just physical ailments but deeper messages from your body, urging you to listen.

I've been where you are—feeling stuck, overwhelmed, and unsure of the next step. But I'm also proof of what is possible when you embrace healing from the inside out because I get to live it now. That's what I want for you."

My coaching blends cutting-edge science with compassionate support, offering tools like NLP and trauma-healing techniques to address not just symptoms but the deeper causes behind them. It's a holistic approach that delivers lasting change. Imagine waking up each morning with boundless energy, a clear mind, and the confidence to face any challenge. That's the life I help my clients create—and it's one you can have, too. You are not alone in this journey. I've walked the road of pain and transformation, and I am here to walk alongside you. Let's rediscover the vibrant, powerful woman within you—because you deserve to thrive and live life on your own terms.

HEATHER HANSON

Heather Hanson, celebrated as the "Gut Health Paramedic," is a best-selling author, dynamic speaker, and leading wellness expert renowned for her transformative Digestive CPR and Mindset Revive Frameworks. With over 26 years in healthcare, Heather is dedicated to empowering individuals—especially women facing bloating, fatigue, brain fog, and weight gain—to reclaim their health and vitality through a holistic approach that addresses the body, mind, and spirit.

Heather's journey to becoming a wellness advocate is deeply personal. Having triumphed over autoimmune thyroid disease using her own methodologies, she understands the frustration of feeling unheard by conventional medicine. Her experience drove her to uncover the root causes of health struggles, combining expertise in digestive health, hormone balance, detoxification, and mindset shifts to help others heal on a cellular level.

As a speaker and author, Heather inspires audiences to reject the idea that poor health is a life sentence. Her passion lies in helping clients understand that symptoms are the body's way of communicating deeper issues. Through her personalized coaching, she creates clear, actionable roadmaps that empower clients to break free from cycles of pain and limitation.

Heather's work emphasizes the importance of connection, hope, and a plan. She believes that true healing happens when individuals feel heard and supported. Her clients experience profound transformations—not just in their health but also in their confidence, energy, and overall well-being.

Whether on stage, in her writing, or through one-on-one coaching, Heather's mission remains the same: to guide others toward a life of thriving, not just surviving. Her powerful message continues to resonate with those ready to reclaim their health, unlock their potential, and live with passion and purpose.

Website: https://linktr.ee/redheatherh

7

INTUITION AND INSTINCTS

HAYLEY CHAMBERS

Animal Crazy Kid

Animals have never been "just pets" to me - they've always been family, teachers, and a source of endless fascination. From as far back as I can remember, my life revolved around creatures great and small. As a little girl, I would fill my days collecting lizards from the garden, carefully placing them in a makeshift terrarium, assigning them names and personalities, and then setting them free - only to catch them again the following week. My curiosity knew no bounds. I devoured books about animals, glued myself to wildlife documentaries, and meticulously kept a diary of every species I dreamed of one day owning. My scrapbook, filled with clippings of sprawling farms and animals from magazines, wasn't just a pastime; it was a vision board for the life I was determined to create.

It wasn't a phase - it was a complete obsession! One that my teachers acknowledged (every story or creative writing activity involved animals as the main characters) and an obsession that, thankfully, my parents were happy to accommodate. We always had a family pet, and at one stage, when I was only about three years old, I followed the family dog 'Deefer' - a scruffy little terrier mutt - down the road and into bushland for a long walk on my own, causing my parents to engage the entire neighbourhood out looking for me. Just before the police were called, Deefer came trotting out of the grass with me following close behind. My mum was frantic! I don't ever remember being scared or worried - Deefer and I were taking on the world!

As the years went on and I became a teenager, I swear to this day, the only thing that kept me on the 'straight and narrow' and away from the many delinquent ideals that I could have succumbed to were my animals, especially my dogs, and horses. I always had something waiting for me back at home that needed feeding and taking care of. Animals kept me grounded. They helped me through those difficult puberty years when I was trying to fit in somewhere but always felt a bit different. But the animals - I could understand them, and they seemed to understand me more than the humans surrounding me.

Later in my life, I realised that my "not fitting in" was actually undiagnosed ADHD, which goes misrepresented in girls as we are very good at masking. I was excellent at being a 'copycat' on the outside, but inside, my mind was usually whirling from one thing to the next, except when I was with my animals. When I was working a horse, riding, or training a dog, the world slowed down for me. My brain was able to do one thing at a time, and I would feel grounded, present, and complete clarity. In my early thirties, I discovered archery - specifically horseback archery - and I found another thing that could slow my mind down. The feeling of galloping on a 500kg horse and shooting bows and arrows - I still cannot believe how fast my body is moving upon that horse, yet how slow and clear my mind can feel when I perform this ancient martial art. The trust I can put in my horse, and I just know that he is looking out for me, and I'm looking out for him.

I never had an issue with the animals, ever. I found my intuition would kick in, and often, I would just know what I needed to do to help that individual. I couldn't always explain it clearly to clients when I was doing a handover of their animal that I'd spent hours training - in the equestrian world, we call this *'feel'.* Feel is something you simply cannot teach. But it was only later in my career, when I focused on helping people with their challenges, that I realised how important this *'feel'* would become and how ignoring my intuition and '*feel*' would change my life forever.

Passion Turned Career

Animal Instincts Australia began as a horse and dog training business but evolved as I shifted focus to the Disability and Mental Health sectors, using animals as the core of my facilitation. After 18 years of working with animals and their guardians, I realized it was the people who needed the most support. While animals came naturally to me, people were more complex - and I thrived on the challenge! I've always been drawn to "outside the box" animals and helping them thrive, so it felt natural to extend that passion to people with unique needs and challenges.

I love my work. I love my clients. And most of all, I love sharing my animals with wonderful people and seeing the joy that it brings to both parties. I've always been amazed at how animals can change people's energy and bring joy, even in moments of pain. I constantly told people that I had the best job in the world. And whilst there were always challenges in business, I took all of it in my stride because I had my animals by my side.

While I've found success in areas like working with animals and building my business, my personal life has often followed a different, more complicated trajectory. I've always had a tendency to attract individuals carrying emotional wounds or personal challenges - perhaps a reflection of my own desire to help and fix. But as I've grown and gained perspective, I've come to see the crucial difference between two types of people who seek support: those who are ready to take responsibility and actively participate in their own growth and those who remain stuck in a victim mentality, pointing outward to blame others for their struggles. On the surface, both groups can appear similarly in need of help. But time has shown me that while some are eager to learn and make meaningful changes, others seem more comfortable staying where they are, entrenched in their pain and unwilling to acknowledge their own power in shaping their future. For the latter, life becomes a narrative of external forces conspiring against them, a story where they play the victim while expecting others to fix what they themselves won't face.

With animals, I can meet them where they are at, and with each and every step, we begin to trust each other and build a relationship together. They help me out, and I help them out. There is no deceitfulness, no resentment, no jealousy, and they are able to live in the present moment. I feel empathy for their path and enjoy helping them become more confident and more content in their life.

My ability to listen to my intuition and instincts with animals has almost always been spot on. With people, however, the biggest lessons were yet to come......

The Catalyst - April 2023

I'd always dreamed of having a springer spaniel, but my tendency to attract rescue dogs meant purebreds rarely came my way. However, a breeder I'd helped rehome many pups for offered me a special gift in return - a beautiful little puppy named Dodge. With soulful eyes that seemed to pierce through me, he felt like an old soul, as though he'd been here before. I felt incredibly lucky to have him, and his soft, sweet nature made him an instant joy. In the first few weeks, I broke all the "puppy rules," letting him sleep on my bed and snuggle with me, feeling that he was destined for an extraordinary life as a therapy dog and one of our best mates.

One night, Dodge became unresponsive, and we rushed him to the vet. Though breathing, he wouldn't wake. The next morning, the vet informed us that he had passed away from a seizure, likely due to poisoning, based on his bloodwork. We were devastated. This sweet little boy, who had brought us joy for a month, was gone. My son was heartbroken, and we were left grief-stricken and puzzled. After examining our property, we suspected a tree with potentially poisonous berries might be to blame, though no other dogs had been affected in our years there. We removed the trees and tried to move on. Given Dodge's short time with us, we didn't share his death with clients, many of whom were navigating their own challenges. Instead, we simply told them, "He's not here now," sparing them unnecessary detail.

Two weeks later, my son and I attended a horse event. I was running late, and though I usually brought some dogs with me and hesitated, thinking I should make an effort to bring some, I decided it would be easier to leave all five at home. We were also fostering three puppies at the time. After taking care of all the animals and giving our adult dogs bones, I headed to the event. I sent a message to our staff chat, inviting them to visit the event if they had time. Upon returning at lunchtime, I unloaded the horses and let the dogs out of their kennels. After our past experiences with brown snakes, all our dogs lived in off-the-ground kennels while we were away to keep them safe.

One of the dogs was Gal. Gal came to me as a 'secondhand dog', and the running joke was always that her umbilical cord never stretched far from me. She was the matriarch of our canine pack and had raised puppies herself, being pregnant when I adopted her as an adult. We had also kept two of her gorgeous pups, Ace and Rosie. It was not surprising to anyone around me that Gal was my girl! I loved and adored her and her me. We went almost everywhere together. She was my shadow. I'd always wanted a brown kelpie, and she was just beautiful. Instead of bouncing out of her kennel like usual, she was listless and had vomited on her bedding. She looked so unwell, and I instantly suspected pancreatitis from a fatty bone.

I kenneled the other dogs and rushed Gal to the vet, where they suspected pancreatitis. After transferring her to the overnight emergency clinic, they recommended fluids, medication, and a change of diet. When they took her from my arms, I hugged and kissed her, telling her I loved her and would see her soon. It was the last time I saw her alive. Later that night, the vets called to say she'd had a seizure and, while alive, was unresponsive.

Around the same time, I noticed our other dog, Arlo, showing signs of illness. Arlo, a bold and energetic Jack Russell Terrier gifted to my son for his 4th birthday, had always been the tough boss of the pack, even surviving two brown snake bites.

With heavy hearts, we rushed Arlo to the vet, leaving our other dogs and foster pups at home. My partner reassured me Gal would recover, but my intuition told me otherwise. When we arrived, the vets admitted Arlo for tests, and I was faced with the devastating decision to euthanize Gal. She lay lifeless on the table after a massive seizure and hadn't regained consciousness.

I was overcome with grief - screaming, crying, and utterly shattered. We took Gal's body home, planning to take her to the pet cremation service in the morning. That night, the vets assured us Arlo was stable.

His tests were clear, and he remained bright and alert, giving us hope amidst the heartbreak.

I told our staff what happened and that I would be unavailable at work that week. Our clients also had worked with Gal often in their therapy and coaching sessions, and so many people had built a love for and bond with her. I knew our clients would ask me where she was, and I was absolutely not ready to have that conversation. I was an emotional mess.

The day after Gal was euthanized, and on our way back from the pet crematorium saying goodbye to my beautiful girl, I received a phone call from one of my staff informing me that one of the foster puppy boys, Cloud, had also experienced a seizure and was non-responsive. We raced home to pick him up but also picked up every dog on our property - Cloud's two siblings, Haze & Rain (foster pups), and our other dogs, Ace, Rosie, and Georgie. I remember looking over at this Coach, who was also in tears and exclaiming, "What have we done to deserve this? What the hell is going on?"

My world was falling apart, and my worst nightmares were becoming reality. We rushed Cloud to the nearest vet, hoping to save him, while taking our other dogs to the emergency clinic, where Arlo was still admitted. We wanted all our dogs in one place for overnight care in case more issues arose.

While at the emergency vet, our local vet called with devastating news—Cloud had passed away. Blood work was done on all the dogs, but little Haze and Arlo had started to decline. Things weren't looking good.

My parents came to pick up my son and I thought it would be best for him to say goodbye to Arlo in case he didn't make it. His blood work now was showing liver failure, and his levels had gone from great to awful very quickly. The vets were also puzzled as to why all of these beautiful dogs were getting so ill without a history of problems.

Unexpected Farewells

I was in shock; the staff was shaken, and clients were arriving confused about the missing dogs. I hadn't eaten in almost 48 hours, and though devastated, my partner stayed strong for me and the remaining dogs. Ace, Rosie, Georgie, and Rain were cleared by the vet and brought home, but we left Haze and Arlo in care. I cuddled Arlo, hoping he'd recover his bright spirit, but deep down, I knew we'd lose him. His weakness was heartbreaking, and I dreaded telling my son.

At home, we were hypervigilant, not letting the dogs sniff or roam unsupervised, checking every sigh or sneeze. My anxiety was overwhelming. Then the call came - Arlo had a seizure and passed, and Haze was deteriorating rapidly. At the vet, we made the heartbreaking decision to euthanize Haze to prevent further suffering. The vets agreed it was the kindest choice.

Here I was, a "successful animal-assisted therapist" who would do anything for her animals, holding my 11-year-old son's 4th birthday present in her arms, wondering what the hell was happening in our lives and losing so much faith as the moments passed.

Our local vets offered to do autopsies on the foster pups, and we took Arlo to the pet crematorium, where they were shocked that we would ultimately bring 5 dogs over a period of 2 weeks. All of the vets were confused and in tears, racking their brains as to what had happened to these beautiful dogs.

"I don't know how to move forward from here," I said to my loyal friend and staff member. And I genuinely didn't know how. I've always been a ridiculously positive person in my life, despite challenges, and, to be honest, I probably tended to look at most people and situations with rose-colored glasses. I had previously overcome a divorce from a loveless, deceitful marriage and had built my businesses from the ground up. I was always inclined to see the blessing and lesson in each situation, even the really difficult ones that life had thrown at me over the years, usually in my personal relationships with partners or friends.

Despite my drive and determination in every aspect of my life previously, here I was with little faith left, and everything felt hopeless. I didn't know how to get through each day. I'd lost five dogs in the course of 2 weeks, four of those over 48 hours. Same blood work. Same symptoms. As far as the vets were concerned, the same poison. I was an emotional mess.

To say our clients, families, and care teams were supportive during this time would be an understatement. Not only was I devastated, but I was also fearful of the state of my growing business. How would our clients cope? How would they handle knowing that 5 dogs they'd worked with week in and week out had all died so unexpectedly? To this day, words couldn't possibly describe what my clients did for me. When they would see me, I would receive hugs and kind words, and some beautiful little people who normally struggled to show emotions and sometimes even kindness to other people would share their compassion in the way of touch, handmade cards, hugs, tears, fundraising for me and even giving me some of their own pocket money to help with our growing bills. I was so touched and reminded every day that it wasn't always me helping them; THEY would become my therapists during this time. I will be forever grateful for them just being their amazing, authentic selves and simply holding so much space for me and my team when we were all struggling to process the enormity of what was happening to us.

A week or so later, I went camping for a few days to get the dogs off our property and get away from all the traumatic scenes I had experienced in those days prior. I remember one night, I was outside and saw the biggest shooting star I'd ever seen before. I instantly thought about Gal, Arlo, Dodge, and the foster pups. I asked them over and over, *what happened? Where are you? Why aren't you here now?*

On this trip, little Rain, the last foster pup, suddenly fell ill, sending me back to the emergency vet with a car full of dogs. Thankfully, after an overnight stay, the vets determined it was stress from the many changes and the tension of the ordeal. Young pups don't handle constant upheaval well!

To say I was stressed, anxious, depressed, hypervigilant, and in fight, flight and freeze mode is an understatement. My body was racing, and I felt constantly sick physically, emotionally, and mentally.

The Truth Uncovered

Before this event, a long-term staff member with mental health challenges became increasingly difficult to manage. Their work ethic had declined, and attempts to address the issues led to complaints to their other therapists, resulting in constant meetings about their problems. I ignored my instinctive discomfort when they arrived at work despite knowing I no longer wanted them there. Terminating their employment was complicated by their mental health needs, so I restructured their tasks and schedule to reduce disruption to the business and staff.

However, my nervous system was constantly on edge as I continued to endure each shift with them.

After the dogs were killed, we emptied every bag of food, every bag of bones, every treat packet, went through our own pantry, every plant on the property, every bowl, toy, and piece of bedding. We disinfected all of the kennels and everything that the dogs could possibly have access to. Our local government research agency continued over many weeks to run tests to find what poison had killed our dogs and began to rule out anything on our property. During this time, all of the staff exchanged stories of previous weeks and compared notes of various interactions with each other. The same conclusion continued to be met. This staff member, whom my intuition had told me was becoming a big issue, helped an accomplice of theirs enter our property whilst I wasn't at home and baited and killed our dogs. The local police, along with an ex-detective on staff, all agreed that these people were the culprits of this event as the 'balance of probabilities' was directed towards them without a shadow of a doubt.

The guilt I felt for not listening to my instincts shattered me. And to this day, is a lesson I will never forget.

Succeeding with Sorrow - Heavy Hearted Dreams

Our goal was always to buy a larger property, one where our family could thrive and the business could expand. Although we lived just outside Toowoomba with amazing landlords, we were still renting. After the tragic loss of our dogs, I declared to my family, partner, and friends, "I'm moving; I can't stay here." Our home was near a highway, and despite installing security cameras, we felt constantly on edge, especially when people drove by slowly. There were just too many painful memories at this property now. We needed more space to ensure the business and our lives could continue safely and securely.

We had no deposit. But there were no more excuses. We ended up in the hands of an incredible small agri-business banker who took us on and helped us in getting a loan. If he's reading this, I hope he realises how important his contribution was to us in succeeding in our move and changing our lives.

The end of April 2023 was when our dogs were callously murdered, and by the end of September 2023, we had secured a loan and were moving into our own 103-acre property. It had been like living in a hurricane of survival mode for those months.

However, never in my dreams (or nightmares) did I ever think the REASON I would be buying a place would be because someone I knew had killed 5 of my dogs.

We made the mammoth move - so many animals, infrastructure, and organisation went into this effort. We shut down the business for only one week, whilst my partner and I worked night and day to get the ball rolling again. We had signed up for a MASSIVE mortgage (different kind of stress!), so I couldn't afford to close down for too long.

Whilst I was still in hyperdrive and knew that I hadn't dealt with all of the trauma, I at least felt like we were moving forward somehow. One of the first nights at the new property, I stood outside and looked up and saw a massive shooting star - again, all I could think about was Gal, Arlo, and Dodge, reminding me that they were also here for this. Keep on going!

Within a week of us moving, I discovered I was unexpectedly pregnant. I was 41 years old and had a now 11-year-old boy. We had a huge mortgage, and whilst I knew whatever happened, I was sure we could overcome it, listening to my intuition - my inner voice told me that something wasn't quite right.

My partner was so excited as it would be his first child, and whilst he wanted us to at least tell our closest family, I was reluctant. My instincts were telling me not to get too excited. The doctor and my partner kept assuring me that many women have children in their 40s and that there was nothing to be concerned about.

However, upon the first pregnancy scan, I knew that the news wasn't good. The baby had no heartbeat, and I was having a miscarriage. My partner was devastated, and whilst I was upset, I wasn't surprised.

My dogs had been killed only 5 months earlier, we'd endured the stress and hurdles of finally getting a loan, moving to a new property, trying to be a good mum, and now this, a miscarriage. I felt like everything was crashing down around me. During this time, I advised my staff what was going on and asked them to just do their job and explained that I simply didn't have any capacity to support them with any of their own dilemmas or issues in life at this time. About 10 days after finding out I was miscarrying, I was rushed to emergency with a massive bleed, spending a night there whilst they administered medication to hopefully complete the miscarriage. However, lo and behold, a week or so later, following another ultrasound, I was advised that things still hadn't moved along, and I was to spend yet more time in hospital with surgery for a curettage. I was really questioning why I was being 'punished' by the universe in this way. When I could in the past see lessons and blessings, all I could feel now was trauma, depression, and melancholy.

Just before my surgery, I received an unexpected resignation from a long-time staff member who had been with me from the start. While I awaited my procedure, she informed me she would be using her sick leave for mental health reasons and would not be returning. This news was a blow during an already difficult time. I needed to set boundaries for my health and asked for some space, but it seemed she took this personally and chose to step away. Soon after, another colleague, a close friend of hers, also resigned.

Another staff member and dear friend of mine bluntly told me, "Hayley - you have created a culture of saying YES to your staff and everyone around you, even when you should say NO!" And she was right. I had always given so much of myself to everyone around me. My staff, clients, partner, everyone. And yet, it always meant saying no to my own self-care. I had treated many of my staff like clients who needed my help, and I celebrated what I thought was a great 'family' culture. However, even my administration assistant said to me, 'Hayley, you do so much for everyone else, and when you just need a little help and patience because you've had a rough f**king year, where are they?" She was right.

I entered into 2024 with four staff down, one contractor up, and a ton of trauma. Happy New Year!

The Danger of Distraction - Intuitive Lessons for the New Year

Determined to recover lost time and tackle a hefty mortgage, I launched into 2024 at full speed. With minimal staff, I stretched myself thin, working long hours and burning out. Despite coaching others on self-care, I knew I wasn't following my own advice. Yet, with mounting bills, I felt I had no choice but to push through.

I regularly worked 6-7 days a week, often having to send my child to his grandparents, who, as always, were understanding and helpful. I told myself I'll keep doing this till Easter, and then I'll re-evaluate my situation and maybe slow things down.

Truth be told, if the next big STOP sign in my life hadn't happened, I wouldn't be writing this story now.

As Easter weekend 2024 approached, almost a full year after losing my beloved dogs, a staff member with ongoing performance issues needed help purchasing a horse. Once again, I set aside my personal time to assist them. Instead of spending the day recharging with my son, I loaded him up, five dogs, a few extra kids, and the horse float and drove two hours to perform a pre-purchase horse inspection - a favour I'd often done for others in the past.

As a long-time equestrian, I know the importance of being grounded, present, and mindful when working with horses. They have an incredible ability to sense even what we may not be aware of within ourselves.

Despite this knowledge, I made a regrettable mistake. In a hyperactive state, I ignored my better judgment and decided to mount a "quiet school horse." The result was far from quiet - I was bucked off in a dramatic rodeo-like fashion, sustaining a badly fractured and dislocated ankle. I had to be airlifted from a small country hospital to the Toowoomba Base Hospital for treatment.

When I was first asked if I wanted to ride, my intuition and instinct immediately told me to decline, and I initially said, "No, thank you." However, when the owner reassured me the horse was quiet, I second-guessed myself and changed my response to, "Well... why not?"

I ended up with a trimalleolar fracture - an ankle broken in three places, including a snapped fibula and a separated tibia. Two surgeries, two weeks in the hospital, and a minimum 12-month recovery with no horse riding ahead. If I reinjure it with the two plates and 13 screws now in place, amputation could be considered.

Yet, thank you, Universe! This forced break (literally) pushed me to reassess my life, business, boundaries, self-care, and work-life balance. Like it or not, I was finally forced to rest.

I was home from the hospital and had 6 weeks on crutches. During this time, I lost yet again another staff member - the same staff member who I'd helped out that weekend. Again, this is another case of my boundaries not suiting their responsibilities and their personal needs. However, I am so grateful for the lessons that I've learned.

Animal Instincts and Intuition - A New Chapter

Every time I ignored my intuition or excused red flags, I faced the consequences. It wasn't punishment from the universe but a reflection of my choices. The universe operates as it does, leaving it up to us to listen to our inner voice or disregard it - and to live with the outcomes of those decisions. Working with animals has always brought me a sense of peace and connection. I instinctively understood them, and they seemed to understand me. My intuition in those relationships was unwavering. However, when I began ignoring my instincts with people and took on responsibilities that weren't mine to carry, everything began to unravel.

Since Easter 2024, I've learned not to ignore that intuition. I say no regularly. I've put boundaries in place for my own self-care and well-being, and I don't feel guilty or worried about other people's responsibilities or their opinions of me when I place my own boundaries and speak MY truth. What I've learned is that we don't need a reason to say no or tell someone that 'this is not right for me,' and there is no need to apologise for that.

I share my story to inspire you to trust your inner voice without apology and to embrace your natural intuition - your innate "animal instinct" - with confidence. Live in the moment as animals do, grounding yourself in the present, and trust in your own wisdom and embodiment. Animals are unapologetic for how they feel and how they live THEIR lives.

This way of living is truly liberating. While I'm still healing from the loss of my beloved companions, I feel their presence as my guardians, guiding me to honor my inner voice. Let their message be yours too: your instincts and intuition are powerful, and they are never, ever wrong. Trust them - and trust yourself.

Hayley Chambers

Hayley Chambers is a transformative coach, counsellor, author, and speaker with 25 years of expertise in personal development, coaching, and the animal industries. As Managing Director of Animal Instincts Australia and Outback Equines, Hayley has redefined empowerment through animal-assisted therapy and coaching. Her programs integrate evidence-based strategies with the intuitive wisdom of animals, helping individuals build resilience, overcome challenges, and unlock their full potential.

Inspired by her personal journey through grief, loss, and the pursuit of self-care, Hayley has learned the transformative power of trusting her instincts. Animals played a pivotal role in her healing, grounding her in the present and teaching her to embrace life's unpredictability. These same animals now empower her clients, fostering growth and self-discovery in alignment with Hayley's philosophy of connection.

Hayley's programs cater to diverse audiences, including children with disabilities, women seeking empowerment, and professionals in high-stress industries. Delivered from her picturesque farm in Queensland, her workshops combine innovative methods like equine-assisted therapy, team-building, and leadership development.

A passionate advocate for human-animal connections, Hayley's programs also support the rehabilitation of rescue animals, embodying her commitment to social enterprise. Her work reinvests in the community, promoting accessible, inclusive services and fostering well-being for people and animals alike.

Through her workshops and speaking engagements, Hayley inspires individuals and organizations to reconnect with their intuition, foster resilience, and embrace authentic living. Her compassionate approach and dedication to creating life-changing experiences make her a sought-after speaker and facilitator. Living her passion alongside her son and a team of extraordinary therapy animals, Hayley advocates for the transformative power of human-animal connections.

Website: https://www.animalinstinctsaustralia.com

8

NO MORE SECOND PLACE

MANDY MERRIFIELD

Happy Friday

Woosh!

Off went a morning text to my best friend: "Good morning, happy Friday!" with a sunshine emoji finishing off the message.

After being sober now for about 18 months and having recently landed a new job that was the highest paying gig I had ever had, I was pretty damn grateful and optimistic about life.

Ding.

"You know, when you send me messages like this, it puts me in a bad mood for the rest of the day. You know I am NOT a morning person."

What

The

Fuck

Vanessa and I had been best friends since 1984.

We had met when I was 10 on my first day at Queanbeyan Public School, and had been as thick as thieves ever since. Sleepovers, formals, being the first person we told when lost our virginity, trips away, school band together, being number 1 and 2 in all of our classes throughout our schooling days, being those girls who always got picked last in class team sports, school camps. She was my biggest protector when I went into a back brace with severe scoliosis; visiting each other in university years, trying out make-up, drinking port from her dad's stash on the top of the fridge, just hanging out on weekends, happy being us. I remember my first-ever sleepover at her place at the age of 10. Her dad had given us sausages for breakfast, and I promptly threw up. A story revered for 30 years. Vanessa was the matron of honour at my wedding, she is my daughter's godmother. She was the sister I never had, I thought we would grow old together.

Ness had always been forthright. She enjoyed shock value. I told her not to say "fuck" in her wedding speech. Her wedding to an American. Americans who she hated loudly and mouthed off about throughout high school; they were "crass, egotistical and self-centered" so she said.

When she met, started dating, and married an American, no one was allowed to remind her of these opinions.

She didn't listen to me about the wedding speech either. Fuck was said several times.

Ness sending me a message like this didn't actually shock me as much as you might expect.

What happened next shocked me more.

"Yes," I texted back, "but you know that I AM a morning person, and maybe after 30 years, it would be nice for us to compromise."

Did I just stand up for myself?

Goodbye Best Friend

Since getting sober, I have been on a bit of a rollercoaster of self-discovery.

What had led me down the neck of 8 bottles of red wine a day?

Why my kids leaving me wasn't enough to stop me from drinking?

When I lost my job, why wasn't that the wake-up call I needed?

After lying on the floor for 3 whole days, unable to move, paralyzed with depression - why, when I came out of it, didn't I ask for help?

When my hair started to fall out, when I was covered in unexplained bruises, as my skin started to peel off, when my body shook uncontrollably all the time from delirium tremens, when I couldn't hold a pen when I couldn't walk down a set of stairs without holding on for dear life, the dizzy spells that left me disoriented, when I realised that I hadn't showered for a week when I couldn't remember the last time I put food in my mouth... why didn't I realise that something was really wrong?

The day I stopped drinking, I had $1.17 to my name, I had destroyed my career, I was over ½ million dollars in debt with no way to pay it back, and the worst of all, my precious daughters had left me. My oldest daughter left about 18 months before I hit rock bottom, going to live with her dad permanently. She was about 14 and a very straight-talking teenager who was done with me. The hate in her eyes and her parting words stung "I am sick of living with a zombie for a mum." I oh-so-wish those words had stung enough for me to do something about it.

They did not.

I continued in my alcohol haze, trying to convince myself every single day that I was in control of this thing.

I was not.

My youngest daughter left to go and live with her dad as well, about 3 months before rock bottom arrived. She was 13. I remember her curled up in the corner of her bedroom, crying her little eyes out. Big gulping sobs. She looked so little, sad, and helpless in that bedroom in the country home I had bought after my divorce. "I don't want to leave you Mum, but I have to."

Her tear-stained face should have pulled at my heartstrings, those maternal protective mamma bear ones.

They did not.

I had broken her heart and I had let her down. I don't know how many times I had promised her that everything was going to be okay.

And it wasn't okay, not by a long shot.

So, my baby left me. And rightly so.

To this day, I don't know of the level of trauma she endured as I slipped further and further down into alcoholism. This is something I will never forgive myself for.

After I got sober, both girls returned to my life for a while - though they never lived with me again, not even to this day. It was an uncomfortable relationship, they were waiting for me to fuck up again, to have another drink, to let them down as I had so many times in the past. The air was a tightly drawn piece of string... ready to snap at any time during the awkward milkshake dates; eventually, the milkshakes dried up, and there was only a phone call here and there. But I still had contact, which meant I still had hope.

But I hadn't been the mum they needed me to be, and this will haunt me until the day I die.

My life had disintegrated before my eyes. Addiction does that to you.

And now, it seemed my best friend of thirty years and I were disintegrating too.

And funnily enough, I was ok with it.

I'm Not Good Enough

As I let go of the Band-Aids and masks that alcohol had given me - the things so many women cover up - the needing and wanting to fit in, the being able to have the courage to think we are actually good enough, to mistakenly think that we are just like everybody else, the confidence to be truly ourselves; I had started to find a new respect for myself.

And as I started to build a life that was really and truly me, I started to shed a lot of other things that didn't serve me – people pleasing, pretending to like things I didn't, being happy to speak up loudly about what I had been through, and not actually giving a shit about what other people thought of me.

And where had these things come from in the first place?

I think I had been this way because I had always been different.

I was born with one and a half lungs, my heart had moved over in my chest to where the other part of my lung was supposed to be. I nearly died at birth and was always a sick little kid. There were so many things I couldn't do.

Fourth grade. All the kids had cool backpacks, I had a brown, old-fashioned school case; I hated it. Why couldn't I have a cool school bag like everyone else?

We lived right across the road from the little school, on a quiet street. I could have easily walked the 5 meters across the road to home in the morning and afternoon, but Mum walked me. By fourth grade, at least, she would just stand on the lawn and make sure my brother and I got across the road safely. I now know it was because I was so precious to her, but at the time, it was mortifying.

Picking up my brown school case at the end of the day one afternoon, walking down the hall with three of my closest friends - they were talking about a team they had joined; the first game was on Saturday. I excitedly asked what we were doing. We did everything together.

Some of the mums had put together a netball team. I wasn't invited to be a part of it. I was so sad. And I felt so left out.

This wasn't an unusual feeling. Mum often had to come and get me at lunchtime when I was 6, 7, and 8 - so that she could "paddle" my back to get the gunk out of my lungs. It meant that I missed lunchtime; I was left out of the girl talk, the marbles, and all the other things normal kids did at school. Friendships aren't made in the classroom, they are made in the playground.

Paddling my back to loosen the phlegm hurt. Mum would turn over one of the purple vinyl dining chairs so I could stretch my little body out over it, and she would paddle with her cupped hands for at least half an hour every day. The phlegm loosened, but I was never able to actually spit it up; I just swallowed it back down. I think Mum got frustrated and sometimes a bit angry.

"I'm not good enough," my inside voice mantra that I didn't even know existed when I was 6, 7, and 8. But it was there... a little old chestnut that was lodged firmly in my head. I wasn't even good enough at spitting up phlegm, for Christ's sake - I couldn't even do that.

"I'm not good enough:" it was a second skin. A part of me just as surely as the sun rises and falls every day. It was just who I was.

Twelve years old. I was called back into the school nurse's office after our vaccinations. All the other kids were laughing at each other, the boys punching the girls on their arms where they had just been jabbed. But here I was, sitting on a chair while the school rang Mum. The nurse had detected a severe curvature in my spine, and less than a month later, I was in a fully moulded back brace. It went from just above my bottom at the rear to over the top of my shoulder blades and at the front - from the top of my pubic bone to just under my breastbone. There was also a massive wedge underneath my left armpit to try and push my whole body to the right.

I wore that thing for nearly 4 years, every day for 23 hours a day. The skin on my hips was worn red raw, as was the skin under my armpit. The only way to treat it was with an astringent that stung like nothing you have ever experienced. I had to wear a singlet every day - even on 40-degree days. I couldn't swim, not ever. Not on holidays, not down the coast with my nan and pop, not at my best friend Vanessa's house, not at school swimming carnivals, where all the other teenage girls were so cool in their neon bikinis (it was the 80s - neon yellow and pink, and wham t-shirts were da' bomb). The hour that I was allowed out of the brace, I had to do about 30 minutes of exercise, and the other 30 minutes was split into 2 x 15-minute showers.

And there was no point complaining.

It was what it was. I just had to take it on the chin.

I definitely wasn't one of the cool kids.

And I definitely wasn't good enough.

So, as these alcohol Band-Aids started to peel off, one by one, the phlegm of my life started to come to the surface with the help of therapists, doctors, and psychologists - this time, I was able to spit it up.

I was comfortable standing up to Ness. I had figured for a while now that our friendship would probably fade away ever so slightly. We have different lives, different interests, very different opinions about things, different lifestyles, and very different friend circles these days. She thought skulls and skeletons in terrariums were great house décor items, I was more of a Hamptons shabby chic. Even though I have a degree in Political Science, I am not overly interested in the goings on of federal government policy; Ness is staunchly labour, a union rep, and calls her federal minister by name.

We were certainly not the 10-year-old girls who had met all those years ago. And why would we be? People grow and have different lives, different experiences, and different influences.

I loved her anyway.

So even though I was a morning person, and she was not, I was happy to let our friendship settle into its new form organically without any big announcements or fanfare. I wanted to keep the love and the memories, and the laughs and even the tears. They were precious to me.

Life went on. I was traveling a lot for work and was actively seeking a role that would help me relocate from Queanbeyan to Sydney. By August 2019, I had moved to the leafy suburb of Cremorne Point on Sydney's Lower North Shore, and life was continuing to get better and better each day. In October 2019, I celebrated three years of sobriety.

My Epiphany

Huh? Facebook must be down or something.

As I kept driving in the eerie winter darkness around Lake George, I had an odd feeling in my stomach. I couldn't quite put my finger on it and couldn't shake it.

I pulled over.

Checking Facebook messenger again: "You are not friends with this person" was the innocuous subtitle under her name. I flicked over to her profile. It said, "Add a friend".

Again, my immediate thought was that Facebook was down or there was something wrong with the algorithm.

I had moved to Sydney about a month before and was coming home to Queanbeyan for the weekend.

But I texted her anyway: "Hey Ness, I'm on my way home and went to message you so that we could have coffee tomorrow, but it seems we aren't friends on Facebook?"

As I was typing this text message, I held my breath as the three little dots bubbled on my phone.

"I've sent you an email."

"Oh? I haven't received one from you?" I replied.

As I gave her my new email address and waited for the unknown email to drop, I felt like time was suspended. The emotion was rising up my throat and into my cheeks, and I felt a resignation settling in.

And then it landed.

An email that ended the friendship with the person I had known as my best friend for most of my life.

One would think the body blow would have felled me, but it didn't.

I had actively made a decision to let this friendship organically fade into a new form. And stupidly, I thought she would do the same. I had valued the life that we had together. I didn't want the memories soured.

But that wasn't her style.

She had to be in charge.

She was and always had been the alpha in this friendship.

And by standing up to her months before when I had asked for a compromise on our circadian rhythms, I had upset the balance. And that was not ok.

So she put herself back in the driver's seat.

What really saddened me was the knowledge that as I continued to grow love for myself and settle into a version of me that I was happy with for the first time in nearly 45 years, was that I would lose a lot of things.

And one of those things appeared to be my best friend.

This is a story of how I let myself be second, not only with Vanessa but in all aspects of my life. I remember having a habit of saying the most stupid things just to get a laugh from people. And I don't know why I did that. I am a very intelligent woman. But by getting people to laugh at me, I guess I thought they would like me more.

This isn't a story berating my friend.

This is a story of how I didn't love myself enough to stand up for what was important to me. This is a story of me learning to accept myself in all of the fabulousness, all of the flaws, all of the love, and all of the big hope that I have. This is a story of me finally working out that I am good enough.

And how I learned to do that.

The Day

Thursday 13th October 2016. The day.

The day that every single part of my being pushed through and I took my life back.

I had been drinking around 6-8 bottles of red wine for about 3 months now; I had no idea whether it was day or night, whether I was drunk or sober (hint: I wasn't sober), I had no recollection of my life 5 minutes before, and I didn't know how I had got here.

I was 42 years old. I came from a rock-solid local family, I had a degree from one of the top universities in Australia, I had a great job, two beautiful daughters, and a home in the country.

My husband and I had divorced about 5 years earlier. I had realised that the white picket fence life wasn't for me and didn't know how to get out of it. So I went into a deep depression before making some spectacularly stupid decisions which ended the marriage.

Mummy Wants a Wine

I'm not sorry the marriage ended, but I am sorry for the way it ended. If I had my time again, I would use my words.

After leaving my marriage I started to go about re-building the Mandy that I knew was still in there. The independent, sassy, tough, fun, social girl of my uni days. Alcohol had been a big part of that identity.

Funnily enough, as I now reflect on this in my fiftieth year - that 'Mandy' was all a front. Alcohol had given me the courage to be what I thought everyone wanted me to be. It is only now that I am starting to figure out who I actually want to be.

Nevertheless - post-divorce, alcohol came back.

When Holly was born in 2000 and my husband at the time told me that I wasn't allowed to go back to work, my other mum friends and I discovered "mummy wants a wine time at 5 o'clock". This meme was really taking off at the turn of the century, and as I had unwittingly become a stay-at-home mum and very quickly lost my independence, this was something fun to grab onto. And that made it easy for me to have a BIG glass of white wine with the Bold and the Beautiful on Channel 10. And soon, one glass became two, and sometimes three, before my husband got home from work at 6 pm. I guess I was hiding from the reality I found myself in.

I had unexpectedly fallen pregnant with my daughter after 6 weeks of dating, which meant my husband and I never discussed things like what kind of life we wanted, how we wanted to raise our children, careers, and money. And while Holly and Paige are the absolute best thing that ever happened to me in my life, and I would not swap a second of them, nor ever give back a precious hair on their head, my life changed - and his pretty much didn't. He went back to work after a couple of days, worked 6 days a week, and then felt that it was his right to hang out with his mates on a Sunday because he had worked all week. And I was at home. No more career, most of my friends had moved away, no money of my own, and I absolutely lost my whole identity. No more independent, strong, fun, sassy, intelligent Mandy (the Mandy I had curated and thought that I wanted to be). Just a mummy and a wife.

There is nothing wrong with being a mummy and a wife if that is what you want.

But for me, it wasn't very long into the marriage when I started to feel trapped. I had never really wanted to live and stay in my hometown, I had wanted to live a big life and see the world. By the time I had my second daughter, I was severely depressed. This was not something that was talked about out loud in the early 2000s.

Surprise, surprise: drinking doesn't help depression. But it does numb it. So you get caught in a vicious cycle.

As the marriage deteriorated, my drinking got worse - usually a bottle a night for years and years and years.

Eventually, the marriage ended.

Trapped

As I tried to re-find myself after the divorce, alcohol was a constant - because alcohol IS a constant in Australian society. All the marketing, all the ads you see on TV, all the Hollywood movies - every professional woman you see has a glass of champagne in her hand; she is having a martini or cosmopolitan with her girlfriends (Sex and the City, anyone?), or is sipping a whisky as they were working late into the night at their very important job.

My now ex-husband was an integral part of my family. My younger brother's best friend, my even younger brother working for his company. He (my ex) had been around my family since about the age of 13, and even after the divorce, he continued to be front and centre. I didn't ever ask for my family to choose between us, but it would have been nice to have some space for me to rebuild without him.

I didn't get that luxury.

He was invited to every family event, birthday, Sunday afternoon BBQ, and my parents even invited him and his new girlfriend out for dinner on a random Wednesday evening - just because.

The trapped feeling wasn't going away. So I bought a house out in the country to try and give myself some distance between us. My girls hated this, and they went from being with me most of the time to week about with their dad. I got it, and I don't blame them. They were teenagers, they wanted to be with their friends, and they didn't want to commute an hour each morning and evening to school.

But in that off-week, the loneliness set in. And how did I cope with that?

Booze.

And it quickly got worse.

The one bottle of white wine soon didn't even touch the sides, it was just the starter before I got into the red. And the red wine went from one glass to two and then to three.

There were many mornings I was in no fit state to drive the hour into Canberra for work, and working from home wasn't a thing (it would be another 10 years before Covid hit our shores). So my work performance got worse (when I was even able to turn up at all). I quit before they sacked me. And then the drinking escalated.

The 'it's 12 o'clock somewhere' saying would roll around in my head, giving my justification for early afternoon drinking, and then I figured, what the hell was the difference between 11:50 am and 12:05 pm? Once the morning drinking barrier was broken, it was on.

Within 6 weeks, I was drinking to the point of blacking out.

October 2016. I was probably around a week or two from death - either by my own hand or from my body shutting down from alcohol poisoning.

The Time Has Come

I don't know what the switch was, but I remember thinking, 'other people don't live like this.'

Abject nothingness.

I was the only one who could make the decision to turn this around.

I had tried this before. I knew what was coming.

As quickly as I could (and I'll let you in on a secret - it wasn't quick at all), I got a face cloth, a bucket, and a few bottles of water ready.

It was around 10 am in the morning, just before, actually.

Why do I know this?

Because it was too early for any of the bottle shops to be open yet.

There was a glass on the sink. The leftovers from the night before. For weeks and weeks I had transferred 'last night's leftovers' into a new glass, refilled it, and started again. For any red wine drinkers out there, you will know that red wine leaves silt in the bottom of the glass after a while, so the silt had built up over weeks to a slushy grit that constantly occupied my days of drinking.

Down the sink.

There was a splash left in a bottle.

Down the sink.

Not strong enough to have a shower, I changed into a summer dress, one that wouldn't touch me anywhere.

I was going to start sweating.

Soon.

Twenty-four hours of cold sweats and vomiting. Blood red bile. The remnants of weeks and weeks of 'only red wine going down my throat' bile. Until there was nothing left.

And then the bile was clear and phlegmy - like when I was 6, 7, and 8. But this time, it was coming up.

And then real delirium set in.

And hallucinations.

It was now Friday night, I hadn't had a drink since Wednesday evening.

I knew that if I didn't get to the hospital and get medical treatment soon, I wasn't going to make it. But I lived in a little country town; there were no such things as Uber.

I willed myself to get through the night.

I packed a bag. Hot pink. I watched *Australian Story* on repeat on my iPad. An inspirational young journalist from a good family and with a stellar education (just like me) who had secretly battled the booze, too - until she got outed on national television. I kept thinking, "If she can do it, so can I."

Morning came.

It was now or never.

I picked up the bag.

I fed the dog and the cat.

I picked up the car keys.

And then I rang Mum.

"Good morning darling," she sing-songed.

We all answer the phone the same way. My nanna, my mum, my aunty, myself, even Paige.

"Mum, I need you to listen to me."

'Ok'. The sing-song tone immediately changed.

"I am going to the hospital. I am an alcoholic, and I am 3 days sober. If I don't get help, I am going to die."

"Oh my god." On repeat.

I can't even imagine the shock. I had been excellent at hiding my dark little secret.

"But darling, you can't be an alcoholic - you have a degree."

As I explained as shortly as I could (this was taking every ounce of willpower I had) - that "yes" indeed I was an alcoholic, and I understood she was in shock - but that the "Oh my gods" was making me feel judged - I told her that I was ringing to give her advance warning. The hospital would ring my next of kin when I got there, and I needed them to be prepared.

Action stations.

The flip switched in Mum's brain. I will forever be thankful to my parents for that day. There has never been any judgment. Just love.

I had been at a crossroads of life and death before as a baby and as a little kid with one lung full of phlegm.

"Ok, darling, tell me what you need."

I explained that when I got to the hospital, they would take my vitals and likely put me on a drip for fluids and also probably Valium to help with the DTs. They would call her when they were ready.

A phone call to Mum was done; I willed one foot in front of the other.

This was THE hardest thing I had ever done in my life, bar none.

My legs did not want to move.

I spoke out loud to myself.

Move your leg, Mandy.

Good.

Now, the other one.

Good.

Again.

Good.

Again.

All the while, my brain screaming at me: you don't need to do this. You can moderate. Don't be stupid. Just drink on weekends; you can stop at one. Only drink when you are with friends. Just don't drink red wine, only white. You haven't tried hard enough to control this. You can drink just like everyone else; don't be so stupid. Change to cider.

And I kept moving my legs.

One, by one, by one.

The hospital visit went as expected. The nursing staff at the counter told me they had never seen such an organised alcoholic.

I was three days sober, though, and after the Valium and fluids, my parents were phoned to come and collect me.

I stayed one more night in my country home, with my mother by my side. We left the next day. Thankfully, I was able to stay with my parents for the first 8 weeks of my recovery, the revolving doors of doctors' offices, therapists, counsellors, psychologists, and even an AA meeting (which wasn't my thing), trying to walk around the block sometimes, medication and vitamins and tests. Trying to work out how much damage I had done, and ever so slowly putting my life back together.

Hard doesn't even come close to describing it.

Having to tell people that I was an alcoholic, watching the absolute disbelief on people's faces, the lack of understanding of how this could happen to a smart and intelligent woman, the "surely you can just have one?" people, the look from my ex-husband - "I've known you had a problem for years" (gee thanks...); the uneasy conversations with my girls, trying to convince them that I was really and truly done with letting them down. That I was back to being a good mum.

It was a never-ending roundabout of shame, guilt, hurt, and anger. Anger mostly at myself. I wanted forgiveness, but I knew I didn't deserve it just yet, and maybe never.

Imperfectly Rebuilding

February 2019. Awkward phone calls with Holly and Paige were still a thing. The difference now was that there was about 300 km separating us from Queanbeyan to Sydney.

I knew that I needed to get out of Queanbeyan for my own sanity. There was no way I was going to be able to fully rebuild my life into the person I knew was in there somewhere while I was surrounded by the traumas and trappings of my old life.

I spoke to the girls once or twice a week, and on this particular day with Holly I asked a question I had clearly asked before, maybe once, maybe twice, I don't know. She was disparaging, to say the least. I'm sure she thought I was drinking again.

I was not.

When she spat at me, "You've already asked me that, Mum,"; I sputtered back - "darling, I just want to talk to you, and sometimes you make it hard, so I probably go back to familiar topics."

"Well, why don't you tell me about how you and Vanessa aren't friends anymore - tell me about that" she spat at me.

Caught off guard, I tried to explain.

She wasn't having it. In her mind, Vanessa was the stable one, the intelligent one, the one who hadn't divorced her husband, the one with a secure and normal public service job. I was the alcoholic, I was the one that left.

So she believed Vanessa.

I do not know what was said between my best friend and my daughters. But once again, Vanessa had put herself in charge and enlightened my girls to the state of our friendship. I had chosen not to do that - not from a need to protect myself, but for them. I do not push my thoughts or experiences onto other people, I prefer people to make up their own minds based on their own interactions and intuition.

I had taken the high road.

Big mistake.

I don't blame Vanessa. I blame myself. I should have backed myself enough to tell my girls what had happened. But I didn't trust that they would understand, and maybe they probably still wouldn't have - but at least I would have been in the driver's seat.

Holly blocked me. In every conceivable way. Text, phone, email, Facebook, Instagram, Snapchat, WhatsApp.

And a couple of days later Paige did the same.

And then Covid hit the world.

At some point in the ensuing years, Paige suffered from an eating disorder. No one told me.

I got a letter from her. Her psychologist told her that it was a good idea.

In the letter: "I have a mother, and she is wonderful. It is not you."

The old chestnut: I'm not good enough.

Surely this wasn't something I didn't have to prove to anyone? I had given birth to her. I am her mother. I hadn't been a great one for a while there - I am highly cognisant of that... but I had been sober for over 5 years now, and I worked damn hard every day to be the best version of myself.

Thank god for that psychologist, and thank god for Paige's boyfriend - because between the two of them, that letter was the start of us rekindling our relationship.

And I am her mum. And she loves me. And now, in 2024 - she wouldn't have it any other way.

I Love You, Mum

Mum, don't look up. Just keep walking.

What would you do if your daughter said that to you? Of course, you would look up.

And I did.

And there she was. The woman who had been my best friend for 35 years. Walking the opposite way around the lake on a midwinter's Canberra morning, walking towards me with her husband (the American) and her daughter.

Too late.

Awkward.

Vanessa and I exchanged very stilted pleasantries, I think there was a "How are you?" somewhere.

Totally surface.

"And you?" Vanessa asked me.

"I am well, thank you." Being nasty or short was not going to benefit anyone, and that is not who I am.

Having dropped an earring. Vanessa's daughter and husband busied themselves trying to find it, conspicuously removing themselves from this awkward as-arse interaction.

Earring found; time to move on.

"Bye."

As I walked away, so many feelings swirled in my body and my mind.

Sadness for what we had both lost.

Regret that it couldn't be different.

And also a sense of peace.

I was ok.

I am completely comfortable in who I am. My skin fits me.

It has been eight years since alcohol has passed my lips.

In that time I have rebuilt from less than nothing. My life is not perfect, but it is pretty damn good - and I'll take that every single day over the life that I was living as an alcoholic.

My body has returned to full health, and apart from the fun and games of being a 50-year-old menopausal woman, I am fit, healthy, and active.

My daughter Paige is studying nursing, and she is my constant. And I am so proud of her. We speak every day, sometimes twice.

And I show up for her, she is my world.

I show up for those in my family who want me, I show up for my clients, I show up for my friends (a small and valued circle), I show up for my spoiled schnoodle Ivy (who lives a life of pure luxury), and I show up for my work.

And I show up for Holly, too. I send love out into the universe for my beautiful daughter, hoping she knows somehow that it is there.

Thousands of people have been able to move into a better life space, overcome trauma or a bad habit, work through challenging situations, or manage their anxiety and mental health in some small part because of me.

The world of ***self-leadership for women*** is a fascinating one, and so fulfilling to be able to work in. I use my lived experiences, my corporate background in leadership and capability development, and my plethora of studies in positive psychology, hypnotherapy, communication, well-being, and resilience to help women find a path where they can ***discover*** their true selves (minus the expectations of what society tells them they 'should' be doing). Along the way, and as I have done myself - I support women to ***accept*** themselves without judgment (and this means... all of the good, all the bad, all of the fabulousness, the flaws, and everything in between) and to be able to come to a sense of peace with the life we live. When we discover and accept ourselves for who we truly are at the core, we then open ourselves up to be able to ***manage*** our life in a way that is congruent with our higher self, the self that fits our skin, the self that we know - at the heart of it - is truly you. From here, you can continue to **grow** as life goes on.

What a beautiful way to live.

How peaceful.

Such contentment.

Completely fulfilled.

Coaching women with love and compassion brings me untold joy. But if you are one of my clients, don't think I am going to take it easy on you!

I keep it real; I will call you out, I will challenge your thoughts and what you think are your norms, and I will push you out of what you think is your comfort zone to a place you may not even realise is the place you want to be.

And you will love me for it.

"Come on, Mum, let's go and get an ice cream. You did good; love you."

"I love you more, Paige."

MANDY MERRIFIELD

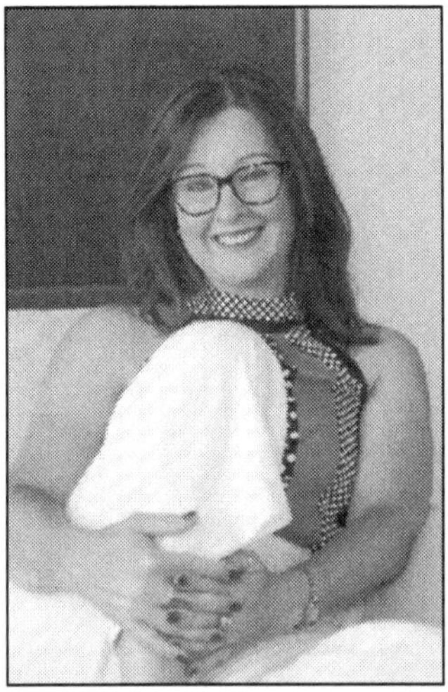

Mandy is a leadership coach who knows what it's like to overcome challenges and transform your life. She has a rich background in corporate leadership and organisational culture, where she helped many people grow and thrive. But after a personal trauma in 2016, she decided to shift her focus to helping individuals find joy, recovery and transformation in their personal lives. She has trained in various modalities, such as hypnotherapy, neurolinguistic programming, timeline therapy, positive psychology, acceptance and commitment therapy, and more. She is passionate about sharing her skills and insights with others who want to create positive change in their lives.

Website: https://www.simplywell.me

9

MY AWAKENING: THE RISE OF THE WARRIOR WITHIN

PAMELA SPENCER

Love is the most universal, the most tremendous, and the most mysterious of the cosmic forces. - Teilhard de Charin

Chasing the light in the darkness

I awoke to the sound of loud knocking at my front door in the middle of the night. Feeling disoriented and groggy. I slowly got out of bed and moved quietly down the dark hallway toward the front entrance, where I heard the noise echoing. I peeked out a long, narrow window next to the door and saw two dark figures standing in the shadows. Feeling shivers run down my spine, I turned the front porch light on. Looking through terrified eyes, I saw two men in uniform standing there with both their badges and guns in clear sight. I was in complete disbelief as one of the officers spoke to me, saying, "This is the police. May we come in and talk to you?" Shaking and trying to pull myself together, I cautiously unlocked the door and asked them to come in.

As they entered my home, they told me their names and asked me my name for identification purposes. As my heart started pounding out of my chest, I asked the officers to please tell me what this was about. They both stood there for a minute, just looking at me. Then, one of the officers asked, "Is anyone home with you?" I told them, "No." Slowly, one of the officers said, "We regret to inform you that your husband was involved in a fatal snowmobile accident tonight." Cold chills ran down my spine. After gasping for air, I said, "Could you please repeat what you just said?" One of the officers repeated it again and then said, "I am sorry to tell you this news." In a sudden outburst of tears, I cried, "MY GOD NO! THIS CAN'T BE TRUE." In this moment of horror, the only thing that kept me coherent was the deep need to see him. When I asked which hospital he was taken to so I could go there, one of the officers said, "At this time, you are unable to." They then asked if there were any family members I could call. With tears flooding down my face, I told them I would call my brother.

With my whole body trembling, I slowly put my brother's phone number into my cell phone to let him know what had just happened. I tried calling him three times until he finally answered. Within thirty minutes, he arrived at my home. My brother is my pillar of strength, and I am deeply grateful he was with me during these dark hours. He had asked where my daughter was, and I told him she was at her best friend's house having a sleepover. Then he asked if he could stay as the night drifted away into darkness, bracing for the impact of what the morning would bring. Morning came painfully and slowly. I needed to call my daughter and have her come home to tell her about this accident. I remember taking deep gasps for air as I tried to call her friend's home phone number. Every time I reached the last part of the phone number that would connect me to her, I kept ending the call. I knew from the moment our 14-year-old daughter came home to learn of this tragedy it would change her life forever. I tried to honor these last moments of her childhood, which had been flooded with love from her happy family. Shaken to the core, unimaginable violent disturbances ran through my mind and emotions as my body went numb, not knowing how to tell her this devastating news.

Approximately an hour later, the phone call finally went through, and I briefly spoke with one of the parents, asking if they could bring her home now. While my brother and I waited for her to arrive, he had placed a phone call to our mother, as she had been travelling out of state and was already booking a flight home.

Nurture, Heal, Elevate

Uncomfortable as it is, I learned that I needed to feel the pain and despair from my loss. At age 45, I had become a widow, and many months following the accident, I had a hard time accepting this truth. I missed him immensely, and though he was gone, I still felt married. In the grace of time, I slowly began accepting the word "*widow*" and the impact that it had in all the facets of my life. At the beginning of this journey, I also had waves of despair for my daughter, who had lost her father at the age of 14. The depth of my grief required time and space to fully process and understand. Moreover, in all honesty, I found that one of the most valuable lessons I learned was the importance of sharing emotions with one another openly, especially the challenging times. This has been incredibly supportive in our healing journey. As a parent, I had been extremely protective of my daughter and wanted to shield her from the pain. I had taught her to find the internal strength of a warrior, but this inadvertently delayed her grieving process. With self-compassion, I later learned that grief is its own teacher beyond comparison.

Loss became my teacher. After years of steadfast belief in myself in embracing healing through realms of loss, I came to understand that grief is the greatest expression of love that there is. In the sacred art of grieving, I found that it is the deepest of passion and connection. This helped in healing every part of me. In times of tears and sadness, there was a rediscovery of the divine love of infinite power it holds. In self-reflection, I understood that no matter how difficult the adversities in life were, it is in the magnificent power that love permeates all. I had slowly built a foundation for my mental fortress as time moved forward. In reflection of what Brene Brown shares in her writing, "Without understanding how our feelings, thoughts, and behaviors work together, it's almost impossible to find our way back to ourselves and to each other," these words helped me in cultivating the beginning of recovery.

As I sat there in deep reflection after the loss of my husband, having realized that I was still in a wave of unpredictable emotions, faith flickered grace and encouragement within. Though grief has no timeline after loss, healing can be tempered as time passes. As time moved onward, feelings of overwhelm slowed. And when I did experience symptoms of heart palpitations and nervousness, I realized the stress and overwhelm began to reveal itself again. At that point, I slowly breathed in and out to calm my thoughts. Whenever I took a deep breath, I imagined a radiant love of light flowing into me. As I exhaled, I envisioned sadness and stress leaving my body. This practice became a quick reset in the most pressing moments of stress and fear, turning the chaos into calm.

I had only taken 4 weeks off from work after the accident. This had been extremely difficult, as I had experienced feelings of sadness and grief, difficulty concentrating, and feelings of isolation. Yet, through these struggles, I felt I also needed to rebuild a sense of normalcy in life for my daughter. So, I decided that going back to work would be a good starting point. What this new normalcy was supposed to look like for her and me, I did not know. What I did know is that I needed to keep the faith and trust in myself in the process of decision making and changes that were yet to come. In the first year I faced fears of the uncertainty in raising a child as a single parent. I vividly remember talking to my mother after my loss, feeling her unwavering support as she listened patiently to my worries about the times I needed help in caring for my daughter with her school schedule and other activities. She reassured me that I wasn't alone and she would always be there for both my daughter and I and reminded me of the unconditional love that she has for us.

Within a couple of months following the loss, I focused solely on the well-being of my daughter and I. Previous to the accident, I was always ready to help others. After the accident, I quickly learned to say "no" unapologetically in all that did not serve my daughter because I felt more protective than ever. The first time I experienced saying no unapologetically was two months following my return to work. A boss had recommended I take a management position to replace the current boss who was planning to retire. I knew this meant longer hours and additional stress, and even though the pay and position were better I was not willing to trade my time in for money. The power of saying no had a tremendous empowering effect on my mental health and built more courage to stand up for ourselves. The choices I made were strategically aligned to prioritize my daughter's well-being and put her needs first. Time for healing became essential for survival for both.

For the first two years following my husband's death, the tranquilizing journey of tears and pain saturated every part of my life. Only later it started to slowly turn into soft waves of peace. Through the slow acceptance of loss, no matter how difficult days were, it is in love that his presence was always felt through seemingly random occurrences like a familiar song or a beautiful bird hovering above me. It is through the presence of an *inner knowing* that permeated the bond we shared. Beyond what I see, the intangible aspects of love, hope, inner peace, and unforeseen forces guided me through my grief journey. Through self-reflection, I realized the adversities and hardships in life have become a teacher of faith, resilience, and self-trust. In the gaining of self-trust, I found comfort in a Buddhist tenet that taught me to allow everything to rise, feel it all, and release what needs to go. Through the voyage of loss, I was finding an inner strength that I never knew I had. In watching the sunrise I felt the promise and miracles that every new day brought. I realized that there are hidden moments of magic sprinkled in between the vortex of peace and awareness. Even the sun itself casts a powerful, bright light of beauty, forcing the shadows to run and hide, and this is how I felt; love started to overshadow my sorrow and pain. In both the adversities and mystical moments in life, love binds all. As I evolved into my deeper authentic self, I realized it was the balance of vulnerability and honesty that was crucial for my personal growth.

A Mother's Wisdom

My mother lost her husband in her late forties and two sons some years later. And she knew all well the journey I would endure. Yet, in her walk of faith, she had taught me profound lessons. Her guidance helped in the understanding that there is no timeline when we are experiencing grief and healing. It is in the cherishing of the memories we hold dear to our hearts, they too will both hurt and heal on our journey of loss. I remember one quiet evening at home while watching a movie. I felt empty inside. I missed him being here. Then by taking a deep breath, I became fully focused on the present moment, and a sense of closeness filled me. This moment taught me the secret to the unseen is truly in the present moment.

The invaluable wisdom that my mother taught me about the importance of being financially independent and prepared me for the future without knowing just how instrumental this advice would be. As she raised four children on her own, being a single parent, her drive, tenacity, and times of struggle, she succeeded. Though she did not have a college education, her work ethic and inner strength guided her in positive financial decisions. I recall many times over my teenage years of growing up in her sharing the importance of obtaining a college degree in a career that I truly enjoy to have financial stability. I am forever grateful for this wisdom, as being a financially independent female continues to provide a sense of security, autonomy, and empowerment, allowing me the opportunity to give myself a future life of security and freedom.

At the age of twenty I registered at a local college to be a registered nurse. A few years into my career, I chose to return to college to obtain my master's degree as a family nurse practitioner. Little did I know that this would provide security and flexibility for my daughter and me. Additionally, having financial planning with a financial advisor significantly helped with my goal setting and decision-making.

Unlock Your Power

> "Women, whether subtly or vociferously, have always
> been a tremendous power in the destiny of the world."
> - Eleanor Roosevelt

Some of the most significant adversities experienced become an intricate part of personal and spiritual growth. I have learned, though, that healing is non-linear. With grace, I feel a renewal to my wounded soul. "Healing grace" became a transformational gift in my emotional wellbeing.

The strength behind the love of family and friends ripples through every aspect of my life. Their impact continues to foster joy in all its wonder in the corners of my heart. In honouring the relationships in my life, these bonds continue to cultivate a sense of belonging and provide loving support.

And of life's treasures, a few years after being married to my husband, our daughter, was the most precious gift that life had blessed us with. Looking back, the moment we heard the news that we were going to be parents was the most majestic time of our lives. Our daughter had truly been our magnificent miracle. She continues to teach me just how magical life can become, no matter how intense the challenges are. In holding our visions close to our hearts, we have the power to move forward in a loving space. The unbreakable bond between a mother and child is sacred.

Love is deeply personal. I slowly accepted the things I could not change. The narrative of "I don't know what to do" turned into "I am honouring my authentic self and choosing to align with positive actions, which helped to recharge my inner power. I realized that saying, "I don't know what to do," tied with self-doubt, had diminished my power. This occurred as I felt overwhelmed by the sheer tasks involved in managing rental units we owned that my husband had been in charge of, including repairs. I had developed limiting beliefs when I was a young girl that *I was not good enough,* from social expectations to gender stereotypes. Through personal growth, I replaced limiting thoughts with empowering positive affirmations and began believing in all my capabilities.

Yet, we may not know what to do in an exact moment but trusting your intuition and allowing space to move in it will always guide you to the right course of action. I am continually checking in with myself, asking, "What would best serve me at this moment?" Carefully choosing the words and narrative, I allow my inner voice to tell myself. You are own author of your own story; no one else can write it for you. The power of words tied with thought and emotions will create your internal landscape, so be careful with what you tell yourself. Allow yourself to feel all your emotions, love them, honor them, the process, and then release them, but be careful not to feel trapped in the lowest thoughts you tell yourself. You are so much more than any limiting thoughts you tell yourself in these dark moments of doubt.

Choose to break the endless loop of a 'less than' narrative created from your past or uncontrollable circumstances. Stay curious even while diving deeper within yourself and your own dark corners of truth. Approaching self-exploration with an open mind, I ask myself probing questions about my experiences. In acknowledging the uncomfortable emotions, I actively seek understanding rather than immediate answers. And in times of catching myself feeling stuck, I strive to gain an understanding. It is our sole responsibility to go out in the world and find beauty in things that bring inspiration and joy. Be kind to yourself because we are our own best friend, teacher, and savior. In reflection of this truth, one of the first steps I had taken began with the courage to say "yes" to anything that spoke to my soul and lit my heart on fire. "Yes," I can do what I put my mind to. The power of one word, "Yes," and believing in yourself can change everything.

"You are One decision away from changing your life." - Alex Hormozi

The Magnificence of Dreams

"I lead from the heart. Not from the head." - Diana, Princess of Wales

I had fallen deeply asleep one evening and had a beautiful dream. I was illuminated with powerful wisdom. As I dreamt, I felt as if I had been floating through a constellation of vastness and yet I had a strong sense of being connected to the universe. It was the encircling of the softest, white golden light surrounding me that I had ever experienced. A deep sense of peace immersed itself in every part of my being. A peace that so warmly and softly flowed into every part of my body. This dream felt infinite. It felt as if infinite loving energies expanded into all the knowledge I had been searching for in the voyage of embracing empowerment into a whole new expansion. I then ever so softly heard, "You are so loved." When I awoke, I felt more peace within myself than I ever had experienced in my life. My faith became stronger, and embraced the limitless blessing that life had gifted me. Part of my life that I had known may have ended, but my internal self-love and curiosity for life sparked a new beginning for the unknown mysteries that lie ahead. The power of positive dreams is magical. In harnessing the power of my dream, I softly felt it revealed wisdom and intuition that may not be as easy to access during waking hours. Whether it is in the mysteries of dreams or miracles in life, the unseen can be powerfully transformative.

Through meditation, it brought a state of calmness and internal peace as if drifting into the healing of Mother Earth. I then knew everything would be okay. This practice helped to shift thinking to the present moment. In the experience of the present moment, the mind of chatter quiets. This is a conduit of truth that started to unravel untruths that I had been telling myself. In my earlier childhood years, I had limiting beliefs that kept telling me, "I'm not good enough." From birth, women had always been locked into a narrative of limiting beliefs and harsh criticism that had been taught to us by humans of a higher power in authority. I constantly compare myself to others in terms of external and internal validation. The frequent negative comparisons to my peers had caused me to feel like I was not smart enough to succeed. Ingrained in my womanhood, the external world had taught me to look for validation outside of myself when, in truth, our power lives within each one of us. Foolish invisible rules that once limited growth no longer have a stronghold. Do you have any limiting beliefs? If so, how are they affecting you?

The reclaiming agency over my thoughts helped to reframe my thinking and release this self-limiting inner critic inside. In pivotal teachings, I have learned from Dr. Joe Dispenza that our brain can adapt and heal even from the adversity of trauma. Through his research and expertise, he discovered that we can accelerate our healing process by choosing to commit to the daily practice of meditation and mindfulness of the thoughts we tell ourselves. In the awakening of the power of the mind, I began increasing these practices as they are life-changing.

Through research, it is proven that neuroscience can change our brains just by thinking differently. For the first time in years, feelings of worthiness and self-confidence softly whispered, "You are worthy." In the stillness of thoughts, my intuition became enhanced. I felt an inner knowing that life is being supported in more ways than I thought possible. And what you choose to focus on, your energy follows.

In the restoration of the mind and body, I continued to evolve through different facets of healing. I committed to complementing both my morning and evening practices with journaling, affirmations, transformational books, meditation, and yoga. In the beginning of practicing yoga positions, the one position I found most difficult was the Savasana pose, the most challenging pose, the art of surrender. I had learned to surrender instant judgments in my mind with limiting thoughts of not being good enough. I slowly realized through the repeated practice of this pose surrendering meant letting go of all that had not served my highest good. I then released control and started to believe in myself. I had trust and faith in the future in what was to come. This pose consisted of lying in stillness on a mat, and I became engaged in the here and now. As I continued to practice this pose, the experience taught me that when I connected to the present moment, I was immersed in it, thus, past thoughts had faded away. Moreover, I gained an understanding of letting go of worries, anxieties, or any attempt to influence situations beyond my power in the time I connected with them. In reflection on surrendering during yoga, I learned to detach from distracting thoughts and honor my mental tranquility.

I slowly learned to relax my nervous system, which operates more of the flight or fight response. Prioritizing self-care through the mind and body connection had helped me to deactivate the fear I had been living with and create new channels for self-love. There are many different ways to show up for yourself. Whether it is through self-care like pampering, movement like dance, yoga, or walks in nature, creative expression like journaling, art or words of affirmation, or new experiences like trying a new hobby. Life unfolds with positive shifts when you give back to yourself. Furthermore, as I continued with my yoga practice, it became an intricate part of exploring and honoring my inner connectedness. It not only reduced stress, but it also helped me to restore my mind-body-spirit alignment. The magic of yoga has many layers that elevate our truest self. In the compassionate decision of wellness, yoga has become a beautiful instrument for calming all within. In the softness of connecting with the ebb and flow of life that is always moving, living in the present moment has become a conduit to grounding myself and in the transformation of personal growth.

"How you love yourself is how you teach others to love you." - Rupiah Kaur

Empress Energy

> "There are two powers in the world; one is the sword, and the other is the pen. There is a third power stronger than both, that of a woman." - Malala Yousafzai

Empress Energy is learning to trust my decisions, honor my emotions, and cultivate an environment where I can thrive. And in cultivating genuine self-love, you naturally foster the most positive and fulfilling relationship with yourself. Do you find yourself honoring your emotions?

Self-confidence and personal power equipped me with both mental and emotional fortitude. Furthermore, as a woman holds her own power, she preserves to protect all that is important to her. Despite many challenges, redefining my strength became one of my powerful assets. Author of *Joyful*, Radhi Devlukia, shares in the connectedness with feminine energy, "It evokes our creativity, our emotions, and is receptive. Feminine energy is important, it's the energy that helps you feel grounded and nurtured and helps you to connect to yourself, God, and others around you deeper."

Diving into the turquoise waters of Fiji was more than an adventure; it was a leap into the unknown, a testament to the courage I had nurtured through my healing journey. As the vibrant coral danced below, I felt alive, free, and ready to embrace life's beauty. For my daughter, age 22, this trip had been a celebration of her graduation from college and into her career.

> "Take off your armor; dare to be vulnerable, dare to unwrap yourself, and dare yourself to be yourself" - Maria Shriver

Rebirth. From Darkness to Living a Joy-filled Life

In self-revolution, I became a seeker of the soul and self-love. From the darkness of storms to the Divine's unshakable grace and power of healing, supernatural, miraculous gifts filled me with awe.

In discovering insights into healing further and examining the power of the mind and healing of the heart, I embraced the teachings of Dr. Joe Dispenza. He shares that our brain has the remarkable power to reorganize and form new neural pathways in our brains. He compares new patterns of thoughts we repeat to ourselves, like walking through a field of tall grass. In continuing to walk down the path the grass slowly bends and forms an easier pathway. I am committed to choosing new and uplifting thoughts that, over time, create new pathways of thinking. Today, I begin each morning by honoring my mind and the magnificent support and power it holds. Today, I am committed to paying attention to my mental health. Each morning I allow myself to sit still and become aware of my thoughts and emotions as I set powerful intentions for what I want the day to bring. "I am so grateful for the love that is constantly flowing through me and to me. I release all that no longer serves me and embrace the limitless potential within. Thank you for the ease of today and all the new opportunities that it brings. Thank you for the love and inspiring connections that are meant to find me. I am embodying and honoring my most authentic self. I am in a place of alignment, growth, and expansion. As I love, trust, and believe in myself so deeply that pure magic exists when free-falling into the unknown." Intentionally start your day with self-love and in a mind of expansion, watch the transformation of the day unfold, allowing yourself to unlock and attract your greatest potential.

In the echoes of where my lost journey began, I now find a renewed sense of life and hope rekindled within me. The uncertainty that once felt like suffocating weight transformed into the exploration of new possibilities. Each step had been a leap of faith guided by intuition. The universe began revealing glimpses of a new landscape that is exciting and alluring. The beginning of my healing voyage felt like a daunting unknown. Yet, with courage, trust, and belief in myself, the future became uplifting and filled with wonderful opportunities. I actively explored new interests, set new goals, and cultivated new passions that enriched my life. The discovery of my new passions has made a positive impact on women in this world by creating a safe and empowering environment where their voices are heard and respected.

On a warm sunny day, my plane landed and my daughter had picked me up at the airport in California. This was my first visit since she relocated for a new career. This was my first time experiencing the majestic coastal forest. I found myself surrounded by some of the world's tallest trees. I marveled at just how magical nature was and how beautiful the sun-drenched sky glistened rays of gold through the treetops in the stillness. Mother Nature, in all her glory, had secrets of balance and harmony. I thought to myself, just as these big trees stand tall in their strength, they need light to encourage their growth; they endure the changing of the seasons yet endure the forces of nature in never-ending time. It was a moment of clarity that Mother Nature always endures, and I will do the same. Then, looking up into the bright blue sky, I felt a sense of openness and serenity. I had been fully immersed in the peace and tranquility it offered. I felt a calmness filling me and felt a deep connection with nature and all its glory. It felt like I had been experiencing a magical meditative experience. I felt overwhelmed with joy. In the brilliance of life, I, too came to embrace the changing of seasons in my life.

In seeing beyond the sunrise, we all have the power to create the best versions of our lives and of ourselves. What would you see, and how would it feel? It is in our voyage of evolving that we can say 'yes' to reigniting our inner spark of choosing the experiences that lead us to more joy and contentment. I continue to celebrate life and all its magnificence. I choose to live a life with passion. Through the energy and excitement of thriving, I have an unwavering commitment to help other women speak their truth fueled by self-love.

"When you want something, all the universe conspires in helping you achieve it." - Paulo Coelho

In embracing my inner warrior, I discovered that life's greatest challenges often hold the seeds of our greatest transformations. Now, I invite you to say 'yes' to your own journey, trust in your resilience, and know that the light within you is enough to guide you forward.

"She said, 'I'm just not giving up. The woman I'll be in a few years from now is counting on me.' And the world shifted." - Nakeia Homer

Pamela Spencer

Pamela is a Resilience Alchemist, a visionary holistic health and wellness leader dedicated to serving women around the globe to triumph over limitations. As a passionate family nurse practitioner for more than 3 decades, she is a catalyst of mindset and energetic transformation, thus awakening the power of the divine feminine within. She is the founder of Empowering Women & Wellness Solutions, an author, motivational speaker, and life and health coach. She advocates for women's rights in equality and in living in the unquestionable power they hold.

In her journey of immense challenges, trauma, and loss, she transmuted her life with resilience and spiritual revolution. Through personal milestones and self-discovery of challenges faced, it is in the miraculous moments and blessings bestowed that are the true gifts in disguise.

Pamela is a leader of incredible power and authenticity. She awakens women to their truth and to honor the power they have within themselves. With the depth of her knowledge, wisdom, and fire of compassion, she helps others in their voyage to live unapologetically and in the boldness of their hearts desires. She embraces the spirit of resilience, the awakening of her full feminine power, and the transformative power of following her passions.

As a warrior in self-revolution and that of living fearlessly, she mentors women through courage and self-discovery of their greatness within that are ready to be awakened and harnessed.

She cherishes motherhood and family and enjoys yoga, traveling, time in nature and in all its wonder. Life is to be experienced in all its fullness and magic. Your life is calling you to live in your magic of dreams, passions, and exploration of self-revolution.

Website: https://Empoweringwomenandwellnesssolutions.com

10

THE LIFE OF AN ARKANSAS COUNTRY GIRL: TRIUMPH, TRAUMA, TRUTH

DR. ARGIE NELL NICHOLS

As I sat there on that old wooden bench, feeling so alone, very scared, but so proud as I was leaving a two-week leadership camp on Lake Michigan, full of dreams and plans for my future self. My life was overflowing with excitement for the future. After all, I was only fifteen and had received the honor of a lifetime from the governor of Arkansas - Young Female Leader for Arkansas.

Wanting to share with my entire family my joy and happiness, I set my old rugged suitcase down by my feet, knowing I had to call home. I looked around for a phone booth. Locating the booth, I grabbed the suitcase and made my way over. Peering over my shoulder, I noticed there was only one other person in the big, empty bus station in downtown Detroit, Michigan. Oh well! I will be just fine. I know I will make that next connection and finally make it back home to my family.

I proceeded to the phone booth, leaving the suitcase just outside, well within my view. The booth was barely big enough for me, let alone the suitcase. I made a collect call, hoping someone would accept the charges since it was so very late at night. It took the operator three different tries before Mother answered the call and accepted the charges.

I started babbling about a flat tire on our transport school bus from camp. It made me late for the first bus connection, and I was stuck in downtown Detroit for another 2 hours. I would be really late getting back to Waldron, Arkansas, our little rural hometown.

I expected my mother to be just as excited to hear from me as I was to hear her voice. I had been away from home for two weeks, and I was rather homesick. This was my very first trip away from home all by myself. I expected her to say, “So glad to hear from you. Don’t worry. You will be just fine. Dad and I will be there to pick you up. See you soon.” As the deafening noise of the phone being slammed in my ear rang loudly, I felt the tears beginning to well up. That was NOT what I expected at all. Her response was, “I don’t care if you ever come home.”

It took me several minutes to regain my composure and leave the phone booth. I slowly made my way back to the end of the bench. There was no stopping the tears at this point. I sat there holding the suitcase in my lap, trying to hide my face and the tears.

Remember that one other person in the entire empty bus station? I now believe she was an angel sent by God to comfort me in just that moment. In a still, small voice, she said, “Honey, I don’t know what is wrong, but I will help you.” As I put down the suitcase, the most beautiful lady put her arms around me. Her hair was silver, and her smile made my tears slow down. She asked if I was hungry and if I could use some water. She purchased a stale sandwich and a bottle of water from the machine over by the phone booth. That just might have been the best sandwich I ever ate in my entire life. She sat with me for the next two hours, making small talk, and then made sure I got on the correct bus to get home.

You guessed it! There was no one at the bus station to greet me or take me home. Thank goodness the lady running the small station knew me and called my Uncle Jack to come get me. He and my Aunt Hazel lived a few short blocks from the bus station. I spent the night with them, and they took me home early the next morning. The love oozing from those two made me feel so welcomed and loved. Now to figure out what I had done so horribly wrong to make my mother mad at me. My thoughts began wandering back to my younger years as I went about my chores.

Life Down the Frost Lane – Triumph Younger Years

Imagine a picturesque countryside, nestled in the heart of a small community, where the Frost Lane winds across the river and through fields and forests. It's here that you can find me, a bright and curious young girl brimming with enthusiasm for life's simple pleasures. My family, with their warm hearts and strong values, shaped my love for nature, community, and all the wonders that surrounded the ranch.

My days are filled with exploration as I venture through the fields and meadows, chasing butterflies and catching glimpses of the vibrant wildlife that call Frost Lane home. From the enchanting chorus of chirping frogs from the nearby pond to the gentle rustling of leaves in the breeze, my world is alive with the symphony of nature's harmonies.

As we delve deeper into my world, we also encounter the vibrant cast of characters who inhabit Frost Lane. From my very best friend and brother, Dwayne, who shares with me the infectious laughter and love for outdoor adventures, to the wise Cherokee grandparents, who share stories of the community's rich history and impart valuable life lessons, my friendships form an integral part of my journey.

Together, my brother and I embarked on escapades that fostered a sense of camaraderie and community. Whether we're organizing charity events, building treehouses, or simply gathering around a crackling bonfire to share tales, our bonds grew stronger, and our amazing adventures created lasting memories. Oh, but wait! It is almost time for our parents to arrive from working their stressful jobs in town. We need to get to the house as fast as possible. We need to make sure all our chores are complete, so we won't be in trouble. We must not displease our parents because the yelling will start, and there will be hell to pay.

We made it just in time and pretended we had been there most of the day working on all our chores. I quickly grabbed the basket and headed to the hen house to gather the eggs. That was my last chore for the day and this was the perfect time to complete the job. My brother was taking the trash out to the burn barrel. Perfect timing once again. We thought we had escaped the fighting, but we were wrong.

As we entered the house, both our parents were screaming at each other. We had no clue what caused the fight, but one thing for sure, we didn't want to be caught in the middle of things. Dwayne quickly went back outside to feed the dog and I disappeared to my hiding place in my bedroom. We didn't even glance at each other.

My special place was tucked away in a corner behind the moon dresser, positioned diagonally in the bedroom, creating a snug hideaway just big enough for me and sometimes my brother. I would retreat there for hours, finding solace and quiet for my thoughts. It was my safe haven.

In my secret spot, I kept a collection of picture books and the new Christmas catalog from Sears and Roebuck's Department Store. I would spend countless hours gazing at the pictures, lost in dreams and imagination. Even though I was too young to read—or so I told myself—the letters and numbers seemed unfamiliar and strange. Unlike my brother, who could read, I felt like I couldn't.

Dwayne, being fifteen months older than me, started school that year. Each morning, he got on that big yellow bus, and I stood in the window waving. I was crushed. Why couldn't I go with him? Why did I have to stay home all alone? Well, I wasn't exactly alone. After my parents left for work, I was to finish my chores and walk up the road to my grandparents' house, just a short hike away. Now, don't take this wrong. I had a blast with Pape and Grannie, but I missed my brother.

My Cherokee grandparents were very nurturing. Grannie was the oldest of eight children, and her mother passed with the birth of the youngest child, the same Uncle Jack that I mentioned earlier. She became the mother figure and raised the other seven children. Papa was the oldest of nine children and grew up working hard to help his family make a living during the early 1900s. They married in their early thirties and gave birth to only one baby boy, my Father. Needless to say, he was just a little spoiled as an only child. Adding to that, Uncle Jack was only about eight years older and moved in with Grannie and Pape when they married. Daddy and Uncle were raised like brothers instead of a nephew and uncle. Together, they made quite the pair of mischievous boys.

My life was still full of adventures, just of a different nature. I spent most of those days in the house with Grannie and we made cookies, pies, and various other things. Occasionally, there was a fishing trip over to the pond where the frogs hang out. Depending on the time of the year, there were always things that needed tending in the garden.

One rainy week, I sat in Grannie's lap as she peddled the old-time sewing machine. Together, we made my very first quilt top. She made very sure I didn't run the needle through my fingers. It has been almost seventy years, and I still have that quilt.

My favorite time each day was when that big yellow bus arrived, and my brother joyfully bounced off the bus steps. I waited for that yellow bus with bated breath and a homemade snack five days every week.

The next hour was spent at the kitchen table, eating our special snacks and going over homework. He taught me everything he learned each day. Dwayne soon realized that I didn't see things like he did. I turned letters around and numbers into letters. We made a pinky finger pact to never tell our parents about my slight dyslexia issue. He promised to teach me how to read and do the numbers correctly. That is exactly what he did. We spent hours and hours under the moon dresser practicing the learning process with handmade flashcards. Two years later, it was my time to also get on the big yellow bus. My life was forever changed.

Arriving at Parks Community School, our small rural school, I really impressed my teachers. I was so very smart in their eyes because I was doing third-grade level work in the first grade, and it just got better and better. I had the guidance of my brother for the next few years until he left for college. No one ever discovered our secret.

Each day of my school life, I tried so very hard to make perfect grades and be the perfect daughter. However, I never accomplished that feat. I was always caught in the crosshairs of the yelling and fighting between our parents. I often wondered what I did wrong or was it something else that my mother was hiding? I did my chores which Dwayne and I thought was just a normal routine for country kids. We never talked back. We never let our parents see our tears. We never gained their praise. All chores had to be completed before any extracurricular activities were allowed. Believe me, when there was a very important softball game on Saturday morning, we made sure to button up all chores and home activities early.

Moving to the teen years brought many additional challenges. I went through that change that all young ladies experience and I was so afraid to tell my mother. So, I just tried to do this on my own, not understanding what was happening to my body. I should have reached out to Grannie. She definitely would have helped me understand.

This was not something that my brother could help me with. I spent my study period at the new bigger town school in the library doing the research. Finally, I thought I had the understanding needed to survive. I was so very sick, and trying to hide that sickness was nearly impossible. I got off the bus at school every morning and threw up. I got motion sickness just watching moving objects. I guessed this was just part of the process, but it was not mentioned in the research books.

Mother finally noticed that I was not eating properly and dropping lots of weight. She finally took me to a very old country doctor but he didn't know. He had never heard of someone being this sick unless I might be expecting a baby. What? I didn't even have a boyfriend and I sure didn't get any sympathy. According to my mother, if I really was that sick and not just pretending, perhaps I should stop all sports and extra activities at school.

For the rest of my school years, I tried to appear normal or conceal my feelings when I couldn't. The arguments and shouting at home, though, continued unabated and escalated. I had outgrown my old hiding spot behind the moon dresser, so I found refuge in the barn instead. There, I could cry in peace. The baby calves became my companions, listening to me and providing comfort through gentle petting and affectionate gestures.

Dwayne left for college the summer I got back from the leadership camp on Lake Michigan but not before hearing what I learned and all the new things I got to experience. We totally shared everything with each other and he was very proud of me for receiving the award. I, on the other hand, was devastated by his departure to college. Who would step up to help with all my studies? Well, no one. I was on my own. Thank goodness, the dyslexia training that I had received from my brother was strong enough to get me through the next school years.

I never understood why Mother reacted so strongly when I was awarded the leadership trip. I often questioned if she harbored resentment towards me or if she envied my achievements. For the next three months, we lived in complete silence. She didn't speak to me until well into the new school year. I still wonder today what I might have done to upset her so deeply. Perhaps I was seen as the "problem child." With Dwayne no longer there, I felt constantly on edge. At home and at school—where Mother was now the secretary—I had to tread carefully at all times.

Most of my friends couldn't relate to my life, and they didn't really try. They spent weekends going to movies, shopping, or hanging out and drinking with boys in parking lots. Despite this, I did have a memorable experience at the Junior/Senior Prom and Dance during my junior year. My date, a boy who saw beyond my country roots, asked me to be his girlfriend.

Mother was a chaperone at the dance, so there was no chance for any mischief. Later that year, I was elected Student Body president and pursued the role of state Beta Club President, striving to live up to my leadership potential. Strangely, the more I succeeded, the more distant and disapproving Mother seemed. I yearned for her guidance and approval, hoping she would communicate with me about how I could improve and be a better daughter. Unfortunately, that conversation never came.

Going into the summer of my senior year, things got even more tense. I knew she disliked the boyfriend and discouraged me from ever being associated with him. The next thing I overheard during one of the yelling matches between my parents was that I was being shipped off to California to live with my Uncle Paul. She screamed, "I just can't stand to be around her anymore." What brought that on? My head was just spinning with no understanding of my faults.

No way! I was not going to California my senior year. I dug my country heels in the dirt and called in reinforcements. Out the back door, I went straight up the road to Pape. With big tears in my eyes, I explained what I had just heard. In his very calm voice, I heard, "Sissy, don't you worry one minute. I will take care of this." And that he did. I never asked how or why, but I didn't move to California. Thank goodness Grannie never heard this, or there might have been some type of war at the ranch. Being her only granddaughter left me in an excellent place most of the time.

Young Adulthood - Trauma at Best

Upon graduating from high school, I began my university journey on a full academic scholarship. While it was difficult to leave behind my supportive grandparents and the life on the ranch, I recognized the opportunity for growth and the chance to explore a broader world. The transition was both emotional and exciting as I moved beyond the familiarity of home to pursue new academic and personal challenges. I believed that going to college and starting my adult life would ease my mother's burdens. I imagined that by excelling academically and focusing on my future, I could help reduce the tension at home. I convinced myself that, with me out of the house, the constant conflict would subside, and our lives would be filled with more peace and joy. At the very least, I hoped to escape the turmoil and the constant shouting. My strategy was to immerse myself in my studies, striving to give my parents more reasons to be proud of me, even if I couldn't directly resolve the issues at home.

I didn't travel home too often because I had no car. I could beg for a ride with my high school friend when he decided to visit which was not very often at all. And, then it happened. The phone call of all phone calls. I was called home. Grannie had a massive heart attack and was no longer with us. My fragile life was shattered. How could I go on living? I wanted to die and be with her. That was my first thought of taking my own life.

I couldn't bring myself to leave Pape and go back to college. That same weekend, my boyfriend told me he had found someone new. I had hoped to lean on him for support, but he wasn't there for me. He didn't even come to the funeral.

I was devastated. First, I lost Grannie— the woman who had shown me unconditional love and safety. Then, my boyfriend abandoned me in my darkest moment for someone else. It shattered me completely. I felt so broken that I didn't want to go on living.

Pape insisted that I go back and finish my first year of college with just a few weeks left in the spring semester. I did finish, but the grades were not very good. I spent that summer in a deep depression. Then, low and behold, HE, yes, the former and only boyfriend, showed up at the house. Such an apology I received! He was so sorry he had not heard about my Grannie. Truthfully, the other girlfriend had just broken up with him, and he was lonely. He just could not be alone and promised me the moon and the stars in the sky. If I married him, he could cure all my sadness. He would get me away from all the yelling and discontent. What a plan! I was just stupid enough and also very lonely that I agreed to the plan.

The sunset wedding took place at the ranch the weekend before our second year of college began. It was well attended and very beautiful. I did everything except make the cake. All the dresses, the flowers, the decorations, and invitations were created by me. I was working on a very tight budget that was only supported by me. Mother never approved of the relationship or the wedding.

I transferred universities and changed majors. Our senior year, over spring break, we welcomed our first and only child. The birth was beautiful and went perfectly. However, our little boy came home for only 2 days before he was rushed back to the ICU, where we spent the next two weeks in the critical care unit. The trauma was intense for all of us. Mother and Dad finally came to visit about a week into the stay. I guess they wanted to see their first grandson in person. Finally, all of us went home and this little boy got to see his Mom and Dad graduate college.

That joyful union was not so joyful and lasted almost seven years before the divorce. The ex-husband remarried shortly after the divorce, and I stayed single for almost 15 years. My son, Josh, was the most important thing in my life. There was no change with my mother. Her favorite saying was, "I told you so". Josh and I moved back to the ranch because Pape was very sick. I wanted to be just as close to him as I could be, and I wanted my son to know how beloved Pape was to both of us.

At the young age of 27, I was diagnosed and treated for ovarian cancer. Perhaps this was why I had been so very sick in my younger years. The doctors were very surprised that I was even able to have a healthy baby. I still suffered from the symptoms of the diagnosis and treatment. My health was nowhere it needed to be.

My mother once again played a significant role in my life, though not in a positive way. As my health was deteriorating and I needed her support more than ever, she betrayed me in a way I never expected. Without my knowledge or consent, she and my ex-husband made an arrangement to send my son, Josh, to live with his father for the rest of his school years. I was blindsided when, one day, Josh didn't come home from school. There are no words that can fully convey the pain of losing my child in such a manner. In many ways, this felt just as devastating as losing my grandmother to an unexpected heart attack years earlier. My heart was shattered, and I often wonder how I didn't just give up at that moment.

My mother went into great detail, explaining why she believed this decision was the best for both Josh and me. She argued that I could focus on regaining my health and no longer had to work so hard to support a child. Her reasoning was rooted in the idea that Uncle Paul had fathered a child at a young age and never had the chance to be truly involved in his son's life. She didn't want Josh to grow up without a strong relationship with his father. In her words, "I had loved him for the first 10 years, and now it was time for his dad to raise him." Nothing about this made sense to me, and it sent me into another spiral of deep depression. For the second time, I found myself questioning why I should go on living. Without my son, what reason did I have to continue?

The sadness in my heart and soul was devastating. I didn't get to see my son for several years. I mailed a card or letter every week, but I learned later he never received any of them. When I would call, he was always outside playing, never home or could not come to the phone. I took a teaching job and moved as far away from the ranch as possible. There was no communication with my parents.

The Truth is Yet to Unfold

As the truth is about to unfold right before your eyes, you will learn many things as I have over the years. By the time you are reading this, I will be nearing my 70th birthday. I have lived a very blessed life growing up on the ranch. I had the best grandparents that any person could have. They were my true support system throughout my life. I had the very best friend, my brother Dwayne, who was my superhero. I do not regret any decision that I made in all those various years. Would things have turned out differently? Of course! But...I have no regrets.

Being scared in downtown Detroit in the late 60s probably was a good thing. However, it was many years later that I learned and read about the racial riots going on in that city. Buildings were burned - mainly in the downtown area near the bus station. People were killed just because of their color. None of that even concerned me that late night as I met an angel - an angel of color who loved this little white girl with fiery red hair from Arkansas. The advice from Pape rushed back into my memory. Pape said to me many times, "Always treat people like you would like to be treated. The color of their skin never matters. Kindness will always serve you well." I live by this advice still today.

I was and am still very dyslexic. My brother, at a very young age, helped me understand this issue. Back in the early 60s, no one understood this nor how to work with this issue. Dwayne understood and helped me learn to read and do math. It is not cured because, as we now know, there is no cure. My brain now understands how to function, and I still struggle with this issue. Thanks to my brilliant brother, all my success is owed to him, along with all my good grades.

The fact that we had chores at such an early age was a true blessing. We knew how to work, how to meet deadlines, how to manage time, and how to enjoy life full of nature. There was no task too small or too large for either of us. The most valuable lesson we learned was how to trust and support each other no matter what the situation. The real truth was that both of us started our first savings account before we were five years old. Oh yes! I got 25 cents from each carton of eggs sold. What a great start to finances. We were never left alone. Pape and Grannie were within view at all times and could hear us holler/laugh at any given moment.

The cancer diagnosis turned out to really be an autoimmune disease tied to my thyroid. Back in the late 50s and early 60s, this was not even a thing that doctors understood. I did go through radiation for no reason. Now that the truth has been discovered, I am living in a healed body, or at least, I now know how to control the issues. I am also lactose intolerant, and our only drink of choice was milk. Thus, throwing up every day in my early years.

Josh graduated high school and returned to my home that very same day. We have never been separated again. He and I still support each other today. He is happily married, a strong Christian man, and the father of two very wonderful children, my grandchildren. He lives less than 20 minutes from my current location.

Now, let's get down to the real 'elephant' in this story. I cannot fully answer all of your questions, and I will never know the truth. Both of my parents have passed. There was never a time for the "talk" from either parent. There were never the words "I love you" shared with me or my brother. We were not perfect children by any means, but a simple "I love you" or "Thank you" could not have hurt.

After their deaths, Dwayne and I finally had a heart-to-heart. He experienced the same spiteful treatment as me. Until then, we were unaware of each other's struggles. We had deep conversations about past events, often shedding tears. Some things defy understanding or justification. Maybe we were the two-and-a-half kids each family needed to fit the standard of that era.

Turning Our Trauma into Personal Peace

That conversation with Dwayne brought us both solace. Though it occurred just a few years back, we agreed that our childhood struggles would not define us. Together, we confronted various emotional challenges. Dad and Uncle Jack were troublemakers, making Grannie's life unbearable. Despite it all, she never complained or revealed her hardships to us because of them. Then Mom entered the scene, inheriting those same issues of shouting and conflict.

Mother was the pioneer in her family to pursue college. She enrolled in business college for just one semester before Daddy insisted she return to him and the ranch. With his recent Army draft, he feared losing her to someone at college. She sacrificed her education dream and married, only to find herself alone as Daddy departed for training camp just a week after their wedding. With her family having moved to California for work, she found solace living with Pape and Grannie. Daddy's illness led to a medical honorable discharge, bringing him home after a brief three months away.

Mother often harbored resentment towards Daddy for compelling her to abandon her college aspirations. She had envisioned herself as a business major specializing in bookkeeping, but Daddy's insistence on her returning home thwarted those dreams. Despite this setback, Mother's intelligence shone through, and upon returning home, she secured a position at Arkansas's largest timber and lumber company. From a young age, she efficiently managed the office, overseeing a team of employees who reported to her.

During this time, Mother earned significantly more than Daddy, which might have stirred some jealousy in him. Around this period,

Dwayne and I were born. Daddy insisted that Mother return to work shortly after our birth, leaving us to be raised joyfully by our grandparents.

Mother always emphasized that her children deserved the best education. She was determined that neither of us would end up like her, feeling trapped on the ranch. Many of the arguments stemmed from this conviction. It wasn't so much anger directed at us but rather her fierce defense of our educational opportunities. That's how we interpreted our upbringing and later years, finding solace in each other's understanding.

But... on that day of our conversation, Dwayne and I gained a broader perspective. Our lives were rich with blessings, achievements, friendships, and cherished memories. We never experienced hunger, physical abuse, or sexual abuse. Drugs and alcohol were never part of our lives, and we never lived through a war. Both of us grew into strong leaders deeply connected to our communities and with a profound love for our families. Our careers have been successful, and we had exceptional educational opportunities. The kindness instilled in us by our Cherokee grandparents profoundly influenced our lives. Kindness, we realized, is truly the key to a happy life.

Those who read our story need not worry or feel dismayed about our upbringing. It molded us into resilient adults who now lead loving families of our own. Each day, we ensure our children know they are deeply loved and respected. Dwayne and I live our lives in tribute to the values instilled by our grandparents, who showered us with daily affirmations of love and specialness. The strength we gained from our past experiences enriches us as we navigate this remarkable world.

Everyone faces personal challenges, but we believe in overcoming them and finding our place of love and fulfillment. Each of us possesses greater strength than we realize. Never underestimate your worth and the impact you can make. I choose to spread love and kindness, aiming to make this world better for even just one person. If I achieve that, I feel I've fulfilled my purpose here on this beautiful Earth.

"I am exactly who I need to be at this moment."

All your past actions are teaching moments for your present self.

Every lesson takes you to the present moment, to exactly who you need to be.

ARGIE NELL NICHOLS

Dr. Argie Nell Nichols is a seasoned entrepreneur, educator, lecturer, and author with over 45 years of experience in both education and business. Driven by a deep commitment to family and faith, Dr. Nichols is passionate about empowering students and women entrepreneurs to realize and achieve their personal and professional goals.

A dedicated educator, Dr. Nichols has spent more than four decades shaping the lives of students across various educational levels. Her approach to teaching is informed by her own diverse life experiences, blending practical knowledge with a genuine desire to foster growth and success. As a result, she has helped countless individuals achieve their academic and entrepreneurial aspirations.

In addition to her educational work, Dr. Nichols is a sought-after speaker, traveling the world to inspire and motivate leaders and entrepreneurs across industries. She draws from her extensive career in direct sales, where she has consistently achieved exceptional success, earning multiple seven-figure incomes over the course of her career. Her entrepreneurial journey also funded her college education, reflecting her resilience and dedication to both personal and professional growth.

Dr. Nichols' entrepreneurial legacy is rooted in her family's rich history, as she and her extended family continue to own and operate an Arkansas Century Ranch, a property that has been in the family for over 138 years. Through her leadership, she exemplifies the values of hard work, perseverance, and the importance of nurturing meaningful relationships—whether in business, education, or her personal life.

A true testament to the power of faith, family, and entrepreneurship, Dr. Argie Nell Nichols is committed to making a positive impact on the lives of others, helping individuals unlock their potential and achieve long-lasting success. Dr. Nichols specialized in Financial Leadership and teaching women to leave a financial legacy for their families.

Website: https://www.financialleadership.life

11

HOPE IS A STRATEGY

BARB MCATEER

The Promise of Forever

With sixteen more years of life experience, including a twenty-year marriage from which he was now divorced, and two grown children living near him in Germany, my husband Werner had a lot more insights to the future than I at 29 years of age.

He knew of financial, health and emotional challenges as well as the impacts of deep loss and heartache. He also knew better than I about what was required for us to build a marriage that would sustain us until death do us part. So, when Werner laid out all the things he could imagine the universe taking us through; I remained adamant that my love would be unwavering and assured him that I had the type of strength it takes to prevail through all obstacles.

I had no idea how much that promise would demand of me. Over the next 34 years, I would navigate a constant marathon of adversity, punctuated by sprints of crisis. This relentless roller coaster tested my resolve and reshaped my understanding of strength, love, and hope.

Werner's complex health issues made the ache in my heart from losing our father when I was seventeen resurface. Dad was just 42 years old when he lost his battle with lung cancer, leaving our mom to carry on with four children ages between 8 and 17.

I realize now that she was the "HOPEMeister". Amid her own anguish, she told us, "what doesn't bring you joy won't bring you sorrow." She assured us that what we felt then was the pain of all the joy that loving had brought to us. It was a price you pay. But it was worth it. Many years later, we'd come to understand that and agree that she was right.

She was incessantly telling us that "who we are is not a product of what happens to us, but rather who we are is a RESULT of how we respond to what happens to us".

She also brought a therapist into our home every week for a few months to help us process our grief. At 17, I was about as interested in leaning into this sorrow as I would be about having bamboo shoots pushed up my fingernails.

But our mom was not swayed by our reluctance or even the emotional outbursts that came with our disdain for this therapeutic practice. She continued to encourage us to *stay curious*, to *build knowledge, to seek support & imagine a future* where we would thrive.

I would just do the same now as I embarked into my married life.

You see, we are not BORN with RESILIENCE. Resilience comes from adversity. I would just reactivate my learning on how to lean into adversity the same way I learned to lean into grief.

I now see that THIS was the beginning of our lessons in HOPE.

The Trials Begin

The tests of my commitment started before we were married. Werner had a stroke in 1991, and I headed to Germany to be with him in the hospital. Just 5 years later, In 1996, he would have his first open-heart surgery. The doctor projected a "20-year life expectancy" on that triple bypass.

Ironically, it would be exactly that long before he'd need the second heart surgery during which he would flatline twice on the operating table; it would take two tries and 15 days to get his body to release the fluids that would enable the surgeons to close his chest back up. All while they kept him in a fentanyl coma.

I recall looking at the 3 IV poles filled with bags of dripping medicines and *feeling nothing but fear*. All I could think about was how this traumatic experience would haunt him. The doctor told me, with utmost certainty, that Werner would have no recall of anything including much of what would follow in the initial weeks of recovery after his "awakening". He also assured me that I would never be able to forget this part of the journey.

Try as I might to mitigate those memories from returning to my mind, they still so often invade & create that same sense of dread that the story would end there. I never prayed so hard that it would not. I made deals with God; I offered whatever I could in exchange for giving us more time. There was more to say & I was seeking certainty that Werner knew how much I loved him regardless of how unconventional our marriage had become. I also hoped and prayed that he and our daughter Madi would find a way to express their love for each other and offer forgiveness for their own shortcomings as humans.

Werner had already faced incredible and unending health challenges. A stroke to the occipital artery in 1999 while I was still on maternity leave would render him unable to drive again until enough physical therapy would enable him to overcome the blind spots to his peripheral vision.

A heart attack in 2000 during a return flight from Munich to San Francisco and another one in 2001 while in Tahoe for a wedding we never did get to attend were almost commonplace in our lives.

In 2003 I would go to our dear friend Paul's 50th birthday celebration with my brother Kevin while Werner remained at home with a drip IV of antibiotics recovering from surgery to close an open wound on his leg which was exacerbated by undiagnosed osteomyelitis for 30+ years. My mother and in-home nurses would take care of the surround sound support I needed to look after Werner and our child. I would reactivate this recipe of cobbling together the resources needed so that I could participate in social activities and experience some joy & laughter.

I would learn to live a form of *single parenting* that was not a result of death or divorce, but rather it was my destiny to do so with my husband technically right by my side.

A Life of Constant Vigilance

I became expert at using my sense of humor as my shield when "fighting" as Werner's Caregiver and Health Advocate and while I had been described by some as a "force to be reckoned with" I began to use that force to protect & preserve my husband and my child.

Between surgeries, life continued, but it wasn't easy. Werner faced one health crisis after another. He would be hospitalized repeatedly in 2015, 2016, 2017, 2018 and 2019 due to more strokes, hypoglycemia, hyperglycemia, pneumonia, falls and other events.

He would evade death by a much narrower margin in 2020 when he was among one of the first to contract COVID. I was living in Cambridge MA with Madi at the time, having taken a job just two months before the pandemic shut the world down. For three months, I coordinated his care from afar, making life-or-death decisions over the phone. When the doctors asked if he should be intubated, I drew on past experiences and said no. Later, his cardiologist told me that choice likely saved his life.

By the time Werner returned home months later, his short-term memory was severely impaired, and his ability to manage his diabetes had deteriorated. Assisted Living became a necessity, and once again, I found myself navigating an impossible choice: how to provide for him while also being the mother Madi needed me to be.

It seemed inevitable that every time the phone rang, day or night, it would be another catastrophic event; and I would go into stealth FIGHT mode.

I was "intense" 24 x 7. I was intense at home, at work, at play, in the garden & even while engaging in my version of relaxing out by the pool listening to music. I was constantly in a state of high alert; always preparing for the next thing the universe would make me swerve around to avoid a collision.

I realize now that I was purposefully avoiding being completely present in my life or aligned with my feelings. This act of denial was my preservation. It would take years before I'd be strong enough to start unravelling all that and allow myself to feel the emptiness, the grief and the loneliness.

Parenting through Intricacy

"When my child told me, 'I am a girl trapped in a boy's body,' my world shifted. I didn't have answers, but I had love— and hope. That hope guided me through the fear, the learning curve, and the darkest moments when she struggled with depression and suicidal ideation. I realized that I needed to create a safe, affirming home where she could thrive."

We were preparing to attend my brother Kevin & his now husband's civil union in Vermont in the summer of 2005. I went into my child's room; to begin our nightly ritual: reading a book, singing a song I would make up while swaying in the rocking chair and if needed laying down in the bed until usually I fell asleep first.

We were talking about our upcoming trip and how much fun it was going to be to see the cousins then all I could hear was the fear in my child's voice about being scared. About monsters being under the bed and in the closet.

It wasn't the first time I'd heard these concerns, so I went to the closet and made sure nothing scary was lurking inside and then I crawled around the floor looking under the bed and was absolutely shocked to find a butcher knife from our kitchen lying there in plain sight.

I looked at my sweet child holding the knife and asked "why is this here? What's going on lovebug"? That's when I heard my precious angel say the words I will never forget for as long as I live: "Mama, I don't know how you can love me; I am a girl trapped in a boy's body."

That was 20 years ago, & I was speechless. I didn't know what that really meant, I didn't know what I was supposed to do or say. I could only tell my child that I can and do love her and that I always will and that my heart would ache forever if she wasn't here in this world with me. Then we just sat in the rocking chair together until she fell asleep.

All I could think of at that moment was how much I loved this child in my arms. And all I felt was fear because I had no clear visual for what I would do next.

So, I did what I always do when I'm stuck or confused; I called my mother. While I didn't consciously know it then, SHE is the one that instilled HOPE in all of us.

I reiterated what I had just been told and my mother said, "OK Barbara I'm not sure exactly what this means but you just need to do your job, and we'll figure out the rest. Your job is to love your child".

Speechless again, I thought, that's it? You are my beacon, my guide, my inspiration and that's the best you've got for me?

From that day forward I became intentional about creating space for HOPE that would allow me to *discover my COURAGE & enable me to CHANGE. Because it was ME that had to evolve.*

And so began the work to uncover the facts, not the misinformation. In my quest to understand what all this meant, I became a voracious reader. The knowledge I acquired came like a slap in the face. I learned that 82% of transgender individuals have considered suicide & 40% have attempted it. The highest number of suicides comes from Transgender Youth.

The Trevor Project

https://www.thetrevorproject.org/

I learned about Gender Dysphoria. According to the Diagnostic and Statistical Manual of Mental Disorders, Gender Dysphoria (DSM.5), is defined as a "marked incongruence between a person's experienced and expressed gender and the one they were assigned at birth".

Gender Dysphoria is the psychological distress that results from this inconsistency.

A 2017 chart review from a transgender clinic in Cincinnati found that among youth aged 12-22 with a diagnosis of gender dysphoria, 58% had another psychiatric diagnosis, and 30.3% reported at least one suicide attempt.
https://pmc.ncbi.nlm.nih.gov/articles/PMC6903884/

Our child would suffer in this lethal combination of comorbidity AND experience suicidal ideation for the better part of her life. One attempt nearly occurred right before my eyes. I came home from work one day to find Madi in the bathroom holding a handful of pills telling me she couldn't take it anymore. She didn't want to live. She couldn't take the pain of it. I could only think in that moment of the sessions I'd had with my therapist who kept advising me to stop trying to control everything; that I'd have to accept that Madi's life was hers: that IF she intended to kill herself, one day she just might. BUT that it was her life, her choice.

Holding those thoughts in my mind, I simply said to her, "Madi, someday I won't be here to have this conversation with you, but you need to know that I want you here on earth everyday. If you can just hang on to the HOPE that things will get better, they will....but if you can't I will accept that..."

She tilted her head back and threw the pills into her mouth; but spit them out before drinking from the glass of water on the counter. And then we cried and cried until there were no more tears left for that day.

I only stopped waking up each day worried she would take her own life 4 years ago when she turned 21. On that birthday, she asked that we change the spelling of her nickname Maddie to Madi because she didn't want the word "die" in her name anymore.

I learned that only 1 in 3 transgender & nonbinary youth found their own home to be gender-affirming. Maybe my mother was right that loving my child was THE JOB I had to do.

I also realized that coming from the most open-minded, accepting and forward-thinking home didn't mean I was easily able to adjust to this new Parenting Handbook I was creating for myself. I didn't even know I had a vision for my child until she spoke her truth & gave me the insight to see what she saw in her future and it was bleak.

She didn't believe she could be loved; she didn't love herself, she was experiencing suicidal ideation at 6 years of age.

I learned that support was hard to secure because my "tribe" was not filled with the knowledge or experts that I needed. Nothing in my Playbook for Success was going to help me with this.

My Neurodiverse Child

The support needed for Madi came with more insights....

Nothing happens in a vacuum. Madi is not just "transgender":

She is artistic, empathetic, she is Irish, she is funny...

She was also diagnosed with ADD, General Anxiety Disorder, Autism, Chronic Depression, PTSD, Insomnia, Anorexia....

So while many of you may not be raising a transgender child or a neurodiverse kid, you are undoubtedly all part of a Village of people that are raising children in a world that is just NOT SAFE.

I mean, I didn't think about the possibility of school shootings when Madi was a child. I had other negative thoughts that caused my fear. Today it's different; I don't believe there is any really SAFE SPACE for our children.

I read the Global Economic Forum's Global Risk Report for 2024 & was disheartened to see Social Polarization and the Erosion of Human Rights as 2 of the top 10 threats.

We need HOPE now, more than ever. We need our parents, teachers, CEOs and geopolitical commanders to be leaders in HOPE. We all need this VISION of a better future to provide us the COURAGE to do the things that frighten us to be part of the CHANGE in the world.

I didn't always have the COURAGE to drive change. Sometimes Madi had to literally show me what COURAGE looks like.

Like when she was in middle school and went to the Friday night dance all decked out in her female clothes, makeup and earrings. I dropped her off and she walked into the school with her friends, and I immediately started the intervention on my brain to make it stop repeating the negative thoughts I was having about all the things that might happen to her that night.

Thankfully, my friend Linda was with me so we drove around a bit and talked a lot. I was able to express my fears that the bullying that took place in the school would penetrate its way into this night. But alas, just a couple of hours later I was back to pick up Madi and a couple of her friends to bring them home and learned how those wonderful young boys and girls literally created a human shield around Madi that evening. Keeping her in the center of their gathering along the walls of the building. So there wasn't much dancing but there was safety in their friendship. Madi is still connected with several of those friends, and I will live the rest of my life in gratitude for their love and loyalty.

Terrible, unimaginable things had already happened.

I was delicately managing my relationship with my husband while trying to influence his relationship with Madi during this time. I wished for more of a partnership, but I also realized Werner was doing the best he could & had to fight his own demons and health challenges. To "be there" for me or Madi wasn't possible.

Werner was always the practical one, guided by logic, facts and objective analysis. Werner had expressed to Madi his confusion and dismay about how or why she'd want to leave being a boy to become a girl. I believe that Werner was truly seeking to understand when he asked this question; it was however, the least affirming thing he could have said.

I have always been the emotional one guided by feelings, intuition and subjective experiences. It was easier for me to accept what I couldn't understand. Unlike Werner, I hadn't had to bury my first-born son as he did in his first marriage. I had only to accept, advocate for and love our transgender daughter.

Be that as it may, my biggest character flaw is being ***TRUST STILL.*** *I believe that all humans are well intentioned at the core. I TRUST that people you bring into and let stay in your life won't bring harm to you or those you love. I have been terribly wrong about that.*

I had outsourced the job of caring for our child while I was working full time because although her father was home, he was unhealthy. There had already been too many strokes, heart attacks and events of hypoglycemia & hyperglycemia that had happened while Madi was in his care. But entrusting your precious child to someone doesn't mean they will be safe. In Madi's case she was a victim of sexual abuse under one nanny's watch. I will never forgive myself for missing those signs; for not knowing until it was too late, for being Trust Still.

Once aware, I did all I could to protect Madi and ensure this person would never be responsible for another parent's' child. But even the restraining order wasn't enough to undo the damage that had been done.

Indoctrination in HOPE

I once again went back to our "HopeMeister" to garnish insights & develop HOPE.

It was then that our Mom moved to California to surround us with her love and wisdom. She didn't plan too far ahead after I told her, "I need you out here with me for a while." She simply packed a suitcase and got in the car with my brother Brian who would take her to the airport.

On the way, he told her in a couple of short sentences about what had happened. She said only, "Okay Brian, that's enough. I don't want or need to hear more; I'm going to California and that's all that matters". My sister would come out shortly after and help to set up an apartment for our mom after we'd had some of her things, including her car, shipped across the country.

My Mom reminded me of the steps to create a winning plan. She would say, "I can only tell you what I know from my own experience". She was a polio survivor and had raised four children on her own. She clearly had experience with adversity. She consistently reminded me that having HOPE doesn't mean all will be ok. BUT having HOPE as your strategy meant you would create a plan to build the strength that would enable you to persevere through the roller coaster of life.

Hope is itself, not an emotion. *It's a way of thinking or a state of being.* Which means it can be taught. I realized that I had to HOPE that I could develop the skills to not only raise our daughter but to keep her safe given I'd already failed once in doing so.

Of course, my marriage was also impacted. Both Werner and I felt filled with rage but also guilt about not being able to keep our child safe in her own home. We stayed in California but moved to a new house in the East Bay in 2006, seeking to free ourselves from some of the harsh thoughts about what Madi had been subjected to. My Mom moved again to another apartment in the town next door to us. She was always such a flexible type of person, always going with the flow, now that I am almost the age she was then, I wonder how she ever did it all with such joy, humor and conviction to teach me how to do the same.

I never understood why Werner drew an analogy for me when I first was pregnant with Madi. He had two grown daughters in Germany and as a parent he was clear that once there was a child, that human being would be the priority. He went on to play out a scenario that IF the three of us were ever in a boat and it capsized, and if it was clear that we could only save one other person that we would promise to save Madi vs. each other. At the time it seemed so morbid and unnecessary to talk like this; to force me to agree. To bring it up several more times over the course of our lives. I wonder now if he'd had some sort of premonition or if perhaps, he just knew more than I about living through hardships.

When Madi was in her deepest darkest state in 2015, at the age of 16, I made one of the toughest decisions of my life. We were living in NJ, having moved back from California in 2008 when I was in between jobs. There was too much turbulence, and heightened emotions in our home to be healthy for any of us. I had to focus on saving Madi. So, Werner moved into a Continuing Care Community in NJ. As I was creating the plans for this move, Werner's doctor at the time said something to me I will never forget. She said: "Barbara, Werner needs support, he needs services and an infrastructure to help care for him BUT your daughter needs YOU. There is no one else that can do this job."

I cling to these words to this day in the hope that was the right decision.

HOPE as a DISCIPLINE

You too CAN turn HOPE into a discipline & make it your Playbook for Success.

1st thing that is needed is an INTERVENTION to stop the loop of fear statements.

When I was ruminating in my head the fear that I couldn't do what I needed to; I had to tell myself I can do this. In my case, the "this" was ENSURING that my daughter knew & felt that I loved her exactly as she is. AND to keep her safe. Because the knowledge I was accumulating supported my greatest fears; that the world was not safe, and she might one day take her own life.

My goal was simple: Madi would be one of the 3 transgender youth that lived in a gender-affirming home. But the world was not aligned, and I didn't know how to navigate that & help Madi do the same.

The 2nd part of the process is to RECALIBRATE / REBOOT. There is a need for the body to rest and relax so that the brain can function as it should. We know that it is the body that absorbs all the incoming signals before they reach the brain.

An example of this is when we walk into a place and feel our heart race or a tightness in our chest. We sense danger. We feel fear. Our brain registers "unsafe situations". These often visceral responses are then processed through the midbrain (prefrontal cortex) which interprets the perceived threat.

The challenge when all this is going on is that we don't have complete access to our brain. The frontal lobe, responsible for Executive Functioning. Impulse Control etc. is not yet doing its job; allowing us to apply reason, organize our thoughts and create a plan. The threat assessment that is taking place cannot differentiate between a Threat Level 1, 2 or 3.

As a Certified Gallup Strengths Coach, I now understand why this RECALIBRATE & REBOOT part of the process was so difficult. Gallup Strengths is basically a journey of self-discovery and intentional development focused on using your innate strengths.

Activator & Achiever are in my top 10 Strengths, which means that I naturally forge into ACTION with a sense of urgency AND the Achiever in me creates a strong inner drive to do and achieve more. It means that I don't like to "talk about the plan" but rather get started to quickly reach the finish.

My mother was constantly reminding me to execute this 2nd step RECALIBRATE & REBOOT before jumping to the 3rd step in the process which is FOCUS ON THE FIGHT: the execution of the plan.

This was a real challenge for me. My mother would remind me to do the things that help my body relax like going to the beach, enjoying a long walk in nature and listening to my music.

There were neurophysiological things happening to me over and over during the next 15 years as I lived within FIGHT OR FLIGHT response mode. The strength you garnish from steps 1 & 2 creates the ability to EXECUTE your plan.

When I skipped the 2nd step, my health suffered. At one point, I developed such high levels of cortisol in my body that my doctor had to prescribe meds to get that back under control.

So, imagine the impact of this happening to our transgender youth who literally take their lives in their hands each day they go out into the world. Hence, why I became intentional to set HOPE as my Strategy.

The Power of Visualization

I have never experienced neglect or abuse or any crime of humanity against me. The adversity that I have faced has come in the form of a barrage of continuous health issues and complex parenting experiences that resulted in major transformations of the vision I had for my life.

Werner's health issues continued, and I walked the path as an ambitious career woman, the parent of an at-risk child and a wife to an unhealthy husband that was determined not to let the world see me fail in any of these roles or to hear me complain.

I first learned the power of visualization in my twenties when I told my mother I wanted to work at a company that I only knew of because of the large sign on top of their building near the George Washington Bridge. "Start visualizing it," she said. "Imagine what you need to do to make it happen. Then go make it happen." The following summer, I was hired at that very company. The experience taught me that hope, when combined with action, could make anything possible.

Over the years, I used visualization to guide my life: envisioning a loving marriage, a fulfilling career, buying a home, becoming a mother, and creating a safe and happy future for my daughter. Hope wasn't just a feeling—it was a strategy, a way to see beyond the obstacles and focus on the possibilities. Once I could see it, I would put together a plan and then I would execute that plan with veracity.

My mother often told us: "you can be anything you choose to be." Therefore, I began to see myself as unbreakable but adaptable, resilient yet stealth, full of energy, enthusiasm and love yet calm in the face of misfortune.

I didn't know until many years later that THIS is exactly how you *manifest your destiny.* It is precisely how my daughter would survive years of depression, anxiety & suicidal ideation. This belief in visualization was the beginning of my commitment to build a discipline of HOPE as an antidote for adversity AND to create the life I wanted for my husband, our child and me.

HOPE Is contagious. I didn't yet know the root cause of why it worked exactly, but I see now that my mother's relentless ability to HOPE rubbed off on us kids.

A Legacy of Hope

Hope carried me through 34 years of love and loss, parenting and caregiving, joy and heartbreak. It taught me to find courage in the face of fear and strength in the midst of despair. My mother's wisdom: "What doesn't kill you makes you stronger", proved true time and again.

Now, I pass that legacy of hope to Madi and anyone facing their own journey through adversity.

Hope is a discipline, a mindset, and a way of life. Hope is what allows us to face the unthinkable and still believe in a brighter future. It's not *just* a strategy—it's the foundation of resilience, the spark that keeps us going when everything else feels impossible.

In addition to my mother, my brothers Brian & Kevin, my sister Kim and their spouses were my partners in life that got me through these waves of destruction. Amazing therapists, doctors and friends like Dana & Paul, Linda & Bruce, and Kari and Scott served as buoys in the water I felt I was drowning in which kept me aligned with the shore.

And always, there was laughter and love mixed in with HOPE.

BARB MCATEER

Barb McAteer is a "rejuvenated" Software Sales Executive. She is the founder of BarbMac Consulting, a Diversity, Equity & Inclusion Consultant and a Certified Gallup Strengths Coach. She is also an expert in HOPE.

Barb has 30+ years experience in Direct & Indirect Sales, Sales Management; Business Development, Change Management, Mergers & Acquisitions, Strategy and Operations, License Management and Sales Enablement. As a Certified Gallup Strengths Coach she has embraced her own Top Strengths; Strategic, Activator, WOO, Achiever and Communication; which is to say she's an "Influencer, a Visionary, a Motivator, a Coach and a Guide.

She's a Conduit of Change for those that seek positive transformation.

She has been described by people she has worked for and with as "authentic, bold and fearless". Some have said she is a force to be reckoned with. Fortunately, the years have taught her that not everyone desires change or has interest to transform their life. Hence, she's committed to investing in people that are ready and intentional about manifesting their dreams. Barb is adept at a) building strategic succession plans, b) assisting teams to enhance their efficiency to improve the outcomes and c) leveraging an organizations' tapestry of talent.

Her superpower is in her ability to quickly build trust and create safe spaces for people to be vulnerable and begin the work to utilize their resilience. The "how" she works is important for clients that want someone with high energy, enthusiasm, empathy & humor.

Website: https://www.linkedin.com/in/barbmcateer/

12

TRANSFERRING TRAUMA TO PURPOSEFUL JOY!

NIOBIS QUEIRO

The room is dark and cool. I'm wearing my favorite purple PJs, a waffle fabric that makes me feel warm and happy. All is quiet except for my salt lamp providing a gentle sienna glow. I open my eyes, inhale deeply, hold my breath for a count of five, and release slowly. It's time to rise.

I quickly bounce up and walk into my living room, focus on the large round rug in the center. I sit facing the four ceiling-to-floor windows, awake but burdened by the many pending deadlines. I put my AirPods in, pull out my phone, and open the Missing Link App, selecting the stress release therapy component. As the sun rises, I'm transported to a calm space, following guided breathing and listening to 1990s jazz. The music takes me back to my youth, a time of freedom and invincibility. Eyes closed, I feel the warmth of the sun's rays hugging me as it climbs the sky, filling the room with light and filling me with joy. Good morning, Nio. Let's start your journey.

Three years ago, I was living in beautiful Quincy, Massachusetts, in a golf community with a wooded walking trail as my backyard, leading to the Quincy Quarry with the full Boston skyline as the backdrop—a magical sight. I seemed to have it all: SVP of Revenue for Tufts Medicine in Boston, a thought leader in my industry, Nana to the exceptional Cylas, mom, wife, daughter, and friend. I had the expected trappings: the right house, car, vacations. Little did I know how quickly it could all fall apart.

On a sunny June morning, I had a 10 AM hair appointment. Running late, I quickly showered, put my hair up, threw on a sundress, and did a quick face beat. Bob, my extraordinary husband, handed me my tea as I dashed to the garage. Sitting in the car, waiting for the top to go down, I felt a sharp pain in my abdomen. Ignoring it, I drove 10 minutes to Gwen's Salon. I told Gwen about the strange pain and sudden constipation, and she, the holistic queen, brought me an herbal tea remedy. But the pain didn't pass, it sharpened. I found myself on the bathroom floor, doubled over and throwing up.

I screamed for help. Gwen ran to me, wet a towel with cold water, and placed it on my forehead and neck. I started crying from the pain, "Please call Bob." She called my husband and told him I needed medical attention. Bob was on his way. Meanwhile, I stayed on the floor, finding some comfort in its coolness

When Bob arrived, he sprang into action without exchanging words. He picked me up and took me to the car. Once inside, Bob suggested going to the ER, but I insisted on a cold shower at home. We drove in silence, with me moaning in pain the entire way. Bob helped me inside, and I begged him to run cold water in the bathroom. As I stepped in, I crashed through the glass, hitting the cold ground, feeling both intense pain and relief.

Bob called 911, and it seemed like an eternity before they arrived, though it was only minutes. I lay on the floor, screaming in pain with minor cuts. The female paramedic asked, "What drugs are you on?" Bob responded that I was not on any drugs. The paramedic remained skeptical until two others arrived and began assessing me. They noted my high fever (103 degrees) and covered me with a robe and sheet. They placed a breathing mask on me, and I lost consciousness.

I was taken to a local community hospital, which was a mistake. This hospital focused on delivering babies and fixing broken bones, while I needed trauma care. They administered morphine (to which I am allergic), causing severe reactions. After numerous tests, they identified septic shock and a major abdominal obstruction, requiring emergency surgery.

Bob requested a transfer to Tufts Medical Center, the nearest trauma hospital, where I worked. Dr. Johnson was on call and immediately dispatched the medevac team. During transport, I suffered cardiac arrest, but the team didn't give up. They revived me using Boston grit and brought me to the trauma bay.

Dr. Johnson began surgery, but an hour in, I experienced a second cardiac arrest. They revived me again and transferred me to the ECMO unit. ECMO, a life support system, removed carbon dioxide from my blood and sent oxygen-rich blood back to my body. I was placed in a chemically induced coma for 12 hours to stabilize.

Once semi-stable, Dr. Michael Tarnoff, CEO of Tufts Medical Center, was called to lead my surgery. Dr. Tarnoff had developed the standard for reconstructing the abdomen post-sepsis. My case was fate intervening, as I had a formidable team and a prayer army on my side. Dr. Tarnoff joined Dr. Johnson to start rebuilding me.

After eight hours of surgery, they removed nine feet of intestine and part of my abdomen. The fear was that I might need a feeding tube and catheter for life, if I survived. After surgery, I was too fragile to breathe or manage my organs on my own. After a week in a coma, the team decided to wake me.

The ICU room was packed with surgeons, nurses, and my family. Tubes protruded from unexpected places. My surgeon, who was also the hospital CEO, Dr. Tarnoff, sat next to my bed, holding my hand. He told me, "You are a tough woman." I wanted to ask questions but could only say "water". He began telling me how they put me back together. I saw tears in my family's eyes and wanted to console them. Lying there, I wondered, "Why did I survive this catastrophic event? Why am I here?"

Looking Back to Find My Truth

I closed my eyes hoping it would all disappear and I would be home waking up from this nightmare. But no, it was my reality and I felt my husband touch my face, I know those hands oh so well, they are soothing and magical. I am grateful for him. He was trying to comfort me, so

I opened my eyes to acknowledge him. Then the voices started speaking, welcoming me back. It was a chorus of love and caring. But I was not present in spirit or mind, I was just a body that looked like a science experiment. I scanned the room and noticed more people had arrived from the finance team. I was overwhelmed and my heart was racing in fear. I can't act as if all is well, I can't carry this load on my shoulders. Bob knew it was too much for his wife, he knew that his Nio did not appreciate being seen so vulnerable. He asked Dr. Tarnoff, "Don't you think she needs some rest?" He immediately said, "you took the words right out of my mouth, time for rest." My heart melted feeling great gratitude for my loving husband.

I fell asleep for an eternity but finally woke up late into the night, full of tears running down my face. The wetness was foreign to me as this was a new emotion. I was just human. I couldn't wipe my tears. I had so many IVs that I couldn't bend my arm or touch my face. Tears are strange to me, I pride myself on not having time for frivolous emotions. I refuse pity and lack of self-control. There in the empty room alone with my thoughts, I started to reflect on my past traumatic passages in time. I needed to understand my truth through the journeys of the past.

I've lived a life of continuous trauma. At 19 I lost my sight from a pseudotumor of cerebri (idiopathic intracranial hypertension). I was a senior in college and engaged to be married. I fought through that trauma like a phoenix. I took all my tests and provided my papers in verbal presentation mode and graduated with honours. The wedding went off without a hitch, no one knew I walked down the aisle with low vision. In time I regained 75% of my vision. That is the positive outcome with these tumours", you get most or all of your vision back in time. I never cried or accepted pity, I pushed through, focused on a no-victim philosophy, nothing to see here, just solutions. I made sure not to be a burden to my family and finish my academic goals at the time. I moved on with my life. Got married, had a beautiful son, and built a career. I was golden, I learned that power of disciple and perseverance.

Ten years later, I am divorced from my first husband (often called the practice husband). A single mom with a successful career and fate gives me a surprise on my 30th birthday. What should have been a normal annual physical turned into one of the scariest moments of my life. I was diagnosed with three pituitary tumours (three large tumours in my brain and evidence of a small brain bleed). My doctor referred me to a neurologist for urgent surgery. It took two weeks to get me ready for surgery, and on morning itself I went to the hospital with my parents and partner. It was the first scheduled surgery, I met the pre-op team of doctors and they assured me it was going to go well.

This was expected to be a 4-hour surgery. They took me in and 2 hours into the operation I had a cardiac arrest. The primary surgeon Dr. Puglisse went to the surgical waiting room and informed my parents and my partner, told them that they were able to revive me but I had a major stroke after the cardiac arrest. They were continuing with the main surgery but there were no promises as to what would happen next. When the surgery ended I woke up in post-op with Dr. Puglisse next to me (I was told he never left my side since the surgery). I couldn't form words, I had no vision from my right eye, my motor skills were non-existent, I was in a completely vegetative state. He explained what had occurred and that we would be handling this one day at a time. I did the only thing I could do to acknowledge him. I blinked. The next six months were spent in OT, PT, speech therapy and thanks to my mom acupuncture, cupping and eastern medicine herbs. I never cried, I pushed through, all that mattered was raising my son (Quinton). I had to be a pillar of strength and an example of resiliency. Months later, I went to my post-op appointment not in the wheelchair that I left the hospital in but on my own two feet, I walked into Puglisse's office. When I was called in to go into his office he had the permanent disability paperwork at the ready, but that was not my future nor my present.

I was renewed, I could walk and talk while chewing gum. I had grown accustomed to my permanent vision loss, and learned to navigate the world with no vision in my right eye and low vision in my left, but it was not stopping me. I walked into his office with confidence wearing a sharp, navy blue pinstripe suit with a pixie cut and my first attempt at makeup. I felt like a powerful woman again. I still had some speech issues and my gait needed some work but that was temporary. Dr. Puglisse was in complete shock "What, I'm serious What, How? You look great!" I sucked my stomach in and said what I had been practising for days so my words would land with perfect diction: "Thank you, I am here to ask for my return to work letter". He laughed and said, "let's do that in a month, you've done great but we need to honour your body's need to heal fully." I inhaled and told him, "I'm holding you to that." A month to the day, I was back and got my letter to freedom.

At 19 and then at 30, I handled trauma as a warrior of intentionality, perseverance and resilience. Actually, I was just dealing with the symptoms of the illness and the impact on my nature and authenticity. As I laid in the hospital in June 2021, post the two cardiac arrests and total abdominal reconstruction, things were different this time. This was not to be an autopilot approach to get the body back to function while ignoring the emotions and spirit within me. This time I wanted to understand my why, value, emotions, purpose and authentic self. I could place the situation on a shelf and ignore it. The tears were my shelf crumbling from the weight of avoidance. Honestly, for the first time I was not doing, creating, overcoming, caring, educating or perfecting. I was just being present and vulnerable.

Out of Pain Comes Awareness

A week later, I was given my discharge order. I experienced my first anxiety attack, my blood pressure went through the roof, my heart was pounding so hard it hurt, I was nauseous and dizzy. The doctors were confused about what was happening. My sweet nurse Nancy sent everyone away and sat by me, held my hand and told me it was going to be okay. During this time I barely spoke not because I couldn't but because I did not want to engage with others, I did not wish to carry on a conversation nor perform for others. I realised that when we are sick those that love us and care for us are seeking reassurance that they are providing for our needs, that we are getting better - they need us to let them know it is all ok. But it wasn't ok, and I did not want to be responsible for anyone's emotions. I was scared to go home because I knew Bob was not prepared for how weak I was, nor had he ever experienced my headspace. I didn't want to go home and see visitors. I wanted to just be left alone. But it was my time to deal with Nio and whoever she truly is.

The next day I was home and it was exactly what I thought it would be. My husband wanted me to try more at physical therapy and other prescribed rehabilitation activities. But I was not into it, I did the bare minimum to keep everyone quiet. I was not truly engaged. I woke up one day and thought to myself I need help to figure this out. I called the most zen person that I've ever met, Lora Carr. She was her incredible high-energy self and I spoke in a mere whisper, she clued in and met me where I was. When she too whispered the floodgates opened. As I cried I kept asking for help. I needed a safe, no-judgement place to find myself. Lora said "I got you, we are going to Kripalu." I had no idea what that meant. She laughed and said remember the movie Clueless and the mom was at a yoga retreat that was very exclusive, "I guess," I said. Lora said, "well that was Kripalu. Don't worry, it is the place to find yourself."

Two weeks later we were en route to Berkshire, MA to discover Kripalu; two and a half hours of listening to music and finally laughing freely. The sign as we entered said *The Highest Form of Spiritual Practice is Self-observation without Judgement* - I was home!

Kripalu was incredible. The property was a captivating painting of glorious landscapes, with accommodations simple but inviting. I was greeted as if I was a long-lost friend, which made me uncomfortable at first because I am not a touchy-feely person. But I remembered the no judgement quote and went with the flow. Kripalu is a yoga wellness centre that dedicates its services to transformation of mind, body and spirit. I was exposed to programs that were out of my comfort zone that renewed my soul.

I had signed up for a grief session. This was a meeting of 16 people that were seeking to understand and manage their grief. I went to deal with the grief of the old me that was now gone, so I thought. We entered the room and it was set up in a circle with cushions on the floor. I sat on a chair outside of the circle because I could get down and up from the floor. The coordinator expanded the circle to include me. RATS!!! We sat wondering what was to happen. We were first educated on the many faces of grief and how grieving appears in many different forms. My avoidance of my trauma was my way of handling grief and, though not sustainable, it served me well for a time in my life. We went through some exercises to get comfortable with acknowledging grief. There were two exercises that were life changing: the first was identifying your initial life grief. I never saw it as grief, just a part of my story and the way I grew up.

You see, my family came to America from Cuba when I was 4 years old, through the Red Cross due to health issues my father experienced.

America was where he could get the surgery to regain his sight. My grief originated 4 years later when we were assimilated in the United States as citizens. My mom became ill and I was her translator through it all. I gave her the news that she had cancer. I went with her to the treatments and multiple surgeries, I was the trooper caring for her as she threw up all day after treatment. I prepped dinner, kept the house clean, and made sure to get good grades to not be a bother. My dad worked multiple jobs to pay for her care, my two older brothers just played sports, got good grades and stayed invisible. I was obsessed with being the perfect daughter. That grief session made me aware that I was a Parentified Child. I lost the chance to have a childhood, I went out of my way to please and be perfect in all aspects of my life. I was grieving the child I never was. I did not go to the kid events at school after hours like other kids my age did. I just listened and wondered how it all was. No one knew what my life was really like, so my escape from the great secret was music and dance. I played classical piano from the age of 4 and danced multiple genres including ballet, flamenco to jazz from the age 8. My music and dance were my silent healers. They increased my endorphins and dopamine while decreasing my cortisol levels. All was learned during this grief session. I understood why I reacted to matters in a quick solution-oriented manner and why I never dealt with my feelings and instead focused on making sure everyone else was ok. I finally got a glimpse of my why and how.

Boundaries Matter

The second grief session was about the strength of boundaries and self-care. I lived with an equivalent to a PHD in giving and a kindergarten certification in self-care. This was the toughest for me because I was always the one that people came to for help. In my mind I believed that if I start saying no and practising boundaries and self-care then people wouldn't like me. That may be true for the people that are only around to use you. They will not like you once you acknowledge your voice, needs and boundaries. I deserved a group of friends who cheer, support, challenge me and keep confidence in each other. Nio, you must elevate your friend group kiddo.

The four days at Kripalu opened my insights into who I was and why. I went through a rollercoaster of emotions: anger, frustration, sadness and joy. I accepted them all in my journal, played the piano feverishly at the retreat, I walked into the fire and came out victorious on the other side. I found a new voice in boundaries and peace that liberated my soul. "It is well in my soul..."

We Were Born with Purpose

Kripalu opened the door to my journey of learning. I couldn't get enough of this search for myself and what to do with this knowledge. I went ahead and got my executive coaching certification, Energy Leadership Index Master Practitioner (ELI-MP) and then my Neuroscience therapy certification. I wrote my first book *Joy Notes, Balancing the Trauma with Triumph, a book* about overcoming every form of challenge and finding your joy through the power of music. The book details my story and that of five other women who dynamically found their triumph using music as their catalyst; every chapter is an exploration of the impact of music by genres. Gloria Gaynor (American Songstress and Queen of Disco) wrote the foreword and the chapter dedicated to the disco genre through her personal story. Writing my first book was a major achievement that has taken me to the purpose chapter of my life. I quit my job as the SVP of Revenue Cycle for Tufts Medicine and started my own consulting firm to bring humanity back into healthcare delivery, from patient experience to human-centred executive leadership. I get to speak across the country and share my learning and talents with others. This transition has been one of true enlightenment. I finally have the courage to deal with my emotions and question my limited beliefs to how they currently serve me and fit into my newfound knowledge. Anger is replaced with awareness and joy. As I recovered and had the good fortune to build a successful niche business, I became aware of the worst form of jealousy. This is called survivor jealousy: when the closest to you get jealous of your success post-trauma. This happens because their comfort was in your station of struggle and they feel surpassed and no matter what you do, you betrayed them by not just overcoming but thriving. As small victories came my way, my dad warned me not to let survivor jealousy eat me up. I remember agreeing not having a clue of how it was a real thing. I had family and friends that processed my success in that manner. Though crushing at the time, I understood their perspective and leaned in with love. It is so funny that today my focus is what I can positively bring to the situation and let people process their emotions, and remain there to address the future with them with minimal judgement "still a work in progress - no judgement is really hard".

The Never-Ending Journey

I think the best part of this journey has been my understanding of why. As I explored myself, I awakened to why my father was such a special beloved man. He was always my refuge but I had no idea how much he impacted his community in his 84 years. His amazing smile, kindness and honesty were always a gift to me. He was all those things but of utmost importance he always was authentic and took full custody of himself. He cared for his emotions, spirit and health. He believed that if we weren't whole we could not be there for anyone else. I am leaning into adopting his core values and traits to be the best person I can be.

My dad was a very wise man and a victim of a horrible accident in the required Cuba sugar cane harvest duty. When we arrived in the US, he went directly to New York and the Eye Infirmary for a total eye replacement. Unfortunately, the procedure did not work and he had total blindness in his right eye and minimal sight on the left. Who would imagine that 30 years later I would share the same disability. His journey empowered my journey by example. When the doctor told him he was to be permanently disabled he said "no" and would place duck tape on his face to cover his eye and go off to work in poor conditions at the local textile factory. In time, my mom and dad built their own business employing immigrant craftsmen from around the world providing them a place to practise their craft while being honoured, and respected in a culture of trust. When my dad Tony passed there were hundreds of people there sharing their stories about him and how he led with kindness and inclusion. Twelve languages were spoken at the funeral and the storybook passed from person to person to share a Tony memory. As I read the stories and wrote the thank you cards I was so blessed that he got to see me transcend to my authentic person before he passed, and that from the grave through the funeral storybook I gathered greater learnings. Every day I wake up and pray, meditate and affirm that I will respect those around me, whether I agree or disagree with their perspective. I will honour those I encounter as we are all perfectly made for a purpose and deserve to be acknowledged. I'm completely invested in continuous study and growth. As my father said, I must be wholeheartedly mature and practice radial authenticity at all times in order to be a source of development for others. My purpose is to help others find their truth and untangle their limited beliefs, challenges and traumas.

I manifest my purpose through my dedication to serve as an executive coach guiding leaders to find their authenticity and flow to success. As a motivational speaker and facilitator of transformational retreats, I focus on empowering inner exploration, unleashing the power from within and providing a safe space for "your journey to Unfold". My Joy and Gratitude Podcast is a source of real-life conversations about how to detangle your life by reshaping your path into a genuine reflection of your inner self in authentic flow. Daily, I provide a blog on LinkedIn (Nio (Niobis) Queiro | LinkedIn) of inspirational Joy Notes to boost their professional and personal journey. I continue to extend my message by releasing *Joy Notes - Balancing The Trauma with Triumph* in audible and a translation into Spanish to honour my parents. The first companion book in the Joy Notes series is *The Joy Notes Journey to Thrive over Trauma* a workbook that will be used as a curriculum for my seminars, coaching, retreats and podcast.

This has been an exploration of the twist and turns of my life's journey to finding my purpose. With every trauma there was a learning that developed the person I am today. I learned how to embrace intentionality, determination, perseverance and strength in my first 20 years. The next trauma at 30 made me aware that I am who I believe I can be, I am unstoppable. In my maturity, I found my purpose and joy. Most importantly, I use kindness, empathy and compassion to create a culture of trust. I will continue to use my voice to help others find their inner power.

Life is limitless if you are willing to be present. You too can embrace your inner power by giving yourself permission and grace to put yourself first. Remember your past is proof of your resilience and ability to achieve beyond dreams into authentic purpose.

NIOBIS QUEIRO

Niobis (Nio) Queiro is the founder of The Queiro Group offering Organizational Transformation, AI Management and Implementation, M&A, Advisory Services and Leadership Development Services.

Nio formerly was the SVP of Revenue Cycle Tufts Medicine, a 2.5B health system in Boston Massachusetts. Currently, is the Chief Strategy Officer for Nashville General Hospital in Nashville, TN and the CEO of Queiro Group. Nio is an award-winning author of "Joy Notes - Balancing the Trauma with Triumph. Nio's development and implementation of digital, AI and hyper-automation strategic transformational models was awarded one of the Modern Healthcare Top 25 Innovators of 2021.

Nio uses her to drive change across diverse healthcare delivery channels, hence, bridging the chasm between finance and clinical care with transformational solutions for patients and families to overcome care equity and financial toxicity. She is dedicated to assisting others embrace themselves fully to empower them to reach their goals and purpose through coaching and educational events. She has assisted healthcare providers in growth revenue, implementation population health innovative models of care and sustainability delivering an impact of 8 billion dollars across the provider IDN, Community Hospital and Professional services.

Nio has presented in front of Congress as an industry expert for the digitization of the military service men medical records as the lead of a proof-of-concept project that is now the standard healthcare data exchange for the military.

Website: www.queirogroup.com

13

THE WAKE-UP CALL: TURNING PAIN INTO POWER AND PURPOSE

ANNE-MARIE HUGHES

Some may call it a midlife crisis, I like to call it finally listening to my intuition. For decades I lived in my masculine energy and denied my feminine energy. In June of 2023, I heard the clear intuitive message "your soul contract has ended". I wasn't exactly sure what it meant at the time but it was slowly revealed over the following few months when certain people would leave my life. I was shown that I had a big soul contract with many narcissistic people. The universe was showing me who they were and getting me to place solid boundaries up. It was as if a veil was being removed from my vision; and my third eye was being activated.

Growing Up

I was raised to be a people pleaser, by a toxic patriarchal family on my stepfather's side and later my biological family, who I met in my 20s. As a child holding feminine Christ frequencies and a strong intuition, I became a "people pleaser" in order to fit in with them, which in turn made me a magnet for narcissistic people during the first part of my life.

I was born in Ireland in the 1970s out of wedlock; the child of a young single mother and a much older married man; with an existing family of his own. From the day I was born I was thrown into a web of lies to keep the truth of my biological father a secret. My family was determined for me to never know the truth. It was a journey of being lied to and abused by narcissistic people. This journey blocked my intuitive feminine energy for a long time. The majority of my family tried to shut me down in the hope that I would be too afraid to listen to my intuition, and dare not speak my truth.

When I was aged 4 my mum met my stepfather. Despite my warnings about my stepfather and the horrible things he was doing to me, she married him and organised for him to adopt me when I was 7 years of age and take his surname. A new birth certificate was created so that on paper it would look like my stepfather was my biological father. However, on a soul level I always remembered that he was not my father. I have a photo of me on my Holy Communion Day around the same age I was adopted and I looked so sad. I felt so abandoned by my mum having her do this to me.

The topic of my biological father was never discussed until we were preparing to immigrate to Australia. One day, before we left, my Nana (on my mum's side) took me aside. We sat together at her kitchen table in Wicklow, Ireland. She pulled out a photo of my biological father and explained that my stepfather was not, in fact, my biological father. To be honest, this revelation didn't come as a shock. Hearing her speak the truth out loud felt less like a surprise and more like a confirmation of something I had already sensed. I felt a sense of relief.

I had a tumultuous upbringing. I was abused mentally, emotionally, physically and sexually by my stepfather and different family members, including some female members. I grew up being trained to "suck any problems up" and to "sweep my problems under the carpet". My mum was known for her hand gestures for sweeping things under the carpet. She avoided difficult and uncomfortable conversations with me. In my search for truth, I would ask her questions, but I had been taught repeatedly not to ask questions, to ignore my intuition and feelings, and to suppress my emotions. I was silenced so many times that

I eventually became too afraid to speak at all. During public speaking events at school, my face would turn bright red. I hated speaking in front of people. Later, I discovered that the redness and pressure in my face during those moments were actually the result of energetic attacks on my neck and throat chakra—psychic assaults from certain family members to prevent me from speaking my truth. With a Scorpio moon in my astrological chart, however, it was clear that silencing me in the long term was never going to be possible. A Scorpio moon in an astrological chart signifies a deep affinity for the unseen and the esoteric. As someone born with this placement, I have always been a truth seeker. No matter the challenges, uncovering the truth has and will always be a passion of mine.

For most of my life, I ignored my intuition out of fear. Certain family members constantly told me that my intuition and emotions were wrong, that they didn't matter. What I was really hearing was that I didn't matter. My stepfather would often tell me I was a waste of space. If I had a dollar for every time he said that, I'd have banked a lot of dollars! These words contributed to my feelings of unworthiness and abandonment wounds —wounds that I would later need to heal when I learned Quantum Energy Healing.

Moving to Australia in 1988

I can clearly remember the day that Nana, who was my primary caregiver during my younger years, sat me down and asked me if I wanted to stay in Ireland with her and Grandad, while my mum, stepfather, half brother and half sister moved to Australia. It's important to note that, back then, many grandparents would care for their grandchildren, but this was not officially recognized by government organizations. As a result, Nana did not have any legal claim to me. My mum was able to take me away with my abuser, have him adopt me, and move me to Australia to live with him.

One day, there was a big argument outside my grandparents' house, in my mum's car. Nana didn't want me to get in the car with my mum and stepfather and brother and sister. I remember my mum coaxing me into the car—it was quite an ordeal. I was really confused about what to do, and none of us kids really understood what was happening. Later, Mum told me that Nana had suspected my stepfather of stealing from their shed, but that was just a cover-up. The truth was, Nana was devastated at the thought of me leaving with my stepfather, who was abusing me. She must have been horrified when she discovered he had managed to create an adoption paper for me, along with a new birth certificate. Looking back, I now see that she was desperately trying to prevent them from taking me.

I honestly can't remember when I told Mum that I knew my stepfather was not my biological father. I feel like it was later in life, perhaps when I met my first boyfriend at 17 years. She was telling me not to have sex with him and I shot back at her that she had had sex before she was married. That hit a nerve with Mum as you could imagine. She picked up the sweeping broom and chased me around the back garden.

Knowing what I know now, I can see why she was extremely upset and angry. Shame is such a low vibration. It really holds us hostage to lower timelines and frequencies. I really feel that we need to own our mistakes in order to move on. Hiding details opens us up to a web of lies, secrecy and in my mum's case, also blackmail. We literally give away our power when we reside in shame. It may be extremely difficult at first, but being authentic and speaking our truth is more empowering. It releases you from all shame and guilt. Easier said than done, I know. But essentially, we are all human and we all make mistakes. Holding onto the past in secrecy only has us live a life of a lie. And living this way can make us physically ill. Mum was still carrying the shame of having a child with a married man and out of wedlock. I can only imagine how painful that shame must have been for her and how it affected her reputation, especially in Ireland at the time. Having a child outside of marriage was one thing, but having a child with a married man was another. I can understand why moving to Australia would have seemed like an appealing option for her.

My mum passed away from lung cancer. She never smoked, however when you look at the emotional causes of lung cancer you can see that she held onto so much grief and regret. My Mum died at age 61. Bless her Soul. I feel like a lot of her disease could have been avoidable through healing work. When you think about soul contracts, maybe Mum wasn't meant to do the healing in this lifetime. Perhaps she was setting me up to fulfill my own soul's work instead. It's hard to say for certain. I learned a lot about soul contracts while studying Quantum

Healing, and that knowledge has been incredibly helpful. It's also helped me come to terms with why some of us do the things we do.

I always thought that we moved to Australia because of Mum's Nursing qualification. Mum had mentioned that she had applied for our family's immigration using her qualifications and experience. However it was in the early 2020s that my stepfather mentioned that it was his idea for us all to move to Australia, which may explain why they had to create a fraudulent adoption paper and new birth certificate for me in 1984 prior to immigrating in 1988. With Nana as primary caregiver in Ireland back then and me telling her of the abuse I was enduring at the hands of my stepfather, there is no way she would have consented to him taking me to Australia.

We immigrated to Australia in May 1988 and stayed with Mum's friend for a few weeks until we found a rental in Doubleview, Perth. Us kids started tee-ball and immersed ourselves in the Australian culture. As a 10 year old I was pretty adaptable. I remember enjoying the adventure of it all. Mum enrolled us in Holy Rosary a Catholic School in Doubleview, however once we bought a home in Mullaloo all of us kids went to the local state school. I met so many great kids there, whom I'm still friends to this day.

After graduating high school in 1994, I met my first boyfriend. He wasn't accepted by my mum and stepfather, and before long, they kicked me out of the house for not ending the relationship. After being thrown out three times, I decided to move out permanently with my then boyfriend during my first year of university. We rented a place together, and I began studying primary school teaching, a path my mum had suggested. Teaching was in my astrological chart, which my mum had studied. Little did I know at the time, it was referring to spiritual teaching and much later in life. After a year, I realized that primary school teaching wasn't for me, so I transferred to a business degree. I completed a Bachelor of Business and began working for the Commonwealth Bank.

Not long after, I decided to travel to Ireland for a year of work. It was during this trip that I met my brother for the first time, who posed as my biological father. I was 22 years of age when I met him and the rest of the family. For 25 years I believed that my brother was my biological father. He would send me messages and Christmas cards signing off as

"Dad". I was 47 years of age when I found out that he was not my biological father. I discovered through my intuition and through meditation that he was not my dad, and confronted him. He could not deny what I had discovered. It seemed my brother had decided it was a good idea to masquerade as my father in order to cover up the truth.

Interestingly, when people would ask me what it was like meeting my biological father I would simply respond that it was like just meeting any man, proving that my intuition was on point back then. But this knowledge did not download into my conscious mind at age 22 so the illusion became part of my reality until I found out the truth in 2024. I never did get to meet my biological father as he had passed away in 1997.

The repercussions of growing up with narcissistic parents is that you learn to accept what people say regardless of their intentions. You learn to "walk on eggshells" and "people please" in order to fit in and keep the peace. I had learned not to ask too many questions so as not to disturb the "peace".

My mum and stepfather had a very tumultuous relationship; they fought constantly. My stepfather was always argumentative with me, constantly belittling me to make me feel unworthy and unwanted. Later in life, after my mum had passed and my two boys were toddlers, I took them to visit my stepfather at a café, accompanied by a family friend. During our visit, my stepfather told my boys they were ugly, explaining that it was meant to make them stronger. He claimed that by saying it to them, they would become more resilient and better prepared for when a stranger might say the same thing. This was the kind of distorted mentality I grew up with.

Needless to say, when my boys were born, I made it my business to be a work from home mum so that I was their main caregiver. They did attend some daycare leading up to their school years but it was one day a week to socialize with their peers. I ensured that I was a very present mum so that no-one could interfere with them, as was done to me.

Masking With Medication

After breaking up with a long-term boyfriend in my 20s, I was self-medicating with alcohol and cigarettes, as well as Xanax that had been prescribed to help me with my anxiety as a result of the breakup.

Mum took me to the hospital emergency after a bender of a night when I was hungover and at an all-time low which did not help my case. She spoke to the young Registrar who was over from England on his first assignment. Mum had told him that my stepfather had bipolar and convinced him that I did too. Ironically, my stepdad and I are not blood related and I wonder now if she omitted the "step" part when discussing me with the registrar. My mum was a nurse so I am sure she would have told him that she had the expertise and that she knew best. That's how I felt about her at the time. I thought she knew best so I went along with everything. On that fateful day, I received a diagnosis and began my journey with pharmaceutical medication for an illness I would later come to realize I didn't have. This medication journey would go on to span over 16 years.

Interestingly, one of the psychiatrists I would later see wrote me a prescription for 30 mins of daily walks outdoors and 2 fish oil tablets, instead of the medication for bipolar. Looking back, it is apparent that he knew that I did not have bipolar. Mum sent me back and demanded that he prescribe me the official medication or she would report him. I still trusted my mum at this stage and wanted to please her so taking the medication seemed like the right thing to do. When you are surrounded by liars, you learn to believe the lies. It's a frequency. And you can actually start attracting more liars in your life.

As time went on, the medication I was taking did not seem to work. I had a lot of "breakthrough mania" as they call it. I now know it was my soul breaking through and screaming at me to stop taking the medication.

I underwent 16 years of being on heavy medication; 300mg of one and 200mg of another. The only time I did not have medication during this time was when I was pregnant with my two boys. And I felt amazing!! I was glowing and I was very stable emotionally. In hindsight I feel like my intuition was telling me that I didn't need the medication, by not needing it while I was pregnant. However, after each birth I would go back to taking the medication thinking that I needed it. My mum was always in my ear, making sure that I would take it. I know now that she had her reasons for getting me to take it. She wanted to ensure my intuition was permanently blocked. She still thought that she had made a mistake by sleeping with my biological father. She hadn't done any healing around this. I have no doubt that she was also under pressure from other family members who wanted to ensure that I didn't find out. So essentially, she was being silenced also. And herein lies the generational throat chakra wound.

By the time I was 40 years of age, I had been on medication for 14 years. My boys were now 10 and 8 years of age. It was during this time that I spoke to a very highly esteemed astrologist who told me that I didn't have bipolar and he told me that I had been told a lie.

This was so intriguing to me. I had always loved astrology and I now had this very successful astrologist tell me that "I was told a lie". I honestly could not ignore the call. It still took me a year or so to fully let it sink in and to make the decision to start weaning myself off all my medication.

It started in 2018 while I was living in Western Australia, I met an intuitive counsellor, who was from Ireland also. We connected really well at the time. She never told me to come off the medication but I told her that I was determined to do so. It took me two years to fully wean myself off as they were big doses that I was on. I needed to ensure that I did it very slowly to avoid any side effects. It worked really well doing it this way. I felt light-headed and dizzy at times when coming off the medication, but the essential oils that I was using by Doterra (Balance and Adaptiv) really helped ground me and keep me balanced emotionally. I haven't been on medication since, not even Panadol. I simply refuse to take any sort of pill that is not natural.

During my process of weaning myself off my medication, along with the essential oils, I spent a lot of time walking in nature to help me heal. I set up a dog walking business that gave me the opportunity to walk amongst nature. I absolutely loved working in this business. My adventures with all the dogs was so healing. I learned Reiki to the Masters Level and Quantum Healing, and I would practice it on the dogs on our walks. Needless to say we never had an injured dog in the three years that I operated Ecopooch. None of the dogs were ever injured or bitten by snakes or ticks, and we regularly walked a lot of snake-ridden tracks!! I was learning the power of Quantum Energy Healing.

Moving to the Other Side of Australia

In 2022, I closed my dog business and moved to Brisbane on the East Coast from Perth in Western Australia with my husband at the time and our two teenage boys. Tony had received a job relocation offer to Brisbane, and we decided to take the opportunity. Little did I know, this move would mark the beginning of a major initiation into a new life.

My now ex-husband and I met in Bali in 2004. Tony was a Kiwi living in Melbourne, and I was a Paddy in Perth, as we would jokingly say. Later that year, Tony moved to Perth, and we married in 2007. By the time we moved to Brisbane, we had been together for 18 years. Before leaving for Brisbane, I confided in a friend that I felt I was heading to Brisbane to break up with Tony. It didn't make sense to me at the time, especially since we were moving with our two teenage boys, but I had a strong, undeniable feeling that I couldn't ignore. My intuition was guiding me.

Once we accepted the job offer, we had two weeks to pack up the house and relocate the whole family. During that time, I constantly checked in with the boys, asking if they were happy to go. I was prepared to pull out at any moment if they had expressed hesitation. But they were excited for the adventure and kept telling me they wanted to move.

The move was a lot of fun and we enjoyed all the new beginnings and making new friends. We held so much hope for a brighter future. We definitely made lots of incredible memories. We wasted no time living each day to the fullest.

We met wonderful people and experienced many life adventures, but amid it all, there were also numerous lessons and initiations. It marked the peak of a Quantum Healing journey, with the ultimate goal of us all dismantling our egos, returning to our hearts, and following our inner guidance. It was about reconnecting with ourselves fully, without conforming to society's expectations, and making some significant changes along the way.

My eldest son decided to trade high school for a barber apprenticeship in Brisbane, which he has now completed and loves. My youngest son also decided to trade high school for a full-time electrical role working on-site 3 hours from Brisbane with his dad. He has chosen to pursue an electrical apprenticeship, which he will begin in 2025.

I ramped up my Quantum Healing work and created courses and offerings. I was using Quantum Healing more and more in our everyday lives. I was working very closely with my benevolent spirit guides and connecting to my higher self on a daily basis.

The Ending of a Soul Contract

In June 2023 I joined a Full Moon Lunar Eclipse ceremony that was facilitated by a beautiful soul sister. Odelle was living overseas so I joined her via Zoom in the comfort of my living room. During the ceremony we had a moment to go within and listen to any intuitive soul guidance. That was when I heard the distinct words "your soul contract has ended".

I didn't realise it at the time, but my marriage was about to end and my relationship with various other friends and family members was about to end also.

In 2024 illusions were revealed. My intuition was getting stronger and stronger. My third eye was being activated through my Quantum Healing work and I was able to see through anything inauthentic. I could see the lies that were projected on me throughout my lifetime.

I had been preparing for these impending revelations for the past seven years. My spirit team and soul family had been prepping me with tools and skills to be able to successfully navigate all the lies and deceit that I was to discover this year. More importantly, they were also preparing me with the skills and tools I would need to transmute dense, lower vibrational energy.

In 2024, I discovered that the majority of my family knew the truth about my biological father, and that they had all played along with the lies. It felt like I was the last to know, and it was incredibly hurtful to realize that so many family members had knowingly lied to my face. When I confronted them, they turned their backs on me. To make matters worse, my husband also admitted that he was a narcissist.

Many people ask me today why these people would do such a thing, and honestly, I can't answer for them. I'm assuming that the shame of their father sleeping with my mum was too much to bear, and they wanted to protect his and their reputations. Maybe they also wanted to keep me away from my stake in the estate. It is something that they have never disclosed.

During the two and a half years in Brisbane, I endured many dark nights of the soul. I began to receive vivid images and memories from my past, and a lot of cellular memory started resurfacing for me to witness and heal. I began recalling details of my sexual abuse and how I had fractured my back as a child. I was guided to see different people who would help me piece the puzzle together.

One day, my masseuse pointed out that the lump on my back was likely from a break. She worked with an osteopath, so I made an appointment to see him. He confirmed that I had fractured my back as a child and explained that the reason I arch my back when I lie down is because I had subconsciously trained myself to adopt that posture out of fear of leaning on it and potentially breaking it again. He also explained that the lump on my back was calcified tissue that had formed as part of the healing process for the fracture.

My conscious mind was remembering my sexual abuse. I was shown images through my third eye exactly what had happened at the time, of a man entering my bedroom and approaching me with his penis in my face. Sometimes I would also feel what had happened; the feeling of a finger in my vagina. I would remember hearing him say "we are friends, this is what friends do" and being shown my stepfather. These revelations were coming in thick and fast to be acknowledged and healed. They came in at all times of the day, however a lot of revelations came through dark nights of the soul. They were so uncomfortable at times. I am just so grateful that I had learned Quantum Healing and learned how to transmute the energies that were being shown, so that I could regulate my nervous system back into harmony. I would constantly say "I am Love, I am light" as I lay in bed during these dark nights of the soul. I said this so many times over that two-year period when the nightmares got so bad. I would comfort my inner child and together we would transmute the energy. Timing is everything and I have no doubt that these instances were being revealed to me at a time when I was emotionally balanced and had the tools that I needed.

Deep Healing and Clearing Wounds

I have spent the past 7 years clearing all my wounds using Quantum Energy Healing in order to get to a place where I am now, a place where I can openly discuss these topics, be at peace and not fear being rejected or abandoned. And be able to help others do the same.

Clearing these wounds has empowered me in so many ways. Through Quantum Energy Healing I have been able to bring back fragments of myself that were lost. Self love, self forgiveness and self regulation were, and still are, paramount for me moving forward. I embarked on a journey of reconnecting with and loving all parts of myself so that I could become whole again.

Quantum inner child work was extremely instrumental during my healing journey. Since discovering that my inner child is my intuition, that she essentially runs the show, I know now that if she is not happy and loved and cared for, she will sabotage anything put in front of her.

In order for any of us to be fully successful in anything that we do, I believe we must check in with our inner child and ask him/her what they need. More often than not they will want to experience joy so getting creative with dance, play, art and song is a must. These are the activities that I incorporate into my everyday life in order to stay fully aligned. Coming back to a state of joy is the true essence of life, I believe.

Creating a successful Quantum Healing business required me to heal my core wounds first. These included inner child wounds, past life wounds, witch wounds, mother and father wounds, and sister wounds etc. I had to heal and clear these before I could step into my Quantum Healing work fully. I had to dismantle my ego that was trying to keep me safe and small, in order to remember my multidimensionality. And importantly, I had to start using my intuition and the psychic gifts and abilities that I came here to share.

Once I did the majority of the healing, I was able to start offering healing services for others. I had energies from three lineages, and many sporadic dense energies to work at transmuting. It was a journey that revealed people's true intentions. Alot of people I knew were embodying and channeling dark energies. Some of them were trying to keep me in a low vibration to stop me from using my intuition and speaking my truth, which is where setting boundaries came in.

Looking back, these people were acting out of fear and their own woundings. However, it is this frequency that allows the dark energies into their bodies to take over. Their attachments to uphold a certain image and to hold on to money had many stooping to sacrificing their own family member/s in the process. I was the colloquial sacrificial lamb for many of them. My late step grandma had told me that I was the "scapegoat".

Looking Back at The Bigger Picture

I never look back at anything in regret. I really believe that life happens for us, not to us. It's all part of the journey. Anything that happens along the way is for us to learn from and reach a new level of enlightenment. This is soul contract work. That is why some of the best healers are the wounded healers. The ones that have gone through the fire and can share their experience. I look at some of the most influential people in my life and they have been through the depths of darkness. There is only one way out of the darkness and that is through the light of God, I believe. Keep looking for the light at the end of the tunnel, as it is there. From my experience, I implore people not to fear the dark either. It is your soul wanting you to experience a different frequency, for you to recognize what you do/don't want. You always have the choice as to what you desire. We live in a dualistic world so the choice is always there. And it is through transmuting the dark, that we can finally walk in the light.

It is important to mention that my awakening journey included coming off all medications and alcohol; and I try to eat as cleanly as possible. I have the very occasional alcoholic drink, but it's mainly to celebrate a friend's birthday or a milestone. I really feel that this helped my awakening so that it was more easeful and graceful.

What I now see is that everything that I experienced in my life thus far is part of my soul contract/s. Everything that I experienced up until now was to create confusion, illusion and distraction around the real reason that I am here. I had to learn the lessons and go through all of the initiations in order to step through the dark and into the light at the end of the tunnel, and alchemise all my pain into love, power and purpose. That is not to diminish the excruciating pain of what I had to endure, particularly my younger vulnerable self, but in saying this, I want to offer hope to others walking a similar path that we can heal ourselves from anything.

My purpose is to serve the Most High God by using my intuitive abilities and Quantum Energy Healing skills to help others overcome adversity and heal their wounds, just as I have. As an ordained Rose Priestess, my overarching mission is to help others alchemise pain into love, to step into their power and purpose, and together we can anchor Christ Consciousness onto the planet—bringing forth the frequency of love and harmony.

ANNE-MARIE HUGHES

Anne-Marie is a dedicated Quantum Energy Healer with a deep connection to the divine mission of empowering others that have been through domestic violence and narcissistic relationships. Guided by the most high God, Anne-Marie's work is centered around helping individuals rediscover their inherent divinity and sovereignty. Using the transformative power of energy healing, Anne-Marie's mission is to remind people of their innate ability to heal, grow, and live in harmony with their truest, most authentic selves.

Drawing on her spiritual gifts and extensive knowledge and experience with quantum energy healing, Anne-Marie works with clients to help them release blockages, shift limiting beliefs, and restore balance to their physical, emotional, and spiritual bodies. Her approach is holistic, acknowledging the interconnectedness of mind, body, and spirit, and she uses a combination of energy healing techniques and other modalities to help individuals access their highest potential.

Anne-Marie's work is deeply rooted in her own spiritual journey. She has spent years studying the principles of energy healing and quantum energetics, exploring how energy influences our lives and experiences. Through this exploration, she has developed a unique healing practice that integrates these powerful concepts to help others reclaim their personal power.

Anne-Maries diverse work experience from corporate HR, the modelling industry, hospitality and owning her own small businesses while she raised her two teenage boys allows her to help both men and women of all skill sets and expertise.

Anne-Marie's goal is not just to heal but to empower, guiding each person she works with towards a life of divine purpose and sovereignty.

Website: https://www.annemariehughes.com.au

14

SURVIVAL IS THE RULE. THRIVING IS THE EXCEPTION

AMY SANDERS

The 16-Station Sprinkler System

Sweat dripped across my brow as I paused, shovel in hand, surveying the half-acre dirt yard. It was 1994, the middle of summer, and for six long weeks, my siblings and I had been digging trenches for my parents' 16-station sprinkler system. The ground was rock hard, and we used a pickaxe and sledgehammer just to break the surface. It was grueling work — 12-hour days under the scorching sun—and the end seemed nowhere in sight.

That Saturday, my friends happened to walk by, calling out, "Amy, can you hang out?" My heart leaped. Surely, after all this backbreaking labor, I'd earned a break. But asking my dad was terrifying. At 250 pounds with a permanent scowl, his mere presence intimidated me.

Still, I mustered the courage to ask. "Dad, my friends are here. Can I go with them?"

"No," he said curtly, his face masked with a stern look of irritation. "The work isn't done."

I wanted to cry. My body ached, my muscles burned, and all I wanted was a few hours with friends. But I didn't dare argue. I was just a 14-year-old girl who had learned early on that asking for anything—even something simple—could result in disappointment or punishment.

At the time, I didn't understand that my parents were grappling with their own pain. Four years earlier, we'd lost my sister to suicide—a tragedy that fractured our family. My parents carried that weight, plus those of their traumatic childhoods, bottling up their pain, which spilled over into their parenting. But as a child, all I knew was fear. I walked on eggshells, constantly bracing for the next explosion.

A Life Shaped by Fear

If I heard my mom calling my name, I would immediately panic. "Do I go see what she wants? Or do I hide? Either way, I'm in trouble..." I'd think. As a child, I was starved for attention and craved affection from my parents, but it was withheld. So, early on, I adopted a deeply rooted belief that my parents didn't love me. Often, I wondered why they chose to have so many kids when it seemed like they didn't even like us. At some point, I adopted another deep belief: They had seven kids, so they could have free labor and save money on projects and cleaning. This seemed to make sense logically to my young heart and brain.

I learned that asking for something meant getting in trouble or being labeled selfish. Over time, I stopped asking. It was easier to stay quiet, to go along with what others wanted, and to avoid conflict. I became the "good girl," the peacemaker, the one who never spoke up for herself.

This self-silencing followed me into adulthood. By the time I moved out at 18, I carried deeply rooted beliefs: my needs didn't matter, my voice didn't count, and asking for what I wanted was selfish.

When I left for college, my life changed. I experienced a taste of freedom for the first time. My schedule was my own, and I spent time with friends who valued and uplifted me. For four years, I felt more 'me' than ever before. Life was vibrant and full of possibilities. I loved life and feeling peace. I loved having a busy schedule at school and holding a job where I felt appreciated and valued. But that chapter ended abruptly at 22 when I found myself standing in a snowstorm, staring at an empty engagement ring.

The Proposal That Changed Everything

It was Christmas night, and my boyfriend of three weeks knelt in the snow, asking me to marry him. My stomach dropped, and panic overtook my body. I wasn't ready. In fact, I'd planned to break up with him that evening. But instead of listening to my gut, I froze. My fear of disappointing him overpowered my instincts.

I stalled as I left him in the snow on his knee, searching for an escape. "Did you ask my dad?" I asked, clinging to the hope that he hadn't. After all, it had only been three weeks!

"Yes," he said confidently. "He said it's okay with him if it's okay with you."

Trapped, I hesitantly responded, "Oh, ok...uh...sure," ignoring the voice in my head screaming, "No! Don't agree to this!"

As I glanced at the ring, I noticed something was missing—the diamond. The setting prongs were empty. This isn't how I saw myself engaging with the man of my dreams. But...was he the man of my dreams? I wasn't sure. But I guess if my dad gave his permission to marry me, then I should, too.

That was the engagement.

A ring without a diamond in it, and me saying "sure" to the biggest decision of my life because I didn't want to reject him or upset my dad. In my heart and gut, I knew this wasn't what I wanted, but being agreeable and saying "yes" was ingrained in me. So, I got engaged.

Heartbroken, I looked at the four empty prongs that were supposed to hold a diamond. I knew this wasn't right for me, and I didn't believe he truly loved me. But I agreed because I didn't know how to verbalize the word "no," and it was also as if, subconsciously, I didn't want to be like my parents, who seemed to choose "no" above all other words.

I had gotten engaged, but I couldn't show anyone or celebrate because the ring wasn't done. I put it in my pocket and visited the jeweler a few days later. Diamonds were expensive, and my new fiancé had very little to spend on the ring. The thought of him spending money on me made me feel guilty, so the wedding ring was finished with a CZ. One that rattled in the prongs and broke frequently. A cheap ring. A constant reminder that I wasn't worth the diamond ring most women received when they got engaged or the dream engagement and celebration that usually comes after the question is popped.

The ring became a symbol of my self-betrayal. I had chosen someone who didn't feel right, accepted a fake diamond instead of something real and rare, and silenced my own voice—again.

Loneliness in Marriage

Our relationship was strange from the beginning. We were in the same group of friends and had known each other for a while, but were never romantic. He seemed interested in every other girl but me. It was a casual relationship. No flirting. No deep connection. Just friends. One night, I was caught off guard as he poured his heart out and then kissed me! That night, I was so confused. "After all this time of knowing me, why now?" I thought. Yet, at the same time, I was flattered. He was good-looking, and we shared some common interests, so I was open to seeing where this relationship could go in time. Just three weeks later, he proposed.

During my engagement, none of my family or friends spoke up about how bizarre or quick the engagement had happened, so I just went with the flow. Figuring that maybe this was normal.

Once engaged, I learned that he carried significant debt, had no stable job, and lacked direction. While I had savings, a good job, and heading into my senior year in college. But I ignored the red flags, telling myself this was what I was supposed to do.

After we married, I dropped out of college to pay off his credit cards. I took on extra work, teaching fitness classes at night to make ends meet. Yet, no matter how hard I worked, it was never enough. One day, I paid off his $600 credit card balance, only to find a new $600 bill in the mail the same afternoon. I collapsed into tears, feeling defeated and trapped. My resentment towards him grew a little more everyday.

After a year and a half of marriage, I discovered I was pregnant. I wasn't ready to be a mom, and our finances were messy. But the 9-month clock was ticking. When my parents found out I was pregnant, they weren't happy and didn't want me quitting my job to take care of a baby. My husband was still floating from one job to another, and our only stable income was mine. I felt so much pressure. Pressure financially. "How would we live if I quit my full-time job?" Pressure to please my parents. "Why aren't they celebrating my pregnancy with me?" Pressure to be a mom. "How am I going to care for a little human when I seem to struggle to care for myself?" My pregnancy story was different from my friends. No celebrating. Instead, stress and pressure. When the 9-month clock stopped, I birthed the most beautiful baby girl and quit my full-time job.

And we became even more broke.

Within four years, I had three kids. I was treading water as best as possible with a toddler and two babies on different schedules: a newborn, an 18-month-old, and a four-year-old. I was still teaching fitness classes and creating women's boot camp programs. With the little money I was making and my husband still in and out of work, the bills were barely getting paid. My guilt and feelings of failure felt unbearable at times.

18 months later, my 3-year-old son needed some new shoes. We were still extremely tight on money, and buying new shoes meant taking money from the grocery budget or somewhere else. I talked to my husband about the needed shoes. His response was the same as usual: "We can't afford that right now". That same week, he bought his dad a pontoon boat so he and his dad could go fishing together more often. I asked him where he got the money, and he said he had a secret stash and had been saving it. "Why in the world is a pontoon fishing boat for my father-in-law more important than shoes for his son?!" I thought. Rage rushed through my body, coupled with feelings of betrayal. I felt like my kids and I were at the bottom of the barrel of importance to my husband. Throughout my marriage, it seemed like I was the least important person in my husband's life. What I wanted, even if it was for the kids, wasn't important to him.

The longer we were married, the more we saw his family and the less we saw mine. Even though I missed my family, I didn't verbalize it. It seemed easier to do what he wanted. We'd go to his family reunions, dinners, birthday parties, really anything that was on the calendar. When I got invited to my family events, I often didn't even tell him and would politely decline.

I felt so deprived of attention, love, and acknowledgment in my marriage. I was so incredibly lonely and starved for affection and praise. I did all of the things I thought a wife was supposed to do to keep her husband happy while never asking for much in return. I told him I loved him daily and showed affection. I kept a clean house, did the laundry and yard work, cooked all of the meals, and worked as many hours as I could as a fitness instructor and piano teacher while still taking care of my 3 young kids. All of my efforts seemed unnoticed or appreciated. And in spite of my efforts, nothing seemed to fill the hole in my heart or get him to step up as the husband I needed. I felt like I was an exhausted single mom raising three kids alone but had the handcuffs of marriage. I felt trapped.

The Awakening

In June 2010, a pivotal moment came during a 72-hour relay race on an all-men's team. My husband had signed up but decided not to go, volunteering me instead without asking. For three days, I was surrounded by men who treated me with respect and kindness. They opened doors for me, asked about my needs, and spoke lovingly to their wives on the phone. For the first time in years, I felt seen and appreciated. It was a stark contrast to my marriage and a painful reminder of what I was missing.

I chose to marry who I did, but I was unhappy and lonely. How did I get here? I felt like I was living a life that wasn't mine. I felt so far away from myself and who I was. My life didn't match what I dreamed about as a young girl, and it was like a nightmare that I wasn't ever waking up from. I dreamed I'd have a partner who loved me, played with me, respected me. I dreamed that we would have money and would travel. But this wasn't my life.

But by going to that race, things shifted for me. I started to notice little things...

One day at the gym, two guys told me how beautiful I am and how lucky my husband is. They appreciated how I helped their wives gain more confidence in my fitness classes. I wondered, "Why is it that even guys at the gym compliment me, think I'm pretty, and see value in me, yet my husband doesn't?"

Shortly after, I was in the car with my best friend and her husband. We were running late, and his driving at the speed limit annoyed me. I commented on it, and he replied, "She's my most prized possession, so

I'm extra cautious with her in the car, even if we're late." My heart softened, but I instantly compared this to my own marriage. I couldn't imagine my husband ever saying that. It was a stark reminder of what I lacked.

A couple of months later, on a cruise, I dressed up for a formal night, hoping to impress him. While I was getting ready, he left for dinner without me and later offered no compliments. As I met up with everyone for dinner, my friend's husband, however, kissed my cheek and said, "You look beautiful." I felt both pleased and hurt—the compliment was lovely, but it stung that it came from a friend, not my husband.

All of these experiences showed me how different my life was from those around me. Mine was a life of pain, loneliness, and what felt like worthlessness. But these experiences showed me what I knew I wanted but didn't have. There was complete dissonance in my life, and it was palpable.

As I started turning inward and reflecting on my marriage and life, I asked my friends whether they thought I should have married him. They all said, "No, we never thought you were a good match."

How did I get on this path of unhappiness, loneliness, and heartache? I could blame how my parents raised me or my friends for not speaking up before I got married. I could even blame my husband for the way he treated me.

But the truth is: I chose this.

The life that I created was my fault. Nobody else's.

Early on, I learned to silence my wants and needs to please others. This played out in every part of my life - from accepting my parents' constant "no" to panicking when called on in class. I became an agreeable, quiet girl, always putting others' needs first. But this pattern led to unhappiness and resentment. I felt unseen and unimportant, trapped in a life that wasn't truly mine. I was so used to doing what everybody else wanted me to do that I couldn't even hear what I wanted.

When my dad told me I couldn't hang out after working for 12 hours in the hot sun, I didn't challenge him, explain how exhausted I was, or express how much it would mean to me to hang out with friends. I just accepted his answer (scared, upset, and resentful) and kept working.

When my husband asked me to marry him, my gut knew what was right for me, but I ignored it. Even though marriage is one of the most significant decisions you ever make, I said "yes" to please someone else because I didn't want him to feel bad if I rejected him. I had been conditioned to reject myself before I rejected anyone else.

When I wanted a diamond in my ring, I told the jeweler that a CZ would be okay. My husband didn't make that decision, I did. Then I resented him for it.

I dropped out of college and put my dreams on hold to pay off someone else's credit card debt. He didn't ask me to, but I took that burden on as if he had.

The root of my situation was this: I didn't believe I was worthy of wanting anything for myself.

I was the common denominator here—not my husband, parents, or anyone else. It was me. By being agreeable and not speaking my truth, I allowed these circumstances of financial ruin, an unhealthy marriage, and saying "yes" to everyone else at the expense of myself to rule my life.

In order for my life to change, I had to change.

Choosing Myself

I started making small, simple changes by becoming aware of my actions while experiencing examples of healthier relationships.

I started asking myself, **"What do I actually want?"** and then practicing it.

At first, the answers were terrifying. I didn't know what I wanted because I'd spent my life ignoring my own needs through self-sabotaging. "You're fine," I'd tell myself, or simply, "no, you don't need to do that." This is what I would think, every time there was a decision to be made about something I wanted. I was my own worst enemy.

But I knew I'd have to start doing things differently if I wanted a different life. No one could do it for me. So I decided to treat this like an analogy of the muscle. Working at it daily so that my thought patterns could get stronger. I would pay close attention to my thoughts while also listening to my body. Then, challenge my thoughts and check back in with my body (emotions).

When faced with a decision, big or small, I'd ask, "*Amy, what do you actually want?*" Then I'd dig deeper and ask "why do you want that?"

I would continue to get curious, while peeling the layers back of my wants and needs. This helped me start finding my way back to myself.

I started to make small changes.

I wanted to go to the mall without kids one day, so I did. I went without anybody asking me for anything. No kids pulling on my leg or a set time of when I had to be home. I just did what I wanted.

I started seeing my family more and inviting them to my house. Although I felt like I was breaking rules and being rebellious by doing this, it felt good and empowering.

If I wanted to go on a long bike ride with a friend, I would find a babysitter and go. This was a new concept to me, but it worked! Hiring a babysitter is something I could do more of!

One night, I made a meal that I wanted. Instead of taking orders or requests, I made a meal that sounded good to me. This was so small yet so freeing to do: pick a meal I like instead of being a short-order chef for my family.

One day, I signed my son up for soccer even though I wasn't sure where the money would come from. The money worked out, and he loved playing soccer. I felt like a baller mom for making it happen.

I chose to say "no" to my husband's family reunion one weekend. I just told him " no". And it felt so good! I stayed home and did what I wanted instead of scrambling to take care of our kids camping for three days in a tent in the rain. For the first time, he had to take care of them without me.

Little by little, I made the choices that I wanted, and the most amazing thing happened. Nothing collapsed or fell apart when I said no. The house didn't burn down. Nothing crumbled. When I started to choose myself, my life got easier. My relationships grew deeper. I started to feel more happiness and freedom. I had more bandwidth to give to others. Instead of resenting the time with my kids, I was enjoying it. And my life started feeling more like the life I had always envisioned.

As I kept choosing myself, my self-love and respect grew, something I had lacked. Like that muscle analogy, my confidence continued to get stronger. Learning to trust myself again gave me more energy and more to give.

There was never a sudden "ah-hah" moment that some people experience when they just know it's time to end their marriage. For me, a series of small moments adding up over time opened my eyes to what my life could be. I stayed true to myself and my integrity throughout my journey. As I did, the time came when I felt peace for me to leave and not accept his choices or behaviors anymore.

I was married for eleven years before I gained enough courage and self-worth to leave my husband and choose a different path. Even though I had grown a lot, it was still the scariest decision of my life. I felt like I was breaking up my family and doing the one thing that my religion was against - Divorce. Although there was a lot of judgment, and I lost many relationships through the process, I braved the painful change and divorced him.

From Surviving to Thriving

Starting life over as a single mom with three kids under the age of eight brought new fears and challenges. How would I support the kids? Would I be single and lonely forever? Would I lose relationships? Would I ever find love again? Despite the fear, I stepped into it and faced it. It was empowering and freeing, even though I wasn't sure what the future held for me.

My life wasn't cupcakes and roses the second I stepped out the door. There were parts of it that got really hard. As I continued to turn inward and listen to my wants and needs, some people in my life didn't like the change.

It was a dark time as I went through a grieving process of everything I had lost. I lost my ex-husband, friends, and people within my community at church. I even lost relationships with a couple of my siblings. When you become who you are meant to be, some people will fight it. They can act out and push back because they are used to you showing up a certain way in the relationship. This was my reality, and it can be really hard. You may want to retreat or go back to the way things were. But refrain from it. Stay the course. The most important thing you can do is stay true to yourself.

I learned that important relationships will always find their way so I stopped allowing certain behaviors in my relationships. By teaching others how to treat me, I created a ripple effect of healthier connections around me. Setting boundaries and releasing expectations deepened my relationships, allowing me to love more fully and let go of other relationships that no longer served me.

As I chose myself, the life I dreamed of unfolded. I found love and remarried. My husband and I have built a beautiful life together. I don't have money worries, and the life I once dreamed about is my reality. My husband treats me well, and we are happily married, even though we still have a lot of challenges as we raise a blended family of seven kids.

During my self-discovery, I learned that spending time with people I love brings me the most joy. And we now get to do it all the time. I used to dream of my kids being able to participate in competitive sports and take luxurious vacations, and now it's our life.

Because I decided to start choosing myself and making decisions that aligned with my dreams, my life unfolded, and I have attracted everything I used to only dream about.

I live in a multimillion-dollar home in the most beautiful neighborhood and upscale city. My kids are privileged and live a dream lifestyle. We travel regularly because we have money and time freedom. I have a husband who values me and supports my dreams and goals. If you had told me this would become my life a few years ago, I would never have believed you.

I share this with you from the depths of my heart. Not out of bragging rights but out of the sheer belief that whatever you want is possible. I am living proof. It doesn't matter where you've been or what you have experienced in your past. It doesn't matter how much money you have or don't have right now. Whatever is on your heart, you can build. But you have to *choose it and then take action* to make it a reality.

I'd like to tell you that everything is perfect in my life now. The reality is, it's not. There are still bumps in the road, and I've experienced some pretty significant trauma and trials even since I left my ex-husband. But I am true to myself and practice self-respect. My life is beautiful, and I find joy in it every day. Sometimes, I still get triggered by hearing "no." I still hesitate when I need to ask for help. At times, I fall back into my old ways, but I have learned how to give grace and love and pause to ask myself... "What do I actually want?" "How do I want to spend my time, and with whom?"

Your Turn

Now, it's your turn. What do you want?

When you look in the mirror, do you like who you see? Are you being true to yourself? Do you love yourself? Are you living life the way you envisioned it? Or have you slipped into the same self-betraying trap I did?

Napoleon Hill said, "Whatever the mind of man can conceive and believe, it can achieve."

The choice is yours.

I want you to think about your life as a book. You are the author. Every day you wake up, you get to choose what chapter of your story you are writing. Are you the heroine of your story? Are you the victim? Are you the villain? Who are you, and where are you in your book? How many chapters have you written? How many more do you have to write?

You are worthy of being anything you want to be. You are capable of having whatever you want. The guy, the house, the job, traveling, a healthier relationship with family...literally whatever you want. But you have to ask for it and believe that you are worthy of it.

What if you asked the universe for $500k a year instead of $50k? What if you created a list of that dream partner and then asked for it and started taking action to get that partner? What if you asked for the house and neighborhood you truly want to live in?

The difference between people who are living the life they have envisioned and those who aren't is their belief in themselves and that they are worthy of it.

I'm giving you permission to ask for what you want in life. You are worthy of the life you want. It's waiting for you. All you have to do is ask for it and then create a belief that it can happen for you.

I am living proof of someone who took their power back and created the life I knew was out there for me. I want that for you, too!

I used to accept allowing other people to treat me poorly, and massive amounts of debt. I don't accept that anymore.

I used to accept living in a low-income, small-minded neighborhood. Now, I don't. I am surrounded by ambitious, fun, inspiring people who help me be a little better every day.

What are you accepting in your life that you are ready to stop accepting? If I gave you a million dollars right now, what would you do with it? What are you going to do this year to move towards that goal?

If your life isn't going the way you want it to, I challenge you to get curious. See what isn't working and start to make changes. Small, simple choices over time bring big results.

The only person you have control over is you. You can't control your mom, dad, partner, friends, or neighbors. When we try to, it doesn't work out well for us. We usually end up frustrated with unmet expectations. But you can control *you*. You can turn inward by listening to your soul and move from alignment. You can control your thoughts, which ultimately control your feelings and actions. And that is where the magic happens and brings you the results you want!

If you feel stuck or don't know where to start, I challenge you to find someone who has had success in the area that you are seeking and learn from them. Be coachable and do the work.

You matter. You're worthy. Your voice matters. So speak up, be heard, and go after the life you desire. I'm here cheering for you!

XO,

Amy Sanders

AMY SANDERS

Amy Sanders is a master-certified wellness and life coach and advocate for women's empowerment. For over two decades, Amy has transformed the lives of thousands of women by helping them break free from limiting beliefs, heal from trauma, and rediscover their purpose. She specializes in guiding women through life's toughest challenges—such as divorce, abuse, and betrayal—and empowering them to build thriving businesses and lives.

As a serial entrepreneur who has built multiple successful businesses, Amy understands the grit and resilience it takes to turn a dream into reality. Her journey from a single mom to a self-made millionaire has shaped her passion for helping women uncover their inner strength and align their lives with their true self. Using her Awareness-Alignment-Abundance methodology, Amy helps women embrace self-trust, unlock potential, and create personal and professional success.

Amy holds a BS in exercise science, over 30 fitness and nutrition certifications, and is a master-certified life coach. She combines this expertise with personal experience, having navigated the pain of losing a sibling to suicide, recovering from betrayal trauma, and rebuilding her life. Now happily remarried to her husband Chris, she is raising a blended family of seven while living her dream lifestyle.

Through her work, Amy empowers ambitious, motivated women to move from feeling stuck to thriving. Whether up-leveling your personal life or growing a business, Amy provides the tools, guidance, and inspiration needed to achieve abundance and live a life of alignment, purpose, and passion.

Website: https://amysanders.co/

15

FROM PERFECTION TO PURPOSE: MY TRANSFORMATION OF SELF, AND LIFE AS A WOMAN IN LEADERSHIP

Kristi Brown

Introduction: The Unveiling of My Journey

What inspired you to join the healthcare industry? Most people expect the usual answers: "to help others," "to give back to my community," or maybe a more self-driven one like "career opportunity". Is that what you were thinking? Sure, I've given those answers before, but none of them were truly authentic. They were automatic, conditioned responses—not a reflection of my real motivation for joining the healthcare field.

For me, the answer wasn't about helping others or giving back. It was about survival - and rediscovering myself. This question unlocked years of vulnerability, unmasking a story with no clear ending. Even now, as I share this with you, a woman who, like me, is navigating barriers and struggles to thrive, a part of me still fears judgment. The truth is, I was ashamed, embarrassed, and stuck—suffocating in a mold I had been conditioned to live. I felt trapped, living a life that wasn't mine, constantly measuring my worth against others' expectations. But as I would eventually learn, "you will never be able to find yourself if you are lost in someone else; you will never be able to love yourself if you are in love with the idea of someone else; and you will never find true happiness if you are fueling the dreams of others." These words would become my truth, guiding me toward a life of authenticity, and eventually to a place where success and happiness were entirely my own definition. This is where my real journey began—the moment I chose to step out of that mold and started living for myself.

The Pressure to Be Perfect

From a young age, I was weighed down by the constant pressure to be perfect. As if societal expectations weren't already overwhelming—"Be a strong, independent woman, the world is yours."—I carried the burden of those ideals without guidance, navigating a world that seemed to expect everything from me while offering little support. Don't get me wrong—I'm a firm believer in the women's movement, but the excitement around female empowerment often masked the lack of real training or mentorship for young women entering the workforce. It felt like we were set up to be celebrated for accomplishments we hadn't even learned how to achieve. In my own home, this pressure and lack of guidance was magnified. My mother embodied that enthusiasm for female achievement and reminded me of it often. She was beautiful, with a kind heart, but she carried a burden I couldn't fully understand—she was hearing impaired. My mother, ashamed of her disability, would hide her hearing aids behind her long, golden hair, using it as a shield against the world's judgment. Growing up poor in a household where her deafness went unnoticed for years, she missed crucial developmental milestones. By the time her impairment was discovered in school, there were neither resources nor finances to support her. She never made it to college, never got the education she deserved. Instead, she married my father, a Navy man who offered her a chance to escape her small town and see the world, but the dreams of independence and achievement she once held slipped through her fingers. As a result, she made sure to vocalize the importance of independence and achievement, but aside from words of encouragement she failed to provide a truly supportive structure.

It wasn't just my mother that fueled the fire of these expectations, there was my sister—wild and rebellious. She defied any parental expectations, defied societal expectations by skipping school, and creating chaos amongst our family and the legal system. Where my mother couldn't rise, and my sister wouldn't, I felt compelled to compensate. My mother's unspoken hope that I would become the strong, independent woman she never could be, and my sister's defiance, fueled my relentless drive for perfection. I became the overachiever—excelling in school, behaving perfectly, and constantly striving to be more. I worked harder, pushed further, trying to be the daughter who could do no wrong, the one with perfect grades, a promising career, and a life that checked all the right boxes. I had to be the ideal: the perfect student, the perfect daughter, the one who would make everything right. But as the expectations grew heavier, so did my need to maintain an image of having it all figured out. I felt trapped in a cycle, trying to prove my worth through achievements, trying to be everything for everyone, all while losing pieces of myself in the process. It wasn't just about success anymore—it was about being seen, being valued, and being enough.

As I stepped into early adulthood, perfectionism became both my fuel and my burden. It drove me to succeed, igniting my ambition and hunger for achievement, but at the same time, it clouded my sense of identity. I became disconnected from who I truly was and what my real strengths and weaknesses were. Instead of embracing growth, I shied away from learning new things, afraid of anything that might expose my imperfections. People often say, "get comfortable with the uncomfortable," but for me, perfectionism was the shield that kept discomfort—and growth—at bay.

I sought validation through accomplishments: career success, wealth, and the appearance of having it all together. By the age of 16, I had already become a team captain in sports, a straight A student, involved in numerous programs and affiliations, lead server at the local diner, owning a brand-new car, and community volunteer. Overtime I found myself obsessed with my work in the food and beverage industry because, frankly, I was excellent at it—perfect, even. I thrived in connecting with people, listening to their stories, and building bonds. At the age of 18 I was tending bar and every shift I worked, there wasn't an empty seat available, and my job loved me for it. I loved it too, because it allowed me to excel in areas I was passionate about—customer service , connection, leadership, rules, and regulations. These became the reasons I prioritized work over my studies in college.

Within months I went from tending bar to a head bartender and shortly after, a bar manager, making money, exceeding expectations, and defining success on those terms. But when my grades in college started slipping to Bs and Cs, (something that had never happened before) I concluded that I wasn't good enough—that I didn't deserve to continue pursuing my parents' dream of me becoming a physician. I told myself I wasn't cut out for it. I didn't know how to be resilient. I didn't have a support system, a circle of people lifting me up.

All I could think about was drowning under the weight of the expectations I'd been conditioned to live by, and the flames I was setting to them in the process. Perfectionism had become a mask that hid my true self. And slowly, it began to eat away at my happiness as I battled between work and school. What I hadn't yet learned was that perfectionism doesn't serve you—it only traps you. It stifles your growth, isolates you from your true passions, and leaves you feeling like nothing is ever enough. And for years, that's exactly how I felt. Be cautious of the confidence high you get when you are so doing something so perfectly, for it is the devil in disguise hindering you, and your growth.

Redefining Failure and Success: From Shame to Empowerment

My early career didn't align with my family's dreams for me. I found solace in the bar industry, working hard and excelling, yet I carried deep shame about not pursuing the traditional path of becoming a doctor. I was embarrassed to admit that I actually enjoyed my work because it wasn't what others expected of me. There was also a stigma about women working in the industry being less divine, this perception furthered my shame. But deep down, I knew something had to change. I couldn't continue to define myself by others' expectations—I needed to reclaim my own narrative.

This struggle wasn't just a phase of my young adulthood; it followed me into my healthcare leadership journey, resurfacing every time I was faced with new challenges. I had decided to leave the food and beverage industry to pursue healthcare using the fastest entry point, EMT and phlebotomist. As an entry level employee, if you perform well enough, you get promoted—and that's exactly what happened. Within six months of starting at a new organization, I was promoted. I did the job perfectly, exceeding every expectation. But beneath the surface, I was still battling the internal conflict of defining my own path. Although I knew I was finally on the right track, working as a phlebotomist, I felt called to something different. While waiting to apply for a physician assistant program, my leader encouraged me to apply for a supervisor role. It was an unexpected opportunity, but I took it—and that first taste of leadership became a pivotal moment in my journey.

Despite my success, I struggled with the transition from being the perfect worker bee to accepting and even inviting failure into my daily routine as a leader. Leadership wasn't about getting everything right—it was about resilience, growth, and learning through mistakes. For someone who had clung to perfectionism for so long, that was a hard road to walk. But it was a necessary one. I had to let go of the need to be flawless and embrace the messy, imperfect process of true leadership.

Returning to healthcare was the turning point after years of battling my self-worth and career confusion. At first, my motivation was still rooted in external validation—I wanted to make others proud. But as I advanced, something shifted. I began to rediscover a sense of purpose, not driven by the need to meet others' expectations but by a desire to define my life on my own terms. I realized that success wasn't about perfection, wealth, or fulfilling someone else's dreams. It was about crafting a life that resonated with my values, my strengths, and my authenticity.

At that point in my life, I had already achieved what many would consider impressive milestones. I had a lucrative career in the food and beverage industry, I had completed a college degree, and earned two certifications in healthcare while working at three different hospitals. From the outside, it seemed like I had it all together. But inside, I was deeply conflicted. I carried around the weight of shame—shame that I had a BA instead of the "more prestigious" BS that others seemed to value. Shame that, despite my experience, I was working in an entry-level role. I had allowed self-doubt to overshadow my accomplishments, and that doubt, fueled by perfectionist ideals, held me back from fully stepping into my own power.

The hardest part of this period wasn't the external judgments, but the internal narrative I had created. I was ashamed of where I was because it didn't match the image of success I had been conditioned to believe in. I couldn't see the value in my journey because I was constantly comparing it to others' paths—paths that I thought were more "worthy" or more "complete". The truth is, I had spent so much time trying to fit into a mold that wasn't mine that I had forgotten to ask myself what I *really* wanted, what *really* made me feel alive.

I was so entrenched in my own self-criticism that I couldn't see the lessons and growth that each step had brought me. Every job, every course I had taken, every patient I had interacted with was part of a larger story—a story that I was living, but not yet fully embracing. Instead of viewing my failures or the detours as necessary parts of my growth, I saw them as proof of my inadequacy.

Now, when I look back, I no longer see the past with shame. I see it as a beautiful mosaic of lessons, missteps, growth, and strength. I no longer chase an idealized version of success. Instead, I create it from within, with each choice I make, each lesson I learn, and each boundary I set. And in that process, I am proud of the woman I am becoming—and the journey that brought me here.

This journey—from shame and self-doubt to empowerment—taught me that failure is not the enemy of success. Instead, it's part of the path to finding who you truly are and what you're truly capable of. And in that discovery, I finally found the courage to define success and happiness on my own terms.

Finding My Voice and My Circle

As I evolved, so did the people I surrounded myself with. I began to recognize the profound impact of my support system—the importance of having people in my life who saw me for who I truly was and pushed me forward when I struggled to push myself. This transformation allowed me to embrace my authenticity, to let go of the shame I had carried for so long, and to acknowledge that failure wasn't something to fear. Failure became a natural part of my journey, fueling my growth and strengthening my resolve. Finding my voice, however, is something I'm still coming to terms with. Even now, as I speak in meetings, give presentations, or have crucial one-to-one conversations with leaders and team members, there's always a part of me that remembers the girl whose face turned bright red when she was embarrassed or unsure of herself. As a child, I was teased for that characteristic, and for years, I believed it meant I couldn't be a great leader or communicator. That insecurity followed me into adulthood, making me hesitant to express myself, even when I knew I had something valuable to contribute. For years, I held back in meetings, refraining from voicing objections or offering ideas when others spoke louder than me.

It extended beyond the boardroom and into my bedroom. I didn't ask my husband to actively participate in my career goals or dreams either. He supported me silently—well, not so silently. He's a man with a strong voice, and his frustration eventually grew into resentment as he felt sidelined by my career. But I can't place all the blame for our struggles on him. I had forgotten to include him in my circle, to use my voice to communicate my goals and be honest about my needs. Today, my husband is a crucial part of my support system, and our relationship is stronger because we learned how to share our voices with each other.

In my healthcare role though, there is one person I'll never forget, a woman who became a pivotal member of my circle—a link in the chain of my growth that I will forever cherish. At first, I feared her. She was strong, commanding, and confident. The sound of her heels echoing through the hallway was enough to shift the energy in any room. During COVID she was my administrator, I was a supervisor at the time. She pushed me out of my comfort zone, challenged my thinking, and taught me to be okay with disagreement. And during COVID, operationally there was a lot of that. Most importantly, she believed in me. She opened doors I didn't even know existed and became an unexpected mentor, showing me the power of genuine mentorship and the transformative role it can play in someone's life. Learning to surround myself with the right people and use my voice in both my personal and professional life was a turning point in my journey. It gave me the strength to step into my own power, to advocate for myself, and to redefine what success and leadership mean to me.

Balancing Career, Motherhood, and Marriage

Just as I was hitting my professional stride, motherhood brought a whole new set of challenges. I found myself torn between the roles of mother, wife, and ambitious career woman. I wanted to thrive in my career, but guilt weighed heavily on me. I constantly questioned if I was giving enough to my child, my husband, and my job. This imbalance seeped into my marriage, eroding my confidence and leaving me feeling stretched thin. It was during this time of struggle that I realized I needed to redefine balance and prioritize self-care. Earlier, I alluded to the difficulties in my marriage, and during my rapid career progression—from entry-level leadership to middle management—things were at their worst. Professionally, I was on fire, achieving a role I had dreamed of. I had leveled up, and I couldn't have been prouder. Why was I proud you might ask. Admittedly, a small part of me was elated to have this cloud of success to rest on, maybe I could just relax here a while. Other parts of me thought, my parents would be proud of this right? If I am not serving as a medical provider, surely leading teams that impact the work they do would suffice? Both true, but what was truly at the heart of those thoughts was that I had succeeded in something I had chosen to do, a field I elected to pursue and I enjoyed every minute of my job. Despite the guilt, the turmoil at home, the stress of not doing something perfectly, or the stresses of leading others and organizational goals, I was happy doing it. It was in this period that I knew leadership was my calling, and healthcare leadership would be the path I'd follow for the rest of my career.

Leadership, for me, is about impact—on individuals, teams, and the larger community. In healthcare, this impact is magnified because the decisions I make and the teams I lead directly affect patient lives. Each day, I am not just supporting my team or the organization, but the entire community we serve. While the responsibility is immense, I take great pride in bearing it because of the tangible, positive changes I witness.

I find purpose in moments when team members realize their potential, when our hospital achieves 5-star ratings, and when patients defy seemingly insurmountable odds. In these moments, I feel honored to have played a small part in their progress. It is these achievements that fuel my dedication to advancing and supporting others.

I lead with compassion, transparency, and an unwavering commitment to hard work. This approach has served both me and those I work with, enabling us to build trust and achieve meaningful success. During difficult times—like navigating the challenges of the pandemic—I was proud to be the person entrusted with making tough decisions. It was my responsibility to lead with confidence and to reassure my team, the hospital, and the community that we would get through this together.

In all of this, I am constantly reminded of my purpose: to be a catalyst for growth, empowerment of transformation and change, and a driving support in the lives of others.

Yet, even as I thrived at work, my personal life felt like it was unraveling. At home, I resented my husband for constantly complaining about the time and energy I devoted to my job. To compensate, I poured all my love and attention into my children, desperate not to fail as a mother. In the process, I neglected myself, losing sight of my own needs and desires just to avoid feeling the ever-looming guilt. Work had become my sanctuary, the place where I felt the most alive, the most successful.

Home, on the other hand, was where perfectionism reared its ugly head, where I felt like I was failing—where success seemed out of reach. Multitasking is often glorified as a solution for women balancing the demands of marriage, career, motherhood, and personal fulfillment. But for me, it became a comforting lie, a shield against the harsher reality that I wasn't balancing anything—I was failing. It wasn't until I allowed myself to confront this truth that I began to understand. I had to give myself permission to embrace the ebb and flow of life, to recognize that there are seasons for everything. I had to be okay with redefining success, with acknowledging that my identity, my needs, and my dreams would evolve over time. And that's okay. Change is inevitable, and so is the redefinition of who I am and what success means to me. Once I accepted that, I was able to give myself the grace to prioritize what mattered most in each season and stop trying to do it all, all the time. That's when I began to find true balance—on my own terms.

Letting Go of Perfectionism

One of the greatest lessons I've learned is that perfectionism doesn't serve you. It might push you to achieve, but it also drains your energy and happiness. Success isn't about flawless execution; it's about progress, resilience, and learning to adapt. Once I let go of the need to be perfect, I found greater clarity in who I was and what I truly wanted to achieve.

The moment I realized I needed to let go of perfectionism—and the constant pressure to be the "hardworking" ideal—truly came during a reconnection trip with my husband. After what felt like ages of juggling work, motherhood, and the demands of life, we finally had a chance to escape for a few days. It was just the two of us, a 4-hour drive to a sunny destination, with nothing to do but talk. As we drove, we decided to lay it all bare.

That's when it hit me—how much I had been trying (and failing) to be perfect at everything, in all aspects of my life at the same time. As a mom, I was so consumed by the idea of being the non-present mother that I was overbearing and exclusive of other's involvement in my kids lives. As a wife, I had let my husband fall to the bottom of my priority list, leaving him with little more than the remnants of my energy. I had stopped communicating my needs, and when I did, it was always about work or the kids. For me, I couldn't even remember the last time I did something purely for myself—without some agenda or success metric attached to it. At work, this perfectionism had become paralyzing. As I took on more leadership responsibilities, I became hesitant to make decisions, fearing that any misstep could have larger consequences. I found myself stalling, trying to get everything just right, but in the process, nothing was moving forward. I was holding back from the very growth I wanted to achieve.

It was a lot to hear in one sitting. But my husband was right—he's keeping this chapter as evidence that I actually admitted it! That moment was a wake-up call for me. I realized that trying to be a perfect mom wasn't about doing everything "right" or meeting some impossible standard, I needed to define my own family standard of meaningful presence and time. It was about creating intentional moments of connection with my family. I recognized that my husband wasn't just a partner in life, but a crucial support system I needed to lean on, communicate with, and include in my vision of success.

At work, I regained the confidence I had lost to perfectionism. I stopped hiding behind the need for perfect decisions and started embracing the risks that come with growth and learning. I gave myself permission to make mistakes, knowing that they were part of the journey. And most importantly, I learned that I am worth dedicating space to—just for me. I now make time for Kristi, unapologetically, without guilt. Because I am at my best when I am whole, not when I am perfect.

Creating Happiness from Within

Happiness isn't something you find—it's something you create. I learned the hard way that chasing external validation often leaves you feeling empty. True fulfillment comes when you start defining success on your own terms, doing things that genuinely bring you joy, and surrounding yourself with people who encourage authenticity and strength. By setting boundaries, prioritizing self-care, and being open to accepting help, I began to thrive. I stopped searching for happiness outside myself and learned to build it from within.

The moment this transformation began to take shape was when I made the decision to step into my first leadership role in healthcare, instead of waiting for the "perfect" opportunity that aligned with my parents' vision of success for me. In hindsight, that role wasn't just a job—it was a turning point. I had always felt a sense of shame about my success in the food and beverage industry. There was this lingering belief that I should be doing something more "prestigious" in order to feel validated or worthy of success. If I had trusted in my craft and leadership skills back then, who knows where I might have been? But reflecting on the past through the lens of comparison can be dangerous—and comparison is the thief of joy.

That first leadership role, though, changed everything. It confirmed that leadership wasn't some mysterious quality reserved for others—it was a set of skills that I had the foundation for, and, more importantly, a natural aptitude for. I started to feel a sense of ease in my role that had been missing in previous chapters of my life. I recognized that the people around me weren't just tolerating my journey—they were actively cheering me on. For the first time, I had a true circle of support, people who believed in me and invested in my growth.

Sure, people came and went throughout my career, as they always do. But the ones who truly believed in me and encouraged me remained, and that has been a constant source of happiness. I was finally aligning my passion and skills with my purpose, finding community, and defining my career through my own paradigm—not someone else's. It was no longer about chasing external approval; it was about building a life that reflected who I was and what I truly valued.

Through this process, I realized that happiness isn't something that arrives from external sources or validations—it's something you cultivate, grow, and shape from within. And in doing so, you become the creator of your own joy and fulfillment.

Embracing Authenticity and Resilience

Today, I stand as a testament to the power of authenticity. I've learned that success is not a one-size-fits-all concept—it's something we define for ourselves. True happiness comes from aligning your career, your family, and your life with who you truly are, rather than trying to meet external expectations. I've embraced failure as a crucial part of success, understanding that each setback is simply an opportunity to learn and grow.

Most importantly, I've learned not to give up on myself. There were times when it seemed easier to compromise or conform to others' visions of what my life should be, but I've come to realize that true fulfillment comes from staying true to myself. By breaking free from the external pressures to "perform" or "be perfect," and by embracing authenticity and resilience, I've seen how women can thrive—not just as career-driven professionals, but as fulfilled mothers, wives, and leaders.

As a woman leader in healthcare, a wife, a mother, and a coach, I am deeply aware of the example I set for others. Modeling authenticity is at the core of what I do. I model behaviors like **prioritizing my well-being** and **setting clear boundaries**—showing that taking care of myself isn't selfish, but necessary for my success and the success of those around me. I also model **resilience in the face of adversity**, demonstrating that setbacks don't define us, but rather, how we rise from them does. In my role as a leader, I embrace vulnerability and show my team that it's okay to not have all the answers, but it's crucial to learn, adapt, and move forward together.

In my family, I model what it looks like to **prioritize meaningful connections over perfection**—whether it's dedicating quality time with my children or engaging in honest, open communication with my husband. I show that leadership extends beyond the workplace and that the values I champion in my career—compassion, resilience, transparency—are the same values that guide me as a partner and a mother.

The key to all of this is being true to ourselves, continually learning and growing, and reimagining success on our own terms. By embracing who we truly are—without the weight of external expectations—we create a life that is both purposeful and fulfilling. We show the world that as women, we can excel in our careers and still be the loving, authentic leaders our families and communities need.

"Perfection is the enemy of progress; purpose is the key to fulfillment. Embrace who you are, trust your journey, and redefine success on your own terms and time" - Kristi

Personal Note to My Daughter

To My Beautiful Daughter Harlowe,

Everything I do now is for you. Every step I take, every challenge I overcome, is to create a life where you can see what it means to be strong, authentic, and true to yourself. I hope that through my journey, you'll learn how to navigate life on your own terms, with confidence, elegance, and grace. I want you to know that success isn't about what the world expects of you—it's about living a life filled with love, happiness, and purpose, defined by your own heart and ambitions. I am here to support you, to guide you, and to show you that you can thrive no matter what. I hope you grow up knowing that you are enough just as you are, and that you never have to chase perfection—just be your beautiful, authentic self. When you achieve a life of authentic love, joy, and fulfillment, I will know that I've accomplished the ultimate definition of success for myself: raising you to thrive with strength, authenticity, and elegance.

With all my love.

Kristi Brown

Meet Kristi Brown, a distinguished healthcare professional with nearly a decade of experience in the field. Armed with an MBA and an MS in Science Management and Clinical Leadership, Kristi has seamlessly merged her expertise in healthcare with experience, and unique strategies to achieve progressive leadership promotions, earning her numerous accolades as an award-winning healthcare leader.

Beyond her professional achievements, Kristi is a passionate advocate for women in healthcare, dedicating her time to coaching and empowering fellow female professionals. Drawing from her own career journey, she shares invaluable insights and lessons learned to install confidence and foster success for both their professional and personal lives.

Despite her demanding careers as a healthcare leader and industry coach, Kristi remains committed to her roles as a devoted wife and mother of two young children. Balancing, or as she calls, "scaling" family life with her career aspirations and desire to impact women in this community, she embodies the values of opportunity, drive, and success while prioritizing personal health and happiness for herself and those she mentors.

Website: https://theleap.co/@LeadershipWithKristi

About Women Thrive Media

Women Thrive Media -Women Thrive is a global media platform where every woman has a voice. Where every woman's story is celebrated. We recognise the impact and contribution that women make in the world, and our mission is to build a platform where every woman feels included, celebrated and proud to be part of a community like this.

We started our mission work in 2017 and have since grown to an international platform of over 600k women worldwide. Over the years, we have hosted many amazing and life-changing events, had 100s of inspiring international speakers take our stage, and thousands of attendees' lives changed or impacted by our work.

Now we pride ourselves on being an inclusive platform where women looking for guidance, support and mentorship, can come and connect with others who have already walked the walk and able to share their knowledge and wisdom. Be it through our podcast, events, book, or monthly Women Thrive magazine.

Our mission is to reach 1 MILLION women every year and create a global impact on women's empowerment because we believe that if one woman is given the confidence, tools, and resources to rise, she will go on to empower thousands more. We have seen time and time again when we, as women, come together, the impact and ripple effect is so much more powerful than a woman trying to make an impact on her own.

We hope you join our community, mission, and future events.

www.womenthrivesummit.com
www.womenthrivemagazine.com

Pay It Forward

If you enjoyed this book, please consider passing it to another woman that needs to hear these storis, please tell them:

What was your favourite story?

What are your biggest take aways?

Who do you want to pass this book onto and why?

What was your favourite story?

What are your biggest take aways?

Who do you want to pass this book onto and why?

What was your favourite story?

What are your biggest take aways?

Who do you want to pass this book onto and why?
